ALBANIA *and the* ALBANIANS
in the ANNUAL REPORTS *of the*
BRITISH *and* FOREIGN BIBLE SOCIETY,
1805–1955

Albania *and the* Albanians
in the Annual Reports *of the*
British *and* Foreign Bible Society,
1805–1955

Compiled and edited
by David Hosaflook

Part of the 500/200
Albanian Protestant Commemorative Series

Albania and the Albanians in the Annual Reports of the British and Foreign Bible Society, 1805–1955

Published by the Institute for Albanian and Protestant Studies, courtesy of the Bible Society and the University of London, School of Oriental and African Studies.

ISBN 978-1-946244-14-7

Publisher's Cataloging-in-Publication data

Names: Hosaflook, David, compiler and editor.

Title: Albania and the Albanians in the annual reports of the British and Foreign Bible Society, 1805–1955 / compiled and edited by David Hosaflook.

Series: The 500/200 Albanian Protestant Commemorative Series

Description: Includes index. | Tirana, Albania: Institute for Albanian and Protestant Studies, 2017.

Identifiers: ISBN 978-1-946244-13-0 (Albania: pbk.) | 978-1-946244-14-7 (pbk.) | 978-1-946244-15-4 (ebook)

Subjects: LCSH British and Foreign Bible Society–History–19th century. | British and Foreign Bible Society–History–20th century. | Bible–Publication and distribution–Societies, etc. | Balkan Peninsula–History–19th century–Sources. | Balkan Peninsula–History–20th century–Sources. | Albania–History–1840-1912–Sources.

Classification: LCC DR43 .H67 2017 | DDC 949.602/8–dc23

www.instituti.org

INTRODUCTION

IN 1912, ALBANIA'S FUTURE HUNG IN THE BALANCE.
The Ottoman Empire was weakening, Balkan nations
were rising, and Albania was at risk of being partitioned
amongst its neighbors. In this context the Albanians
declared their independence. They were led by Ismail
Qemali, who became head of Albania's provisional
government. Soon thereafter, the Great Powers
convened the London Conference of Ambassadors to
deliberate on new, post-Ottoman borders in the Balkans.
In the spring of 1913, Qemali himself went to London to
defend Albania's rights. Shortly after his arrival, on his
own initiative, he paid an informal visit to an unlikely
organization: the British and Foreign Bible Society
(BFBS). Why? In his words, to thank them for their help
to the Albanian cause through their Bibles.[1]

Bibles? How had *Bibles* helped the Albanian cause to
such a degree that Qemali felt indebted to the BFBS?
This work begins to answer that question in the form
of extracts from the society's annual reports. By way of
orientation, however, the reader should consider three
foundational elements: the nature of the Bible Society,

---

1 Correspondence, Charles Woods to J. H. Ritson, 17 May 1913,
Instituti i Gjuhë-Letërsisë, arka 3, kutia 1, dosja nr. x, "Pjesë nga
korrespondenca për botimet vitet: 1909–1913".

the condition of Albania in the nineteenth century, and the work the society accomplished for the Albanian people.

The Nature of the British and Foreign Bible Society

The Bible Society was established in 1804, at the onset of an era of unprecedented Protestant missionary expansion across the globe. Because the foundational pillar of Protestantism is *Sola Scriptura* (the Bible alone is the final authority for faith and practice), the first objective of Protestant missions was making the Bible available globally. William Carey, a British missionary with the Baptist Missionary Society, and others like him, were translating the Scriptures into languages of the East, exciting great interest back home in Britain.[2] Several societies began circulating Bibles,[3] but they were targeting Britain and the peoples of the British territories.[4]

Then a village girl from Wales changed the world. Mary Jones wanted a Welsh Bible, but Bibles were a scarce commodity—so scarce that Welsh churches bolted and chained their copies to the pulpit. Mary was informed that Rev. Thomas Charles had Welsh Bibles for sale in the town of Bala. She found ways to earn money and, many months later, walked nearly thirty miles from Abergynolwyn to Bala. Rev. Charles was deeply moved by her story, but he had run out of his limited supply of Bibles. Unable to bear

2 Bitting, C. C. *Bible Societies and the Baptists: compiled from Published Documents.* Philadelphia: American Baptist Publication Society, 1883, 8-10.

3 Joseph Hughes mentions six such societies in *The Excellence of the Holy Scriptures an Argument for Their More General Dispersion at Home and Abroad* (London: Thomas Bensley), 1803, 17-20.

4 For example, there was a "Bible Society" in Britain, founded in 1780, but its scope was the army and the navy.

turning her away empty-handed, he gave her one of the few copies he owned personally.[5]

The next time Rev. Thomas Charles visited London, he related Mary's story to his colleagues on the Committee of the Religious Tract Society, an organization founded in 1799 by Rev. George Burder for the purpose of dispersing brochures and books about the Gospel.[6] Charles urged his fellow members to form a separate society to print and distribute more Scriptures in Welsh. While Charles was concluding his appeal, a Baptist pastor named Joseph Hughes quipped, "if for Wales, why not also for the [British] empire and the world?"[7]

Thus the British Foreign and Bible Society was born. It had a limited focus (it would publish the text of the Scriptures alone, without any accompanying notes or comments) but an unlimited vision (it aimed to publish Bibles in every language possible).[8] The society was

---

5 Canton, William. *A History of the British and Foreign Bible Society*, vol. 1. London: J. Murray, 1904, 465–470. In 1930 the story of Mary Jones and her Bible was printed in Tosk Albanian (*Historia e Maria Xhonsit dhe Biblla e saj*) and the BFBS colporteur Pandeli Sinas reported that "the mountaineers have so much joy perusing" it (1931 BFBS Annual Report). A portion of the story was published also in one of the weekly bulletins of the Evangelical Mission in Kortcha, with a concluding question, "Do the boys and girls of Albania have the kind of deep thirst for the Word of God that Mary Jones had?" (IAPS, "Edwin Jacques" fund, Weekly Bulletins of Misioni Ungjillor, ca. 1935).

6 The RTS began printing Christian tracts in Albanian from the 1820s, and in 1866 and 1867 they printed Albanian grammars in both Gheg and Tosk dialects.

7 Jones, William. *The Jubilee Memorial of the Religious Tract Society*. London: Religious Tract Society, 1850, 46–48.

8 *Address, Explanatory of the Principles, Views, & Exertions, of the British and Foreign Bible Society*. London: J. Tilling, 1814, 3.

passionate about the Gospel of Jesus Christ and the Biblically prescribed duty of Christians to take the Gospel to the ends of the earth, but it believed the self-obvious truth that the Bible was the necessary prerequisite to the evangelism of non-Christian nations. Similarly, in lands with existing Christian traditions, the Bible in the vernacular was a necessary prerequisite to spiritual and theological reform—something the BFBS felt was as necessary in the nineteenth century as it had been in the sixteenth century, when the distribution of the Word of God fueled the spread of the Protestant Reformation.

The Bible Society was not political in nature. It was not an agent of the British government for territorial expansion. It was a massive, privately funded, non-denominational Christian organization that asked one essential question when contemplating whether or not to engage with a particular nation: *Do the people there have Bibles in their mother tongue that they can read for themselves?* Although this question seems apolitical, even impossible to politicize, in truth it did have political ramifications, especially in the Ottoman Balkans. If, for example, it was in a ruling power's interest to keep its subjected peoples uneducated and thereby more easily governed, then any attempt to advance reading and learning was discouraged, especially in the peoples' own vernacular. Similarly, if religion could be exploited by loyalist clerics to keep the masses subservient, then any missionary attempt to increase theological literacy could also become a political problem for the ruling power, and thus needed to be kept in check by the clerics.

Foreign governments viewed the Bible Society as politically expedient if the intellectual rise of minority nations could potentially weaken a rival empire and shift the balance of power in an advantageous direction. From the perspective of suppressed nations within larger empires, the Bible Society could be leveraged as a tool to lift them out of national darkness and international irrelevance through the advancement of literacy. In fact, several non-Protestant Albanian nationalist figures cooperated with and supported the BFBS for this purpose, not because they embraced the mission of the Bible Society.

The atmosphere in the Balkans was marked by frequent conflict between ruling powers, rival powers, and rising nations. Consequently, the Bible translators and colporteurs of the Bible Society had to conduct their work in a highly politicized context. Though they were not politically motivated, the BFBS workers attempted to understand the environments into which they were sent, and wrote copiously about their experiences. Because in some cases they were the only foreigners in certain regions, their writings were sometimes utilized by foreign governments to enhance their intelligence. The missionaries appealed to their countries' representatives when they perceived injustices or when their mission was hindered by local governors. Just as western merchants appealed to their governments' diplomats for protection and for leverage to assist them in accomplishing financial objectives, so western missionaries and their societies appealed for protection and leverage to assist them in accomplishing spiritual objectives.

Such was the nature of the British and Foreign Bible Society: a non-political Christian organization whose singular, apolitical mission of distributing the Bible globally sometimes became politicized as its influence grew in an increasingly complex world.

The Condition of Albania in the Nineteenth Century

The second key to understanding how Bibles helped the Albanian cause is considering the political, social, and religious conditions in Albanian-inhabited territories. The BFBS commenced its work for the Albanian Bible in 1816, fourteen years before the Albanian National Movement began[9] and nearly one hundred years before Albania declared its independence. This fact alone begins to explain why Ismail Qemali and other Albanian nationalist figures felt such gratitude toward the Bible Society. That is, the society was an early contributor to the Albanian National Awakening. Again, national empowerment was not the society's purpose, but it was an inevitable effect, insofar as seeing books for the first time in one's own language tends to awaken national identity and arouse patriotic feelings, however subconsciously.[10]

Although Albanian territories were still under Ottoman rule in 1816 when the BFBS began its efforts for the Albanian Bible, at various times and in various regions the Albanians enjoyed degrees of autonomy, notably in the pashaliks of Scutari (1757–1831) and Ioannina (1788–1822). In general, however, the Albanians were not yet unified or literate, and thus needed an intellectual awakening. Just as the Protestant movement thrived in Western Europe at a time when people desired enlightenment, so Protestantism came to the Albanians at a time when they,

9 See "Rilindja Kombëtare Shqiptare dhe veçoritë e saj dalluese" in *Historia e popullit shqiptar* vol. II, 31–32. In this authoritative resource, Albanian historians periodize 1830–1876 as the first phase of the Albanian National Movement, a consolidation phase that helped the Albanians become self-aware of themselves as a unique nation.

10 Cf. Kyrias-Dako, Sevasti. *My Life* (Tirana: Institute for Albanian & Protestant Studies, 2016), 58–59.

too, desired enlightenment. In the mid to late 1800s, other Balkan nations began unifying solidly around national identities—not merely emerging from the Ottoman Empire but declaring war upon it as sovereign nations. Albania, however, was still struggling with self-identity, debating what level of autonomy they were willing to seek as subjects of the Ottoman government. A majority of Albanians were Sunni Moslems, some of whom held positions in the government and, thus, favored keeping the status quo. But many other Albanians were Bektashi, Roman Catholic, or Orthodox. The absence of a unified national religion delayed their push for full independence and made them susceptible to being divided by the political schemes of neighbors who often utilized religion as a psychopolitical tool.

The Albanian national figure Pashko Vasa (1825–1892) is well known for his call to his fellow Albanians in 1878 to cast away their allegiance to church and mosque, and to rally around Albanianism as a kind of national religion. This was not so much a call to disavow faith in God as it was a call to abandon naivety and refuse to be used as pawns by religious leaders who seemed to be serving foreign governments politically more than they were serving their local flocks spiritually. It must be remembered that when the BFBS entered Albanian history, there was no Albanian Bible or New Testament available to the people. This is almost incredible when considering the many centuries of Roman Catholic and Eastern Orthodox Christian influence in Albanian territories. In 1555 the Albanian Catholic priest John Buzuku published a missal in Venice that included scattered sections from the Bible, but it was not a Bible translation and was not available or understandable to the Albanians in the nineteenth

century. In 1761 the Albanian Orthodox cleric Gregory of
Durrës translated portions of the New Testament, some
more paraphrased than translated, in what is known as
the Elbasan Gospel.[11] This Elbasan Gospel implies that
there was at least a sporadic use of Albanian-language
liturgy in Orthodox churches.[12] In 1770 the Wallachian
scholar Anastas Kavalioti published several pages of
Albanian Bible quotations in his work *Protopeiria*. And
between 1810–1830, a yet unidentified person translated
316 verses of the Bible in the unique Albanian alphabet
of Theodor Haxhifilipi (Dhaskal Todri) of Elbasan.[13] Like
Buzuku's *Missal*, these texts were not in active circulation.
There is some discussion concerning the positions of the
Orthodox and Catholic churches on Albanian liturgy,
but until the BFBS began its work in 1824, there is no

---

11 Zamputi, Injac. "Dorëshrimi i Anonimit të Elbasanit," *Bulletini i
Institutit të Shkencave Shoqërore*, v. 3-4 (Tirana): 64-131. The Scripture
portions known to be translated by Gregory are Matthew 10:32-33,
10:37-38, 16:13-19, 26:1-5, 27:8-17, 27:22-66, 28:9-20; Mark 15:22, 15:33-
41; Luke 2:1-20, 22:4-6, 22:9-13, 23:39-43; and John 1:35-44, 5:1-5, 5:24-
30, 9:1-38, 11:32-43, 13:4-10, 19:31-37, 20:19-31. See the documents,
transcription, and translation at www.albanianliterature.net/authors/
authors_early/gregory_of_durres/gregory_EGM1.html (accessed
October 21, 2015).

12 Giakoumis, Konstantinos. "The Policy of the Orthodox Patriarchate
Toward the Use of Albanian in Church Services." *Albanohellenica* 4
(2011): 137–171. Giakoumis argues that the Orthodox Church "did
not encourage [but] at least did not prevent the first creative efforts to
write in Albanian and use it in services."

13 Elsie, Robert *Early Albanian Bible Translations in Todhri Script*
(London: Robert Elsie and Centre for Albanian Studies, 2016). See also
Islami, Myslim. *Naum Veqilharxhi: Ideologu i parë i Rilindjes Shqiptare.*
Tirana: Kombinati Poligrafik, 1977, 28; Kristoforidhi, Kostandin (ed.
Xhevat Lloshi). *Bibla (Në gegërisht) Kriesa. Të Dalëtë, 1872.* Tirana:
Shoqëria Biblike, 2009, 4–6.

evidence that any one of the sixty-six books of the Bible had been published into Albanian, much less the entire New Testament—and certainly not the Old Testament that contains at least three times more content than the New Testament.

Without religious texts in their own language (the Quran, too, was not yet translated into Albanian), the Albanians, obviously, had negligible theological understanding. On April 1, 1717, Lady Mary Montagu, a baptized Anglican and wife of the British ambassador in Constantinople, wrote a letter railing against the corruption, ignorance, and cruelty of both Eastern Orthodox and Roman Catholic priests, and then mentioned the Albanians:

> These people, living between Christians and Mahometans, and not being skilled in controversy, declare that they are utterly unable to judge which religion is best; but, to be certain of not entirely rejecting the truth, they very prudently follow both, and go to the mosques on Fridays and the church on Sundays, saying for their excuse, that at the day of judgment they are sure of protection from the true prophet; but which that is, they are not able to determine in this world. I believe there is no other race of mankind have so modest an opinion of their own capacity.[14]

Nearly two centuries later, not much had changed. In 1909, Edith Durham described nearly identical religious rites being practiced in both Muslim and Catholic villages, based on superstition, not Scriptures. Christ and

---

14 Montagu, Mary Wortley (ed. Lord Wharncliffe). *The Letters and Works of Lady Mary Wortley Montagu*, vol. 1. London: Henry G. Bohn, 1861, 287–291.

Mohammed, Durham explained, were considered by the Albanians to be "two supernatural 'magic dickies,' each able, if propitiated, to work wonders".[15]

Theological illiteracy was a reflection of the general state of education in Albania. The BFBS reported in 1867 that "amongst the races embraced within the limits of European Turkey, none have been doomed to such utter neglect as the Albanians. They have been left without any education worthy of the name, and, as may be expected, the reign of ignorance prevails." The editors of the BFBS annual reports were intrigued by, and made frequent mention of, the fact that the Albanians were almost without any written literature except the publications of the BFBS itself.[16] Of course, it was a futile effort for the BFBS to produce Bibles for any people group who could not read in their native tongue; as such, literacy became a natural extension of the Protestants' work. In 1886 Alexander Thomson wrote to the BFBS that the Albanians were a "large and utterly neglected Albanian population" that needed education desperately, and he prayed and appealed for people to found Albanian schools.[17] The limited focus of the BFBS prevented it from starting schools or printing basic primers and grammars, but Thomson interceded for these causes, successfully soliciting the help of the Religious Tract Society and the American Board of Commissioners for Foreign Missions.

---

15 Durham, M. Edith. *High Albania*. Manchester, NH: Ayer, 1994 (originally published in 1909), 312–314.

16 1867 BFBS Annual Report, 158.

17 1886 BFBS Annual Report, 161.

The Work of the British and Foreign
Bible Society for the Albanians

In its first one hundred years, the British and Foreign Bible Society translated, printed, or distributed Scriptures in an astounding 412 of the world's languages—an average of four new languages per year. Remarkably, the Albanian language became a focus of the BFBS as early as 1816, just twelve years after the BFBS was established. Albanian was approximately the twentieth project the BFBS undertook. The project began when the Scottish Protestant missionary Robert Pinkerton, agent of the BFBS in St. Petersburg, met Albanians in Vienna and appealed to London for approval to launch a New Testament translation project for Albanian. The BFBS agreed, thus commencing a decades-long work in translation, editing, language development, publication, and distribution. This was no easy task, requiring Albanian translators, editors, a literate populace, and suitable infrastructure, all of which were in short supply.

Without the luxury of a settled Albanian alphabet with which to begin, the translators and project coordinators were forced to be both bold and creative, using their best judgment on orthographical questions in what became a massive and sometimes politically charged linguistic laboratory. In 1824 the Gospel of Matthew was published into Albanian, translated and edited by Albanians—Vangjel Meksi and the Orthodox bishop Grigor Gjirokastriti, respectively. It was published in Greek letters with modifications, because educated Albanians in the South had studied at Greek schools and would understand Greek letters. Furthermore, the publication was a diglot, Albanian in one column, Modern Greek in the other. The

BFBS chose this solution to ensure the maximum potential for readability. After its initial success among educated Albanians in the South, the entire New Testament was published in 1827, also a diglot. The publication of an Albanian New Testament was a triumph for the Albanian people and became a standard text for foreign linguists studying Albanian, putting the language on the world's linguistic map. There was a fundamental problem, though. The Bible Society did not care about the prestige of being a global leader in linguistic research or nation building, but was only concerned with whether or not people could read and understand the Gospel. Hence, they were disappointed to discover over time that their first publications were not generally useful among the majority of Albanians.

Illiteracy was the primary problem that would be addressed in due time. But another fundamental problem was infrastructure. In 1824—the year the Gospel of Matthew was published—Scottish cartographer John Melish produced a map of Albania indicating all available roads, including the approximate amount of hours needed to travel between routes. According to Melish's map, the whole of Albania, including what is today's northern Greece, had only one "made road," three "cart roads," and thirteen "horse roads".[18] Such an underdeveloped infrastructure made Bible distribution impractical. Forty years later, the situation had not improved significantly, the BFBS reporting "the absence of roads and the scarcity of internal productions."[19] As late as 1908, almost one century after the Albanian Bible project had begun, transportation

---

18   Melish, John. *A General Collection of Maps, Charts, Views, &c.* Philadelphia, 1824.

19   1866 BFBS Annual Report, 134.

infrastructure was still inadequate. Sir Charles Eliot described the infrastructure in northern Albania with the wry humor and satirical style of a British travel writer. When a traveler, he wrote, arrives in the port serving Shkodra (Shëngjin), he is "confronted with the problem of how to leave it. The railway has really terminated in somebody's pocket, and has never been heard of on the spot. You cannot drive—because, firstly, there are no carriages, and, secondly, there is no road."[20]

Despite these obstacles, the BFBS remained committed to Albanian enlightenment. In 1860, Alexander Thomson accepted a position with the BFBS as the society's primary agent for the Ottoman Empire and devoted more energy to the Albanian work than perhaps any other field under his watch. Through his close working partnership with Constantine Christophorides (Konstandin Kristoforidhi) and later with Gerasim and George Kyrias, Thomson published new Albanian Bible versions in both Gheg and Tosk dialects, established Bible depots in strategic cities of the North and the South[21], supported schools for Albanian girls, and developed a distribution system with colporteurs who crisscrossed the country by horse or mule, penetrating the hinterlands of Albania with the Scriptures.

In addition to fighting illiteracy and overcoming poor infrastructure, the society faced dangers and opposition. Illness dogged the colporteurs and sometimes took the lives of their family members. Brigandage was a constant threat,

---

20 Eliot, Sir Charles. *Turkey in Europe*. London: Edward Arnold, 1908, 348–350.

21 Depots for Albanian and other language Bibles were located, at different times, in Shkodra (Scutari), Ioannina, Berat, Monastir (Bitola), and Kortcha.

with documented reports of kidnappings and murder. Local
Ottoman government officials sometimes hindered the
Bible Society's efforts and only relented when pressured by
higher authorities. Greek Orthodox clerics also opposed the
work of the BFBS, initially on theological grounds but later,
as Greek irredentism swelled, on political-religious grounds.
Roman Catholics in the North opposed the Protestants
vehemently and consistently.[22] Substandard living conditions
brought manifold hardships to the missionaries who came
to work. There were no Albanian Protestants who could
help them establish a permanent presence. In such an
unfavorable context, even small achievements of the Bible
Society would have been remarkable. Its achievements,
however, would not be small.

Between 1824 and 1908 alone, the British and Foreign
Bible Society printed approximately 55,000 copies
of the Albanian Scriptures, in both Gheg and Tosk, in
twenty-seven unique editions. The society translated
and published all the books of the New Testament and
six books from the Old Testament (Genesis, Exodus,
Deuteronomy, Psalms, Proverbs, and Isaiah).[23] Perhaps
more significantly, they took the initiative to distribute
the books among the Albanian people. It is certain
that the BFBS distributed at least 27,000 Albanian

---

22 The frequency of this complaint in these annual reports renders
any specific reference here superfluous.

23   Gerasim Kyrias (Gjerasim Qiriazi) desired to translate the
remaining books of the Old Testament but died before his thirty-sixth
year. Thanas Sina took on this project but when he became ill Loni
Kristo (Sina's son-in-law) completed it (Roe, James M. *A History of the
British and Foreign Bible Society, 1905–1954*. London: British and Foreign
Bible Society, 1965, 277). It was never published and the manuscript's
whereabouts are still unknown.

books in Albanian territories before 1908, a remarkable achievement when recognizing that there was no Albanian school movement until the last two decades of the nineteenth century. The impact of these publications is more significant than is currently understood by the majority of Albanians and merits greater attention by Albanian educators and historians.

In 1912 the Albanian publicist and political figure Midhat Frasheri wrote: "Certain books of the Old and New Testament in Gheg and Tosk for many years formed almost the entire printed literature of Albania and have made the British and Foreign Bible Society honored and revered among all patriotic Albanians, whether Moslem or Christian."[24] In the sixty-year span between 1824 and 1884—foundational years for Albania's literary awakening and the era of Jeronim De Rada and Dora d'Istria—the British and Foreign Bible Society and the Religious Tract Society were responsible for at least 35 percent of all Albanian language titles. Perhaps more significantly, they published in large quantities and in both of the major Albanian dialects, for mass distribution. Their colporteurs continually traversed Albanian territories with their books, creating literary awareness and a thirst for more learning within Albania, as other Albanian actors were attempting to do the same thing from without, where conditions were better and more safe.

⌒

---

24 Skendo, Lumo. "Albania and the Bible Society" in *The Bible in the World*, July 1912. London: British and Foreign Bible Society, 218–219.

About This Book

Each year the BFBS printed a detailed annual report about its work all over the world. The information in the reports was intended to be a condensed summary of the Society's work, as reported by its agents. The Albanians were first mentioned two hundred years ago, in the 1817 report, and were mentioned in nearly every successive report until 1955. This resource is a compilation of material, extracted from the annual reports, about Albania and the Albanians, but it also contains information about other nations insofar as such information assists readers to understand the context and progress of the Albanian work in the context of the Ottoman Balkans.

For a more detailed study of the BFBS's work in Albania, the Institute for Albanian and Protestant Studies (IAPS) has also published a larger work—the correspondence of the BFBS concerning Albania, extracted from various archives and translated into Albanian by the distinguished linguist and historian Xhevat Lloshi.[25] Additionally, the IAPS has published a companion volume to this work, with a similar title: *Albania and the Albanians in the Annual Reports of the American Board of Commissioners for Foreign Missions, 1820–1924.* The BFBS must be studied together with the American Board in order to understand the cooperation of both missionary societies, the evolution of the Albanian Protestant Movement, and the impact this movement made on the Albanian national cause. The publication of both volumes coincides with the worldwide commemoration of the 500th anniversary of the Protestant

---

25 These are published under the title *Thesaret për gjuhën shqipe të Shoqërisë Biblike Britanike dhe për Vendet e Huaja.* As of 2017, only the first volume has been published, covering the years 1815–1883.

Reformation and is part of a jubilee commemoration for Protestants in Albania, Kosovo, and Macedonia. Other works related to the Albanian Protestant Movement have also been published as part of this series such as Sevasti Kyrias Dako's autobiography, Gerasim Kyrias's account of his captivity as a hostage, John Quanrud's biography of Gerasim Kyrias, and this writer's Ph.D. dissertation, "The Protestant Movement among the Albanians, 1816–1908."

Because the BFBS began its work for the Albanian Bible at the beginning of the nineteenth century and continued working intensely until the communist era, its reports are useful as a running historical commentary and chronology of Albanian conditions predating the Albanian National Awakening and extending well beyond Albania's emergence as an independent nation. As demonstrated by the lengthy index in the back of this book, the extracts herein contain information about a wide breadth of topics and will serve historians and linguists as a fascinating reference work. This book's primary value, however, is to readers who wish to understand the long and adventurous story of how the Albanians received and started reading the Bible in their own dialect, and how something so simple became so significant to Albania's national cause.

Dr. David Hosaflook
Tirana, 2017

REPORTS

OF THE

BRITISH AND FOREIGN

BIBLE SOCIETY,

WITH

EXTRACTS OF CORRESPONDENCE,

&c.

VOLUME THE FOURTH,

FOR THE YEARS

1816 AND 1817.

LONDON:

PRINTED FOR THE SOCIETY,

By Tilling and Hughes, Grosvenor-row, Chelsea ;

AND SOLD AT THE

SOCIETY'S HOUSE, EARL STREET, BLACKFRIARS;

BY WAUGH AND INNES, HUNTER'S-SQUARE, EDINBURGH; AND BY ALL
OTHER BOOKSELLERS IN THE UNITED KINGDOM.

1819.

Title page of one of the BFBS Annual Reports

1st Report, 1805

Pages 3–4

Laws and Regulations of the British and Foreign Bible Society

I. The Designation of this Society shall be "The British and Foreign Bible Society," of which the sole object shall be, to encourage a wider circulation of the Holy Scriptures. The only Copies in the Languages of the United Kingdom to be circulated by the Society, shall be the authorized version, without Note or Comment.

II. This Society shall add its endeavours to those employed by other Societies, for circulating the Scriptures through the British Dominions; and shall also, according to its ability, extend its influence to other countries, whether Christian, Mahometan, or Pagan.

Page 24

If to provide for the temporal exigencies of our fellow-creatures be considered an indispensable duty, to minister to their spiritual wants is a duty of still superior obligation; and of all the modes suggested or employed for this purpose, the supplying them with the doctrines of truth and salvation, is the most benevolent, efficacious, and unexceptionable.

The Designation of this Society shall be "The British and Foreign Bible Society," the sole object of which shall be, to encourage a wider circulation of the Holy Scriptures.

Pages 25–26

The views of the society were made known to the public by the following advertisement:

BRITISH AND FOREIGN BIBLE SOCIETY

A Society having been formed with the above designation, it has been judged expedient to submit to the Public a brief statement of the reasons which exist for such a Society, of the specific object which it embraces, and of the principles by which its operations will be directed.

The reasons, which call for such an institution, chiefly refer to the prevalence of ignorance, superstition, and idolatry, over so large a portion of the world; the limited nature of the respectable societies now in existence; and their acknowledged insufficiency to supply the demand for Bibles in the United Kingdoms and Foreign Countries; and the recent attempts which have been made on the part of infidelity to discredit the evidence, vilify the character, and destroy the influence of Christianity.

The exclusive object of the Society is, to diffuse the knowledge of the Holy Scriptures, by circulating them in the different languages spoken throughout Great Britain and Ireland; and also according to the extent of its funds, by promoting the printing of them in foreign languages, and the distribution of them in foreign countries.

The principles, upon which this undertaking will be conducted, are as comprehensive as the nature of the object suggests that they should be. In the execution of the plan, it is proposed to embrace the common support of Christians at large; and to invite the concurrence of persons of every description, who profess to regard the Scriptures as the proper Standard of Faith.

It may be necessary to add, in soliciting the countenance of the Public, that in consequence of the enlarged means of instruction which the lower classes in this country have enjoyed of late years, a desire of perusing the Scriptures has considerably increased among them; and also that in Wales, Ireland, Switzerland, Germany, Denmark, and other parts of the world, Bibles are greatly wanted, and, in some, are sought for with an eagerness, which, but for authentic assurances to that effect, would scarcely be credited. ...

The Society, which now takes the liberty to address you, founds its claim to your notice, upon the nature of its object; TO PROMOTE THE CIRCULATION OF THE SCRIPTURES AT HOME AND ABROAD; an object, in which every one, who professes the religion of Christ, must feel a deep interest.

The liberal basis of its establishment, also, which unites, to a degree perhaps hitherto unexampled, the zeal and exertions of Christians, of the several denominations, to which the Constitution of this happy Country affords equal protection, will doubtless give additional force to the claims arising from the simplicity, purity, and importance of its design.

It cannot be doubted, that in every part of the United Kingdom, there are many who are actuated with the true spirit of Christian benevolence, and who only want proper opportunities of manifesting it --- The British and Foreign Bible Society now present such an opportunity to them, and solicits your assistance in making it known, as well as your influence and co-operation in promoting the object of its association.

The Society is fully sensible of the happy results to be expected from the combined exertions of the Christian

Community, and is required by a sense of duty to call them forth in the advancement of a work, which it can with confidence recommend to the blessing of God and the support of every good man.

I have the honour to be,

Your most obedient humble servant,

TEIGNMOUTH, President

London, March, 1805

6th-8th Reports, 1806–1812
No pertinent information

9th Report, 1813

Pages 8–9

Appendix, No. IX. Translation of a Letter from ————, Deacon[1], at Scandinari, in the Levant; written originally in Greek.

I was utterly astonished on receiving your last most agreeable letter of the 1st of October, 1811,with four dozen copies of the Holy New Testament in Ancient and Modern Greek. ... The Testament we have found to be most exact The original is correct; and the version into our modern language is very accurate, very accurately printed, and in a very neat form.

It was always a most desirable thing to have in abundance, at least a part of the Sacred Scriptures, in the vulgar idiom, since the learned (viz. Ancient Greek) is

---

1 This deacon is a learned man who studied at Rome; in the college of Sapienza, for some time. (All footnotes are in the original, unless indicated by the editor's initials, "D.H.").

every where so neglected, as to be understood only by a very few. Now we are anxious to know the origin of this fact, because it is in itself so interesting, that we wish to have further information about it; that is to say, how it came into the minds of those great gentlemen in England to print in the vulgar idiom, the Testament of our Lord. For my own part, to tell you how I feel, after reading what you have written, as having been communicated to you by your friend Dr. Naudi: after examining so generous a plan for the dispersion of the Eternal Will of God, and repeatedly reading these excellent Testaments, I find myself impelled to believe, that the Lord, for the sake of his only and beloved Son is determined to reform these our parts, and to communicate the brightness of his light, through your Testaments, into the Levant; where, as you know, there is nothing to be found but darkness, and wretchedness, and perdition. The reading of the New Testament comes opportunely and efficaciously, to repair such serious evils.

Pius VI, of happy memory, was fond of recommending to Cardinal Borgia, at that time Patron of the Society *De Propaganda Fide*, to print the Bible as generally as possible, translating it into various languages: because, he affirmed, that from these, more than from any other means, good might be expected to be done in the parts of the world where Christianity was unknown, or had ceased to be cultivated; particularly in the Morea, Syria, Arabia, and the Isles ...

Pages 10–11

Appendix, No. X [Letter from unnamed author]

At Sea. April 30, 1812

Dear Sir,

Before I state to you, for the information of the Committee of the British and Foreign Bible Society, an account of my distribution of the Scriptures committed to my care this voyage up the Mediterranean; I beg leave, first, to return my sincere thanks to the Committee, for thus honouring me with so important a charge, and so far counting me faithful as to be the bearer of the Words of Eternal Life in so many different languages: so that English, French, Spaniards, Italians, Arabians, Danes, Germans, Greeks, &c. might read in their own tongues, the wonderful works of God. ...

Page 65

From the Third Report of the Connecticut Bible Society, May 14, 1812

Nothing is *permanently* done among the heathen by the most faithful labours of Missionaries, unless the Scriptures can be put in their hands ...In the short compass of six years, the British and Foreign Bible Society has issued from its Depository, in London, more than 325,000 copies of the Scriptures ... The Translation of the Bible into every tongue in Europe and Asia, and the possession of it by every individual, is their benevolent object.

Pages 74–76

[Letter from John Patterson and Robert Pinkerton]

St. Petersburgh, Jan. 26, 1813

It is with infinite satisfaction that we embrace the first opportunity of informing, through you, the Committee of the British and Foreign Bible Society, of the establishment of a Bible Society here in St. Petersburgh. ...

It was truly delightful to see the unanimity which actuated this assembly, composed of Christians of the Russian Greek Church, of Armenians, of Catholics, of Lutherans, and of Calvinists, and all met for the express purpose of making the Gospel of the Grace of God sound out from the shores of the Baltic to the Eastern Ocean, and from the Frozen Ocean to the Black Sea, and the borders of China; by putting into the hands of Christians and Mahometans, of Lamites and the votaries of Shaman, with many other heathen tribes, the Oracles of the living God. Here we had another proof of what the Bible can do, and of the veneration which all Christian have for this blessed Book. We see that it is still capable of uniting Christians in the bond of peace. It is the standard lifted up by the Son of Jesse, around which all his followers rally, in order to carry it in triumph over the whole globe....

Let us pray that the blessing of God may rest upon this Infant Society, and that it may become a real blessing to the empire.

10th-11th Reports, 1814–1815

No pertinent information

12th Report, 1816

Pages 79–80

From the Rev. Robert Pinkerton

St. Petersburg, Oct. 24, 1815

In answer to your important inquiries respecting the Servian,[2] I beg to remark, that the Holy Scriptures have been in the Servian dialect of the Slavonian for upwards of 900 years. This is the translation of Cyril and Methodius, which is used not only in the Russian and Servian Churches, but among all the tribes of the Slavonians belonging to the Greek Church, and is usually called the Slavonian Bible ...

13th Report, 1817

Pages 87–88

Letter of Rev. Robert Pinkerton

Vienna, August 24, 1816

Under the guidance of Divine Providence, I reached this city, on the 12th instant, in good health. During six days' intercourse, with different persons, more or less attached to the cause, I was led to see, that, if ever any thing should be effected for establishing a Bible Society for Austria, the work must begin with Government itself; and therefore, after weighing the matter thoroughly in my own mind,

---

2 These inquiries were made in consequence of an application of Mr. Kopitar, of Vienna, through Baron de Sacy, of Paris, to know whether the Society would be inclined to encourage the translation of the Scriptures into the Servian language by a young man of that nation, employed by Mr. Kopitar.

and earnestly praying for direction from on high, I came to the determination of requesting an audience of the Prime Minister, Prince Metternich, and of laying the matter before him, in all its purity and genuine simplicity. This audience I obtained on the 20th, between three and four in the afternoon. The Prince received me with great kindness and condescension, and heard, with marked attention, what I had to say respecting the benevolent object of the British and Foreign Bible Society, as the agent of which, I had called at Vienna, on my way from Moldavia to Saxony and Prussia, purposely to inquire of Government, whether any thing could be done for promoting the establishment of a Bible Society, for the Austrian States. I farther pointed out to the Prince the great need there existed for the labours of such an Institution, among so many nations subject to Austria. His Excellency replied, "that, though it was a general practice in the Catholic Church, not to put the Bible into the hands of every one, yet he knew of no obstacle to the free circulation of the New Testament." I answered, that the rules of the Society might be so expressed, as to grant a more general circulation of the New Testament among Roman Catholics, without restraining the free dissemination of the Bible among other religious confessions. He then begged me to draw out a plan for the proposed Institution, with my views on the utility of such a Society, for the Austrian empire; to endeavour to have it ready for Saturday next, on which day be invited me to dine with him, at his villa; and to bring the plan along with me, "Because," said the Prince, "His Majesty is to return to town, the beginning of next week, and I desire to have the plan ready to lay before him." I then took my leave of His Excellency, having put into his hand two small pieces in German, and in English, on the object and progress of Bible Societies, and, returning to my lodgings, commenced my labours.

By the information I had collected, during my journey from the shores of the Black Sea to this capital, and the additional particulars obtained since my arrival, I found myself in a manner prepared for the critical and difficult task which the Minister had laid upon me. I have therefore drawn out a memorial, on the design and success of Bible Societies, in general, and on the need and utility of such an Institution for the States of Austria, in particular, subjoining a plan for an Austrian National Bible Society. This, Mr. Kopitar has most obligingly translated into German; and, this afternoon, I hope it will meet with the approbation of the Prime Minister. However, let us rejoice with trembling; God only can remove the many difficulties which still lie in the way, and perfect that which has been thus promisingly begun.

Pages 89–94

Letter of Rev. Robert Pinkerton

Vienna, August 28, 1816

In my letter from Doobosary, I communicated to you the facts I had collected, in Bessarabia, respecting the scarcity of the Holy Scriptures, among the Wallachians, Moldavians, and Bulgarians: I also gave you some account of the arrangements I had been enabled to make in Kischenau, for their relief. In this letter, I intend to lay before you the result of my further researches into the state of the word of God, particularly among the tribes of Slavonian origin, situated between the Euxine and the Adriatic ...

The furnishing of the Albanians with a New Testament at least, in their own language, is an object highly worthy of the attention of the British and Foreign Bible Society. This nation occupies a great part of ancient Illyricum and Epirus, and speaks a language which seems to have no grammatical affinity with the Slavonian, Turkish, Greek, or Latin, languages. Most of the Albanians are professed Christians, belonging to the Greek communion; others are so deeply sunk in ignorance of the principles of Christianity, that they have embraced the Mahomedan faith. Their service is performed in the Greek language, which is quite unintelligible to the people, and even to most of their priests. They have still no part of the word of God in their own tongue; their number is not accurately ascertained, but they are reckoned at between 8 and 900,000 souls. After much inquiry, I find, that a translation of the New Testament into the Albanian, might be executed by some person or persons in the Ionian Islands. I have no doubt, from the conversations I have had with some intelligent Albanians here, that persons, competent to the task, are to be found there. The work ought to be executed under the superintendence of one of the most learned and respectable of the Albanian Bishops; and the expense, both of translation and printing, must be defrayed by the British and Foreign Bible Society. Or, should a Bible Society be established in one of the Ionian Islands, the giving to the Albanians a New Testament in their own tongue, would certainly become an object worthy of its earliest and most zealous efforts. It is true, very few of the people, comparatively, can read; but, not to mention that they might thus be excited to learn what an invaluable treasure would an Albanian Testament be for their numerous priests alone, the greater part of whom are doomed to read the service of their church, during their whole lives, in a language they do not understand! Should this work be undertaken, it ought to be printed with Greek characters; for the Greek alphabet, with the addition of a very few sounds, is by far the best for expressing the Albanian language; and by employing the Greek, instead of the Latin, alphabet, all who can read among them would be able at once to use your Albanian Testament.

Pages 94–96

Letter of Rev. Robert Pinkerton and Project for and Austrian Bible Society

Vienna, September 1, 1816

From my last of the 24th ult. you would see the state of forwardness in which our efforts were, to promote the formation of a Bible Society for Austria. On the day on which that was written, I dined at Prince Metternich's, with Count Stadion, Minister of Finance, and several other noblemen, to whom the Prince kindly recommended me. After dinner, I conversed with His Highness on the subject of the proposed Society, and presented him with the Plan for it, which I had prepared, according to his request. ...

Project of an Austrian Bible Society, presented to Prince Metternich, in Vienna, August 24, 1816.

The most successful means for promoting the best interests of society, have, when discovered, been often found to be no less simple in their nature than powerful in their effects. On contemplating their character, we are led to wonder and regret, that mankind should have remained so long ignorant of such pure and efficient methods of promoting the welfare of the human race. Such is the case with reference to Bible

Societies, in which the simplicity of their principle, and the efficiency of their operations, have excited the admiration of mankind, and combined to scatter many solid blessings among the nations of the earth.

After describing the origin and progress of the British and Foreign Bible Society, and of the different Bible Societies which have emanated from it, together with the patronage extended to them by the Sovereigns of the countries in which they are established, the author thus proceeds:

The establishment of a National Bible Society in Vienna, for Austria, and the numerous nations and tribes subject to her Government, is an event towards which every friend of this cause in Europe, and the Committee of the British and Foreign Bible Society, in particular, look forward with the highest expectations. Such an Institution, among so many millions of Christians, of different confessions, who have the happiness of living under the benign and paternal government of Francis the Second, promises much, not only for promoting a more general distribution of the Holy Bible, and particularly of the New Testament, among the Members of the National Catholic Church, but also for extending the same benefit to so many millions of Bohemians, Slovaks, Servians, Poles, Albanians, Croatians, Carniolans, and others, of Slavonian origin, the greater proportion of whom belong either to the Greek or Protestant churches, and among all whom there exists a lamentable scarcity of the word of God. A copy of the authorized version of the Catholic Bible, in the Polish language, is not to be obtained for money, either in Poland or Galicia; and among the five millions of Servians, of whom two millions belong to Austria, the Bible is rarely to be found, even in the hands of the clergy; and this applies still more strongly to the remaining three millions of Servians, under the dominion of the Turks. The Croatians, who consist of about 900,000 souls, have, to this day, no part of the Holy Scriptures in their language, except the Gospels for Sundays and Holy days: and the Albanians have no portion whatever of the word of God at all, in any language which they understand. Much good is therefore to be expected from the dissemination of the Holy Scriptures, not only among these nations, but also among many other tribes without the borders of the empire, who, professing the Christian faith, under the dominion of the Turks, are unable in their present circumstances, to obtain copies of the Sacred Writings, even for the purpose of supplying their churches and priests. Such, for instance, is the lamentable condition of most of the Wallachians, Moldavians, and Bulgarians, the former of whom speak one language, and possess a version of the Bible in their language, but which is so scarce, that it is not to be obtained for money. For that part of the nation connected with Russia, provision is now making; but for the millions of Wallachians and Moldavians under the Austrian Government, nothing has yet been done.

Not to particularise other important spheres of operation for such an Institution in other quarters of the Austrian empire, it is clearly to be seen, from what has been stated, that no Society in Europe, except the Russian, has such an extensive field to cultivate, as that which the Austrian Bible Society would have. Should it, therefore, please His Imperial Majesty to grant his gracious permission to the establishment of a National Bible Society for Austria, on the principles contained in the following Plan, the British and Foreign Bible Society would most willingly contribute pecuniary assistance, according to their abilities, should this aid be deemed necessary, both to lay the foundation of the Institution, and to aid it in its future labours, for *promoting a more general circulation of the Holy Scriptures, without note or comment*, in the different languages spoken among the thirty millions of people subject to the Government of Austria.

14th Report, 1818

Pages 112–113

No. XLVIII, Letter from the secretaries of the Malta Bible Society, William Jowett, Isaac Lowndes, and Cleardo Naudi

Malta, May 27, 1817

We are directed by our Committee to acquaint you with the formation of the Malta Bible Society, and to forward to you a copy of our Rules and Regulations. From our second rule, you will perceive that we are united with you, and with all Bible Societies, in the fundamental principle of distributing the Holy Scriptures, without note or comment.

The Committee might expatiate largely upon those extensive duties which lie before them; comprehending, perhaps, at no very distant period, the translation and circulation of the Holy Scriptures among people of many languages and tongues. They might also contemplate, with glowing hopes, that share of success which the Malta Bible Society is probably destined to enjoy in the diffusion of sacred knowledge throughout the earth. ...

Pages 112–113

No. L., Letter from the Rev. W. Jowett

Malta, June 10, 1817

From my correspondents in the Ionian Islands, I often receive some account of the circulation of the Greek Scriptures. I am sorry, however, to find, that the sale of them is difficult to effect; and thus it is natural to expect it should be, till men learn fully to prize the true riches.

15th Report, 1819

Pages lxxi–lxxii

The Malta Bible Society, formed on the 26th of May, 1817, constitutes the principal centre of all the operations which are going forward in this quarter. Aided with a grant from the British and Foreign Bible Society, of 500*l.*, together with more than 6000 copies of the Scriptures, in nineteen languages, this Society has opened an intercourse with the Bible Societies in Petersburg, Calcutta, and Bombay; and its proceedings, which appear to be conducted with great judgment, have been attended with good success, not only within the Island, but also in the Ionian Islands …

A Bible Society has also been formed in Smyrna, from the operations of which, much good is anticipated.

16th Report, 1820

Pages lxviii–lxix

The formation of the Ionian Bible Society at Corfu, is an event to which your Committee attach very great importance. It took place on the 20th of last July, in the midst of an Assembly, consisting of Baron Theotoky, President of the Senate (who was appointed its President,) the Greek Bishop Macarius, with a respectable train of his Clergy; the Catholic Vicar-General, with several of his fellow Priests, the Senators of the Ionian State, the Members of the Tribunal of Justice, and many other Gentlemen, "who," (says Dr. Pinkerton) "taken collectively, presented a most respectable assembly of persons of different nations, and belonging to various Christian communions." The zeal of the Meeting was attested by a contribution on the spot, amounting to 1025 dollars, about 250*l*. sterling.

At Constantinople arrangements have been completed by the active and judicious exertions of Dr. Pinkerton, for a version of the whole Bible into Modern Greek, a translation of the New Testament into the Albanian language; and other undertakings, which, it is hoped, may eminently conduce to the dissemination of the word of God among the Christian inhabitants of the Turkish Empire. When it is considered that the plague raged with extraordinary violence during the time of Dr. Pinkerton's continuance at Constantinople, and that he was not infrequently exposed to the danger of infection, your Committee cannot too warmly admire the good Providence of God, which shielded him against the attacks of that destructive pestilence, and enabled him, while surrounded with so many perils, to accomplish so much for the propagation of Divine Truth.

Page xciv

Of the works now in the course of preparation, the principal are: ...

11. A translation of the New Testament into the ALBANIAN, at Constantinople.

Pages 9–10
Letter from Robert Pinkerton

Corfu, July 24, 1819

On the 20th inst. in the evening, we had the satisfaction of seeing upwards of 100 individuals meet in a large hall of the palace of his highness Baron Theotoky, for the purpose of laying the foundation of the Ionian Bible Society. ...

The immediate field of the Society's labours will be the Seven Islands, containing a population of about 200,000 souls. But the exertions of the Institution are meant to be directed to a much greater distance; for, according to the first article of the statutes, the object of the Society is defined to be, " The circulation of the Holy Scriptures, without note or comment, to the greatest possible extent, but especially in the Ionian Islands, and other parts of Greece." The Committee intend therefore to come into immediate correspondence with their brethren in every part of Greece and Albania, and invite them to a cordial co-operation, as far as local circumstances will admit.

Pages 15–16
Letter from Robert Pinkerton

Constantinople, Sept. 25, 1819

Through the merciful protection of God I have at length reached the capital of the Ottoman empire, after a tedious passage of thirty days from Athens. ...

From Athens we directed our course for the coast of the Morea; and, after standing two days' quarantine, landed on the small island of Paros. Contrary winds detained us four days more at that place. This time I employed in collecting information respecting the three islands, Paros, Hydra, and Specia, whose inhabitants are so distinguished in the present day by the numbers of their fine ships, and the extensile commerce they carry on to every quarter of the Mediterranean. What was my surprise, however, when I discovered that the Hydriates, Speciates, and Pariotes were not Greeks, as I had repeatedly read, but Albanians! Our modern Greek Testaments, therefore, can be of little use to them; as the greater part of the men speak more or less the Romaic or modern Greek; yet the language Spoken in their families, and commonly among themselves, is, the Albanian. However, their dialect of it is greatly mixed with Turkish and Greek words and idioms. They told me that it differs very considerably from the Albanian spoken at Jannina. They all belong to the Greek church, and are in the same deplorable state of ignorance about religion as their brethren in the mountains of Epirus. When, in addition to this, we take into consideration, that not merely the inhabitants of ancient Illyria and Epirus speak the Albanian, but that one-third of the inhabitants of Athens, a great part of the population of Attica and of the Morea are also Albanians, and speak the same language, less or more corrupted, the vast importance of a version of the Holy Scriptures in the most commonly understood dialect of that language will more forcibly appear. Of late years, the inhabitants of Hydra and Specia have acquired great wealth by their commercial concerns; but, until the language of their family circles become a written language, and the Sacred Writings are to be read in it, they never can make any lasting advances in genuine civilisation. I found the Pariotes a race of the most ignorant, rude, and barbarous people that ever I was among. How much they need the humanising principles of the Gospel!

Page 18
Letter from Robert Pinkerton

Constantinople, Oct. 15, 1819

It has been my constant endeavour, in the interviews which I have had with the leading men, both clergy and laity, of the Christian population of this city, to give correct views of the object and principles of our Institution, and to produce a union of sentiment among them respecting the different undertakings we had in view, for the temporal and eternal benefit of the Greeks, Armenians, Albanians, and other Christian inhabitants of the Turkish dominions.

Pages 22–23
Letter from Robert Pinkerton

Constantinople, Oct. 25, 1819

One important business has followed so closely upon another, during the short time of my visit to this City, that I have had to labour almost night and day, in order to follow up, with calm and dispassionate investigation, the different subjects which have presented themselves for my consideration. Among these the two following are none of the least momentous: indeed, the first—a translation of the New Testament into the Albanian language, has entwined itself about my heart for these several years past, in such a way that I literally could not get rid of it. And though at Corfu the prospect began to open, and all the hopes of realisation to cheer, yet nothing decisive was there effected. No—I must first visit Athens, learn the vast extent of the Albanian population, suffer the most unkind, and even cruel treatment from the Albanians of Paros, in order rightly to understand the importance of this work, and the great need there was for losing no time in getting it undertaken, for the sake of the numerous tribes of Albanians, who have spread themselves far and wide in the ancient countries of Illyria, Epirus, Macedonia, and Greece. I have now found the man who, I hope, is destined to bestow the great blessing upon his brethren, of giving them the New Testament in their native tongue. His name is Evangelos Mexicos. He has been very highly recommended to me by some of the first dignitaries of the Greek Communion here, as a person eminently qualified for the work. He has already written a grammar in his native tongue, which he showed me.

He is well known to the Greek Patriarch of Constantinople, who has also highly approved of the undertaking, and has promised to send for one or two ecclesiastics well skilled in the Albanian language, with a view to aid Dr. Mexicos in his labours, and render the version as perfect as possible before it is put to the press. We propose to print it with the text of Hilarion's translation, in parallel columns. This will render it more useful in the first instance, as there are such a number of Albanians who are buy imperfectly acquainted with the modern Greek, and of Greeks who understand but imperfectly the Albanian. These will more easily learn to read and understand the precise truths of the Gospel, when presented to them in the two languages, than in either of them separately. He has already translated the 5th chapter of Matthew, and the 1st chapter of St. John's Gospels, and presented me with a copy of them, as the first fruits of this important undertaking ...

May the Almighty direct the decisions of your Committee in the weighty matters I have laid before them! And may the name of our Redeemer be glorified in them, and in all that is attempted by their and your devoted humble Servant.

Page 25
Letter from Robert Pinkerton

Constantinople, October 27, 1819

... The Patriarch Gregory received me with many demonstrations of kindness, and expressed his regret at my being about to leave them so soon. ... I next gave him my agreement with Dr. Mexicos, the Albanian translator. The Patriarch condescended to read that also with seeming interest, and promised to give this work, which he considers of great necessity, every possible support. He further gave his unqualified approbation of the version in Turkish with Greek characters; and finally expressed a desire, that the blessing of the Most High might rest on all these undertakings, which were likely to prove so conducive to the glory of God, and the best interest of the nations for whom they are intended.

17th Report, 1821

Pages 64–67
From a Clergyman travelling in Syria

Constantinople, October 23, 1820

When I look back on my journey, I am constrained to confess that the Lord has indeed been peculiarly gracious to me. Not one untoward accident, not one day's illness, have I been called to suffer, throughout the whole of it. By land and sea, through the fatigues of the desert and the perils of the deep, my God has attended me, and been my guardian and preserver. Oh! May His past mercies ever dwell in my thankful remembrance; and may I evince my gratitude, by renewed devotedness of spirit and body to Him, in whose service I have the high honour and privilege to be employed!

Mr. Leeves is not yet arrived. I rejoice in the prospect of having a companion and co-labourer here. I am about to take lodgings in the Fanál, or Greek Quarter, on the other side of the Port; where I shall spend my winter in revising Hilarion's translation of the Scriptures, the greater part of which is completed. The printer is waiting anxiously for the types, which are not yet arrived. The Albanian translator has finished the new Testament, and has taken it to Salonica for revision.

From the Rev. H. D. Leeves, the Society's Agent at Constantinople

February 8, 1821

With respect to the Albanian Testament, the translation is finished, but Dr. Mexicos is gone to Salonica; as soon as he returns, which Hilarion has written to desire him to do, we must make an arrangement with a reviser. A very competent one is at present residing at the convent of the Patriarch of Jerusalem. In company with Hilarion and Mr. Connor, I have visited him and the patriarch of Constantinople, as well as the Archbishops of Mount Sinai and Salonica. ...

I have thus given you an account of the state in which the works, undertaken by Dr. Pinkerton, stand at present. I have already written to him, to put him in possession of the facts. The arrangements yet to be made, seem to me to be these: to provided a reviser for the Albanian Testament—a thing which is in fair train; to agree for the binding of the New Testament when it comes out, which cannot be for several months *at least;* and to provide another person instead of Petropolis, for the version of the Turkish Testament in Greek characters, which work cannot be undertaken until the corrected copy is sent to us.

18th Report, 1822

Page 50
Letter from Rev. H. D. Leeves

> *Therapia, Constantinople, July 25, 1821*
> I have just seen Hilarion, he thinks he shall be obliged to leave Constantinople for Ternova, in about a month of six weeks. ... I have also put in train the revision of the Manuscript of the Albanian Testament. I have commissioned Dr. Mexicos, to make an agreement with a learned priest for this purpose, whom we have before had in view.

Pages 51–52
Letter from Rev. H. D. Leeves

> *Odessa, November 12, 1821*
> I have taken measures, which I hope may meet with the approbation of the Committee, for the translation of the Old Testament, into the Albanian language. Hilarion has written to an Ecclesiastic at Salonica, whom he represents as very well qualified for the undertaking, and he proposed that this Ecclesiastic should come and reside with him at Ternova, for the execution of his labour. May it pleas the Almighty Disposer of events, that in the midst of the tumults of the world, our works may proceed, and may

be ready for the people for whom they are designed, when tranquillity is restored amongst them.

19th Report, 1823

No pertinent information

20th Report, 1824

Pages xliv–xlv

By the Ionian Bible Society many copies of the Scriptures have been distributed in the various islands. The President of that Institution, Baron Theotoky, has visited this country, and conferred with your Committee. Since his return to Corfu he has written to your President, and observed, "For these ten centuries past, it has been supposed in Greece, that an entire translation of all the books of Holy Writ into our dialect, was a work which could not possibly be accomplished. It is only since the British and Foreign Bible Society favoured us with the transmission of the Modern Greek Testament, that it has been considered practicable to procure a version of the whole Bible, and to become acquainted with its contents. When all these circumstances are duly considered, you will, my Lord, easily conceive how great a value we attach to the gift we have just received, (1,000 Modern Greek Testaments) as well as to those which you formerly made."

Pages xlvii–xlviii

From Adrianople, a physician writes, that he had sold fifty-seven copies; and requests 200 Ancient and Modern Greek Testaments, together with some in the Slavonian, Arabic, Persian, and Turkish languages.

The translation of the Albanian Gospels has been completed, and the copy forwarded to Corfu for the purpose of revision and printing.

Death has removed the original translator, and the two priests who had been selected for the purpose of revising the version; but others properly qualified for the task have been found; and Mr. Lowndes writes, that the work had been examined by four Albanians, who all agreed in stating that the sense was well given.

The principal subject which has engaged the attention of Mr. Leeves, has been the printing of Hilarion's version of the whole Bible in Modern Greek. Difficulties and delays have occurred; but these, however painful, may eventually prove beneficial, as tending to the appearance of the work in the most perfect form.

To Lord Strangford your Society is under the greatest obligations for his unwearied kindness, and for the manner in which he has used the influence of his exalted station, in endeavouring to promote your object. Your President has been requested to convey the sense which has been entertained of the kindness of his lordship. ...

In European Turkey a tour has been performed by your agent, Mr. Barker. He proceeded from Constantinople to Adrianople, and found the greatest scarcity of the Scriptures prevailing in those parts. Portions only of them are to be found in the hands of the priests, either printed or in manuscripts.

Page 70
Letter from Rev. H. D. Leeves

Constantinople, June 5, 1823

One thousand Armenian Testaments arrived from Venice, and a supply of Greek and Italian Bibles from Malta; so that when the books in Greek and Turkish-Armenian arrive from Odessa, I shall be well supplied. ... Another copy is making of the Albanian New Testament, to be put into the hands of the reviser, as soon as a proper one is found. I have written to Salonica on the subject.

21st Report, 1825

Pages xxxvii–xxxviii
Ionian Islands

From the Rev. Isaac Lowndes, Secretary of the Ionian Bible Society, a statement of its proceedings has been received. ... The revision of the entire Albanian New Testament is completed; and the Gospel of St. Matthew has been printed and put in circulation. Mr. Lowndes has mentioned, that a priest of this nation had called upon him to request a copy, saying, that he had received accounts from his country that many there, were anxious to have the work. With regard to the publication of this Gospel, your Committee record with gratitude the following Resolution of the Ionian Bible Society:

> That all expenses incurred by printing, binding, &c. the Gospel of St. Matthew in the Modern Greek and Albanian languages, and what has been paid to Gregory, Archbishop of Negropont, for his labours in revising Dr. Mexico's work, or to be paid hereafter to him for the version of the whole New Testament

in the Albanian language, be borne by the Ionian Bible Society.

To Mr. Lowndes also, as well as to your Librarian, your Committee deem it right to express their gratitude for the important services rendered by them in connexion with this version.

Page lxix
The following works are now executing on the Society's account: ...

Albanian and Modern Greek New Testament, printing at Corfu

Pages 68–72
Letter from Robert Pinkerton

Stoke Newington, September 20, 1824
My being obliged to abandon my tour into Greece and Turkey, and return home, proved a sharp trial to me at the first; but, by degrees, I found my mind reconciled to that which I had not strength of body to perform, and was enabled to acquiesce in it, as the will of God, clearly indicated in his providential dealings towards me. Though I was not permitted to visit Corfu, yet I exchanged several letters with Mr. Lowndes on the affairs of the Ionian Bible Society, the printing of the Albanian and Greek Scriptures, &c. &c. which have already procured from Mr. Lowndes special replies to my suggestions and queries; and these I hope will enable your Committee to determine, with greater facility, what steps are proper to be taken for the completion of these important works. On the 23d of June I parted with my Malta friends, and embarked in the packet for England, in a state of great debility; but the sea air and northern winds, with which

we were favoured nearly the whole way home, tended much to brace and strengthen me.

22nd Report, 1826

Pages xxxv– xxxvi

Malta – Greece

In connexion with the Ionian Bible Society, your Committee may observe, that they continue under obligations to its secretary, the Rev. I. Lowndes, for his attention to the Albanian version. The Gospel of St. Matthew, printed and bound at the expense of the Ionian Bible Society, has been distributed and received with the greatest joy; so that whenever the Gospel for the day occurs in St. Matthew, it is regularly read in the churches from this new version. Another person has reported, that, when the people heard that they should soon have a portion of the New Testament in their own language, they were quite in raptures; and from the report of the Ionian Bible Society, the following extract may be taken: —

The Albanian dialect had never been brought to a written standard till the Committee accomplished it, and printed the Gospel of St. Matthew. By this measure Albania may be regarded as a conquest in favour of the word of God; and the inhabitants, who have lived so many years in ignorance of the Gospel, begin now to read for themselves, or with the assistance of others, that book which contains it in their own language. The printing of the entire New Testament in Albanian and modern Greek commenced in January last.

Page lxviii
The following works are now carrying on: ...
Albanian and Modern Greek Testament

23rd Report, 1827

Pages xli–xlii
Malta – Corfu

From Corfu, the Rev. Mr. Lowndes writes, "The printing of the Albanian and Modern Greek goes on well. The Testament is more than half completed. The Scriptures continue to be distributed in the island; and latterly many volumes have been sold by a Jew of Corfu, who has been twice to Cephalonia, for the purpose of disposing of the sacred merchandise." Zante has been visited by Mr. Lowndes, and arrangements made for visiting the villages in that island.

Pages 59–60
Letter from Rev. H. D. Leeves

Constantinople, November 7, 1826
I am sorry to say I hear of no commencement of the printing of the Jewish Spanish Testament at Corfu, and the press there is in general so sluggish in its operations (being occupied also with other works, among others our Albanian New Testament) that I fear much time may elapse ere it be executed.

Pages 65–67
Letter from Rev. H. D. Leeves

Constantinople, January 18, 1827

Havsa, a small town, six hours from Baba Eskisi, has only about 30 Greek families, who are without church or priest, and, what is rare in the province of Romelia, speak no language but the Turkish. I found here, as masters of a khan, two Albanians, (individuals of which active and enterprising nation are often found in similar situations throughout Romelia), who had heard of the stir produced in Adrianople by Mr. Wolff's visit, and thought the circulation of the Scriptures had been stopped. I told them this was not the case; and my own little stock of New Testaments being exhausted, directed them to apply to Mr. Schnell for a copy, which they promised they would when they went to Adrianople ...

On [November] 17th, I left Adrianople for Ternovo, but was obliged to return thither on the 20th, from the affairs connected with the Jews, of which I gave you a detail in my last. This matter being arranged, I again left Adrianople on the 22d, and the next evening reached Iamboli for the second time. ... Iamboli is a town consisting of about 2000 houses, half Turkish, and the other half Bulgarian, with a few families of Jews. I found at the khan an Albanian doctor, who had come hither to vaccinate the children of Iamboli. He said he had vaccinated about an hundred at this town, and 1000 at Selimnia, where he is established. Before his arrival at Selimnia, three or four years ago, the practice of vaccination was scarcely known.

Pages 77–78
Extracts from Benjamin Barker's Journal

The pashalic of Thessalonica embraces five provinces… It is governed by a pasha of three tails, who has his musselim, or lieutenant, and about 3000 Turkish and Greek Albanian troops, and a civil court, composed of a mulla, cadi, and the ayans. …

Before the revolution, the Greeks enjoyed apparent independence and some consideration; but the cruelties exercised by Aboul Nabout on them in 1822 and 3, greatly depressed them, and they are now much cast down; for he not only killed and tormented them, but deprived them of all their wealth, and reduced them to misery. The present pasha, an Albanian, has been, comparatively speaking, extremely mild to them, so that they begin again to breathe a little.

24th Report, 1828

Pages liv–lv
Corfu

Under the kind superintendence of the Rev. Isaac Lowndes, at Corfu, the New Testament in the Albanian and Modern Geek has been finished. Opportunities have not as yet offered for any effective circulation of this work. One of his correspondents, however, writes to him, speaking of a minister of religion; "I observed this reverend priest felt great pleasure when I informed him, as far as I could, respecting the formation and progress of the British and Foreign Bible Society, and of Bible Societies in all the world; but he felt unmeasurable and unspeakable joy when he received the word of our Saviour in a language understood by his flock." It will be remembered that the Scriptures have never before been translated into the Albanian language.

25th Report, 1829

Pages lii–liii

Another extract from the last of Mr. [Benjamin] Barker's letters, though of considerable length, will require no apology.

> The Rev. Mr. [Jonas] King, of America, who is just arrived here from the Morea and Greek islands, informed me that the schools now establishing in those parts are in great want of books, and will gladly and thankfully receive the New Testament as a school-book. It is his opinion, that we should avail ourselves of this opening to furnish all the schools with the word of God gratis, for the poverty of the country requires this of us, and such an opportunity may not present itself hereafter. In short, all the Greeks now readily receive the New Testament; and where poverty really exists, we ought not, I think, to deprive a family of the word of life; but, on the contrary, see that every one has possession of it. In truth, Mr. King's opinion is, that the generosity of the Bible Societies should now be largely manifested, and that a grant of several thousand Testaments should be made, to be distributed among the numerous poor Greeks in the Morea and Greek islands; not, indeed, to be distributed by every body, but by judicious Missionaries and Agents, or by people particularly known to them, who will make it a practice to visit the indigent families where the word of God will not only be gladly received, but can also be read. Mr. King's investigation in the tour he has just

performed, has led him to conclude, that at the present moment the most effectual spiritual succour that can be carried to that country is the Holy Scriptures, and that the ground is prepared to receive them.

Pages 75–76
Letter of Robert Pinkerton

Paris, September 24, 1828
... I have been at Versailles, and had two long interviews with Dr. Zohrab, our Armenian translator, and editor, on this subject. I found him revising the Epistle to the Galatians for the second edition of his Modern Armenian Testament, now about half printed off. After some consideration, he declared himself willing to become the Editor of the Armenian Bible, according to the laws of our Society. This also gives me an opportunity of proposing to the Committee what has often been on my mind during this journey, viz. to authorise Mr. Lowndes, and the Committee of the Ionian Bible Society, to get the Book of Psalms translated into the Albanian. Probably the Albanian Bishop, who has revised and edited the Testament in this language, will be the ablest person to undertake this work; and the types that were used for printing the Testament at Corfu will serve for printing it also. To render it more useful, Hilarion's version of the Modern Greek Psalms should be printed along with it, in parallel columns.

26th Report, 1830

Pages liii–liv
Your Agent [H. D. Leeves] has been kindly received by the Governor, Sir F. Adam, and met with a renewed cordial reception from the Rev. Mr. Lowndes, who, as it appears in

the above extracts, takes a very lively interest in the work. From the correspondence of this gentleman the ensuing passages are taken, relative to the Jewish-Spanish and Albanian New Testaments. ... Of the Albanian [he writes]:

> In a letter I had from Dr. Korck, at Syra, I learn that the Albanian Testaments sent thither had been all disposed of. He requested an additional supply, which I have sent him. There are also three Americans here at present, Messrs. Anderson, Robertson, and Smith, by whom I hope to send some more. Thus, though Albania Proper is for the present closed against us, the word of God in that language finds Its way to Albanians; and I trust God will bless the reading of it to them.

Page lvii

Of the lamentable scarcity of entire Bibles in Greece, a judgment may be formed, when Dr. Korck states, that he has for two years been looking for a copy, but in vain. It is gratifying to learn from him that inquiries are frequently made for the Old as well as the New Testament. Arabic, Turkish, and Albanian Scriptures have been forwarded to Dr. Korck, various opportunities presenting themselves to him for their distribution.

27th Report, 1831

Page xliv

In a letter dated February 27, 1831, [Rev. H. D. Leeves] writes,

> I am now preparing for my departure to Greece, and hope to start by the middle of next month, taking Zante and Patros in my way to Napoli; from whence I hope to visit several of the islands of the Archipelago,

and perhaps Smyrna, and on my return go through some other parts of the Morea ...

The Rev. J. Lowndes, the Secretary of the Ionian Bible Society, has since informed your Committee that Mr. Leeves actually sailed from Corfu for the Morea on the 18th of April.

Page 85
Letter from Benjamin Barker

Constantinople, May 20, 1830
I am now, thank God, quietly settled with my family at this place, and intend to remain here as long as it will be necessary for me to put our concerns in the same train as heretofore. ...

I am now happy in informing you of the pleasing change that has taken place in the issue of the Holy Scriptures in this capital. No less than 1278 volumes have been delivered from this depot in the course of four months. Of these, 172 have been sold at Caesarea, in Asia Minor, and 60 volumes were bought and carried to Albania, by a Greek, to distribute amongst the poor in that country. Besides these, 220 volumes have been sold by a Greek bookseller, at the Fanal, or principal residence of the Greeks here; making, altogether, 1498 volumes of the Sacred Scriptures sold.

28th Report, 1832

Page liii
Greece

At Argos a new school has been erected, at the expense of government, capable of holding 500 boys; and Mr.

[Leeves] appropriated to its use 100 Testaments. Two visits were made to Napoli; and Mr. L. states, alluding to a previous grant by Mr. Barker:

> I made them a fresh donation of sixty copies, which are not to be alienated from the establishment; and I did this the more willingly, as about 120 soldiers of the regular troops are in the habit of attending the master for two hours daily, as often as their other duties allow them, to learn reading, writing, and arithmetic; and these Testaments will serve as their reading books. On my return to Napoli, six weeks afterwards, I had the pleasure of finding these books in regular use, and that, in addition to the soldiers above mentioned, about forty individuals of the corps of artisans were attendants at the school. A separate school had in this interval been formed in another corps of troops, whose discipline was somewhat different from the regulars, and their dress the Albanian, and which was designed as a model corps, after which the other irregular troops were to be trained. To them I sent a present of 30 New Testaments.

29th Report, 1833

Pages l–lii

In the course of the summer Mr. Leeves made a short visit to Albania, and, with an abstract of his journal, your Committee conclude their notice of his proceedings. He first visited Prevesa, and during his stay of two days sold 50 Testaments and Psalters at low prices, and presented 36 to school, besides leaving a supply with the vice-consul for sale. Mr. L. likewise visited Vonizza, on the opposite side of the gulf: the fortress is occupied by Greek troops, and about 700 families live in cabins in much misery: 60 New Testaments were left here. At Canza, a little village just rebuilt, and consisting of wattled cabins, the priest, and a few others, purchased copies, and some were left for inhabitants, who were only just recovering from the grievous sufferings they had endured from the destruction of their houses by the Turkish soldiery. In Arta, containing a large Greek population, Mr. L. met with much success. He writes:

> Such was the anxiety of the people, amongst whom were several priests, to possess these books, which few of them had seen before, and which, from the lowness of the prices, they understood could only be so sold from disinterested motives, that I could have disposed of a much larger quantity of New Testaments, and of the smaller books, that I had with me; but I was obliged, however unwillingly, to retain a part for the other places which lay before me in my tour, and to send many away with the promise that a fresh supply should soon reach them. These I have forwarded by way of Prevesa.

At Yanina, containing a population of 15,000, Mr. Leeves could only afford to leave small supplies, but he observes:

> A strong desire was, however, shewn to obtain supplies; and I have been pleased to hear that the people are anxiously looking for the books I am preparing to send them. Some English gentlemen, who have since followed my route, have been questioned, both at Yanina and other places, whether they brought books with them, and when they promised supplies would arrive.

Through a Greek gentleman, whose residence is in the mountain of Zagori, but whom Mr. L. met in Yanina, a small supply was sent for the villages in that region. In each of these villages there are schools for reading and writing, and in several of them Hellenic schools. Mr. Clerici, Austrian vice-consul of Metzovo, has had considerable supplies forwarded to him for that town, and its two dependent villages, which lie among the mountains. Mr. L. visited the island of Larissa, and upon inquiring for the school, he writes:

> I found it crowded within with children and grown people, and surrounded by a number of villagers on the outside, who were assembled on the occasion of its being opened, and were viewing, with great curiosity and interest, the introduction of the new system. The master was extremely grateful for the books he obtained of me.

Mr. L. feels convinced that in Yanina and its vicinity a fair field is open in this country for future operations. The village of Dizitza, celebrated by Lord Byron for its noble scenery, was visited, a few copies (all that could be spared) were cheerfully bought, and the people received with satisfaction the intelligence that they would shortly be able to receive a further supply from Yanina. At Argyrocastro Mr. L. left a few more copies, and prepared the inhabitants for receiving more. In this place he says:

> I was received into the house of the bishop, with whom I passed agreeably a day and a half. He is a native of Scio, an intelligent man, and anxious for the improvement of this flock; and he willingly undertook to be the channel through which the Scriptures and other books, of which I brought specimens with me,

should be dispersed through his diocese. He ordered of me, for this purpose, 100 Ancient and Modern Greek Testaments, 200 Psalters, and 60 Albanian New Testaments.

In this place Mr. L. was likewise enabled to make some arrangement for the circulation of the Society's Albanian New Testament. After leaving Argyrocastro, Mr. L. visited Delvino, and thence returned to Corfu, much gratified and encouraged by his excursion.

Of the copies issued by Mr. Leeves, 1336 were supplies sent, after his return, to Yanina, Prevesa, Arta, and Argyrocastro.

30th Report, 1834

Page lviii

Mr. Leeves has requested 200 German Bibles for distribution among the Bavarians in Greece; and has furnished the following account of the issue of copies by him during the past year:

Up to the period of my leaving Corfu, in July last, I issued, during the year, 868 copies of Scriptures. Of these, 203 Greek New Testaments and 106 Psalters were issued for the use of schools in the islands of Corfu, Paxo, Ithaca, and Zante, and in Albania. Of the remaining copies, a considerable portion was put by me into the hands of Baron Theotoki, late president of the Ionian senate, who has been long an active distributor of the Scriptures. Before my departure he sent me 50 dollars, desiring of me a corresponding number of New Testaments, &c., in the Greek, Italian, French, and Albanian languages, at the reduced price at which we sold them at Corfu, which he intended to distribute in Corfu and Epirus, to such persons as were too poor to purchase them. I, of course, gladly supplied him with them, and put into his hands about 80 copies more in different languages without price, that his benevolent purpose might be more widely fulfilled.

31st–44th Reports, 1835–1848
No pertinent information

45th Report, 1849

Pages c–ci
Account of Mr. Barker

The distributions of the Scriptures have been principally confined to the Depots of Constantinople, Smyrna, and Adrianople; and extended by Missionaries to Salonica, Beyrout, Oroomiah, &c. &c. The good work was going on well at Salonica, by the aid of Messrs. Lord and Goldberg, and an Armenian placed there by the Rev. Mr. Schauffler. Mr. Lord writes me under date of the 19th February:

> I have just received an order from Larissa for 50 Hebrew Psalms, and the Armenian has also received an order for Scriptures from Yanina....

46th Report, 1850

Page lxxx
Turkey

On transmitting his accounts for the first half-year, Mr. Barker writes:--

A colporteur sent by the Rev. Mr. Homes, on joint account with me, to European Turkey, obtained, from sales of our Society's books only, the sum of 17£ 5s. 5d. These amounts, though not considerable, are satisfactory, inasmuch as they are proceeds from a country where people spend but very little money for books, and where formerly, we may safely say, none at all was spent in the purchase of the Scriptures.

47th Report, 1851

Pages lxxiii–lxxiv

Turkey

A firman has lately been issued by His Imperial Majesty the Sultan, confirming and enlarging the protection given to all his Protestant subjects throughout the Turkish Empire, and securing to them the full and free exercise of their religion. A document of greater interest and importance is rarely to be met with:

TRANSLATION OF THE FIRMAN OF HIS IMPERIAL MAJESTY SULTAN ABDUL MEDJID, GRANTED IN FAVOUR OF HIS PROTESTANT SUBJECTS

To my Vizier Mohammed Pasha, Minister of Police at my capital, the honourable minister and glorious counsellor, the model of the world, and regulator of the affairs of the community, who, directing the public interests with sublime prudence, consolidating the structure of the empire with wisdom, and strengthening the columns of its prosperity and renown, is the recipient of every grace from the Most High. May God prolong his glory.

When this sublime and august mandate reaches you, let it be known that,

Whereas, hitherto those of my Christian subjects who have embraced the Protestant faith have suffered inconvenience and difficulties, in consequence of their not being placed under a separate and special jurisdiction, and in consequence of the patriarchs and primates of their old creeds, which they have abandoned, naturally not being able to administer their affairs;

And whereas, in necessary accordance with my imperial compassion, which extends to all classes of my subjects, it is contrary to my imperial pleasure that any one class of them should be exposed to trouble;

And whereas, by reason of their faith, the above-mentioned already form a separate community; it is therefore my royal compassionate will, that, by all means, measures be adopted for facilitating the administration of their affairs, so that they may live in peace, quiet, and security.

Let then a respectable and trustworthy person acceptable to, and chosen by themselves, from among their own number, be appointed with the title of Agent of the Protestants, who shall be attached to the department of the Minister of Police.

It shall be the duty of the agent to have under his charge the register of the members of the community, which shall be kept at the Police. The agent shall cause to be registered therein all births and deaths in the community. All applications for passports and marriage licences, and special transactions of the community that are to be presented to the Sublime Porte, or to any other department, must be given under the official seal of this agent.

For the execution of my will, this my royal mandate and august command has been specially issued and granted from my Imperial Chancery.

Hence, thou the Minister above named, in accordance with the explanations given, will execute, to the letter, the preceding ordinance: except that as the collection of the capitation tax, and the delivery of passports, are subjected to specific regulations, you will not do anything contrary to them. You will not permit anything to be required of them on pretence of fees and expenses, for marriage licences, or registration.

You will see to it that, like the other communities of the empire, in all their affairs and in all matters appertaining to their cemeteries and places of worship, they shall have every facility and needed assistance. You will not permit that any of the other communities do in any way interfere with their right or with their religious concerns, and, in short, in nowise with any of their affairs, secular or religious, that thus they may be enabled to exercise the usages of their faith in security.

And it is enjoined upon you not to allow them to be molested an iota in these particulars or in any others, and that all attention and perseverance be put in requisition to maintain them in quiet and security; and, in case of necessity, they are permitted to make representations regarding their affairs through their agent to the Sublime Porte.

When this my imperial will shall be brought to your knowledge and appreciation, you will have this august edict registered in the proper department, and cause it to be perpetuated in the hands of the above-mentioned subjects, and you will see to it that its requirements be always executed in their full import.

Thus be it known to thee, and respect my sacred signet.

Written in the holy month of Moharrem, A.H. 1267 (Nov. 1850).

Given in the protected city of Constantinople.

48th Report, 1852
No pertinent information

49th Report, 1853

Pages lxxvi–lxxvii
Turkey

Your Committee had for some time had it in contemplation to consider the present state of the Society's Agencies in Turkey and the Mediterranean, in connexion with the labours of the Society's Agents, Mr. Barker and Mr. Lowndes. ... They were, therefore, requested to prepare a scheme, for dividing and defining their respective districts, which was adopted by your Committee, subject to revision at the end of two years; it is as follows:

District proposed to be superintended by Mr. Barker:
Smyrna, as a Central Station.— Asia Minor, Constantinople, Turkish Armenia, Adrianople and Salonica, and all Bulgaria, the provinces of Servia, Wallachia and Moldavia,-- the Turkish islands, from the Dardanelles, as far as Rhodes; Trebizond and Erzeroom, as far as Ooroomiah and Jollimirk.

District proposed to be superintended by the Rev. I. Lowndes.
Malta, as a Central Station. — Northern Africa, including Oran, Algiers, Tunis, Morocco, &c.; Egypt; Syria, including Palestine; Greece, including the Greek Islands in the Archipelago and the Aegean Sea; the Ionian Islands, and the opposite coast of Albania; all which are open for the circulation of the Scriptures ...

Mr. Lowndes was directed to pay a visit, at least once in the course of the next two years, to the principal places comprised in his extensive sphere of labour. He was particularly requested to visit Greece... . He was also encouraged to visit the province of Albania, to ascertain the facilities which may there exist for the dissemination of the Scriptures, and the need there may be for printing a fresh edition of the Albanian New Testament.

50th Report, 1854

Page lxxiv
Malta, Greece, &c.

The Rev. Isaac Lowndes, the Society's Agent, has furnished the following general sketch of his operations during the year:—

> Albania seemed to have a claim to my first consideration, and I fully hoped to have gone thither, for the double purpose of endeavouring to put into circulation there the word of God, and of ascertaining what encouragement there may be for printing a second edition of the Albanian Testament, as the former one is exhausted. But the disturbed state of things connected with the Eastern question, by which Albania is materially affected, has prevented my visit thither hitherto; yet I still have this object in view, if it please God, whenever it may be practicable.
>
> With this Corfu stands in close connexion, and when I go thither it may be well for me to see that and some other of the Ionian Islands....

51st–52nd Report, 1855–1856
No pertinent information

53rd Report, 1857

Page cxxi

Malta, Greece, &c.

During the year, I have had correspondence or personal intercourse with one or more individuals at the following places:—Athens, Syra, Smyrna, Constantinople, Balaklava, Alexandria, Cairo, Corfu, Albania, Beyrout, Jaffa, Jerusalem, Salonica, Damascus, Aleppo, Mosul, Diarbekir, Algiers, Bona, Oran, Tunis and Naples. Friendly intercourse is maintained in all these places with persons who take an interest in our work, and the only one in which the word of God has not found entrance is Naples.

Pages cxxxv–cxxxvii

During the year Mr. Lowndes carried out the long-cherished intention of visiting Albania. The Committee have been anxious to ascertain whether, in the present state of that country, there is any scope for a further distribution of the Scriptures. The impressions of Mr. Lowndes were favourable to some fresh effort, and in consequence, and edition of the New Testament in parallel Greek and Albanian, is in course of preparation at Athens. The tour is thus described:—

I left in an Austrian steamer for Prevesa, where I had the pleasure of finding Mr. Saunders, the British Consul, who kindly afforded me all the facility I required in the prosecution of my journey. I took with me four cases of Scriptures in Greek and Albanian, for distribution in different places, and was absent on my tour ten days.

At Prevesa, there are two schools for boys, one of a higher, and the other of a lower order. In the former the attendance is small, but in the latter there are about two hundred scholars. The female school, under the direction of one of our former scholars, had but just commenced, and about thirty scholars were in attendance.

From Prevesa I proceeded to Arta, where there are also two schools of a higher and lower order for boys, in extent and in their general features much on a par with those at Prevesa. There is no female school here, though it is a town of considerable extent.

My next move was to Joannina, the principal town in Albania, and well known as the place where the celebrated Ali Pacha resided, exercised many acts of cruelty and ended his days. Here I visited many schools for the lower orders, and one for more advanced scholars. Most of them are numerously attended, some by as many as one hundred pupils and upwards, and at most of the schools in Prevesa, Arta and Joannina, commodious and suitable rooms have been expressly built. Wealthy Greeks, at different times, have left large sums of money for the purpose of education in Epirus, and thus the ground-work has been prepared. At Joannina, there is a large collection of costly instruments for experimental philosophy, which might be turned to good account, if efficient persons were appointed to make good use of them, but for want of this they are neglected. In Joannina I found two female schools directed, as stated above, by two mistresses. These are both for the lower classes of society, and one of them, attended by about one hundred and twenty girls, is the best school I have visited since I left Malta. The teacher is very efficient, and a portion of her time is devoted to instruction of a superior order.

The higher schools in Albania are, in all parts, conducted by efficient teachers, and the lower schools, professedly on the Lancasterian system, are taught by persons whose qualifications are sufficient, but for want of attention to system, the benefit is small. There is a general and lamentable want of books of all descriptions, even for the first elements; and the cases I took with me contained but a scanty supply where the deficiency was so great. I left one case of Scriptures at Prevesa, one at Arta, and two at Joannina. I found no disposition to purchase, and therefore had to dispose of all gratuitously. All the schools are under the management of committees, and in some instances, I left the books with these individuals,—in others, with the masters and mistresses. I am not certain that they will be put into general use in the schools, partly on account of the paucity of them, and partly on account of the general indifference that prevails and the want of energy in providing books. But the Scriptures I left may be read by those who can better understand them, and may be more likely to profit by them. Since my return to this place, I have received a letter from one of the persons to whom I consigned some of the books in Joannina, who tells me he has disposed of a number of them.

There are no school in Albania in which the Albanian language is taught; nor could this be expected in a country where schools are but few in number, and where no other book has ever been published in this language but the New Testament. At Prevesa it is but little spoken, something more at Arta, and still more at Joannina, and at the last-mentioned place I left the greatest number of Scriptures. In Upper Albania, opposite Panga &c, Albanian is the common language of the people, but I did not proceed farther than Joannina in that direction, as I did not consider it necessary, for it would have been a useless waste of time and expense; and in addition to this, every one assured me that travelling there is not safe at present, travellers being frequently robbed and kept as hostages, till they are redeemed by the payment of large sums of money.

I was happy to find the Albanian Testament is easily understood and valued. A pretty large community throughout the country speak the language, and the word of God, by this means, is accessible to them; and various considerations plead strongly for a second edition of the New Testament.

1. It is the only book that a large number of the inhabitants can understand, and on which they are likely to place value.

2. As it contains the truth of God, the propagation of it is highly necessary, for religious services in the churches are conducted in Ancient Greek which, in general, neither the priests nor the people understand, and consequently, the way of salvation is left in deep obscurity.

3. It is quite problematical how far the measures now to be adopted in Turkey will affect the East in general, and to what extent they may be felt in Albania, as well as in other places. In these parts ignorance prevails to a lamentable extent, and dissatisfaction with the present state of things is widely spread and often expressed. The Turkish population is very small in proportion to the Greek. Persons who reside in Joannina and have the means of ascertaining the fact, assured me, that in that town it is not more than about one in ten, and taking the whole county, not more than one in fifty. A slight turn of events may produce an extensive and permanent change in the country. Such a change

whatever might be its other features, could hardly fail of being favourable to the means of instruction and the spread of knowledge; and no knowledge is to be compared with that which the British and Foreign Bible Society has the means of providing, as this is able, when accompanied by the blessing of God, to make men wise to salvation through faith that is in Christ Jesus.

I consider, therefore, that measures should be adopted for printing another edition of the Albanian Testament.

54th Report, 1858
No pertinent information

55th Report, 1859

Pages 139–140
Turkey

The Committee attach immense importance to Turkey as a sphere of labour, and they are desirous that the action of the Society should be vigorous and expansive....

The vast extent of the Turkish dominions, stretching from the Pruth to the Tigris, bordering upon the Adriatic, the Mediterranean, the Euxine, the Red Sea, and the Persian Gulf; being in close proximity to Russia, Transylvania, Hungary, Galicia, Illyria, Dalmatia, Greece, Persia, and Arabia;—its enormous population, comprising in its European portion not fewer than sixteen million souls, and in its Asiatic territory an equal number, not including the five millions in Africa, that owe subjection to the Sultan's sceptre;—its variety of races, Mussulmen, Slavons, Albanians, Greeks, Armenians, Tartars, and

Jews; the appalling ignorance, the wretched fanaticism, the social degradation and misery that prevail, alleviated here and there, it is admitted, by a tone of religious thoughtfulness, earnest inquiry, and spiritual conversion, —all these circumstances combine to present, on behalf of Turkey, an appeal for sympathy and help, the urgency and importance of which it is impossible for the friends of the Bible to overestimate; convinced, as they must be, that the one great want of Turkey is the Bible—the truth which that Bible unfolds, and which the Holy Spirit graciously sanctifies to the salvation of the soul.

Pages 309–310
Domestic [Death of Robert Pinkerton]

And the honoured Pinkerton is no more ... By this event, the Committee feel themselves at fuller liberty to express their deep sense of the valuable services which he rendered to the Society during the protracted period of nearly forty-three years. ... The labours of Dr. Pinkerton spread over almost the whole of [Europe], nor did they cease until the powers of life and action were exhausted. ... Some of his visits extended to the countries bordering on the Mediterranean, where he laid the foundation of those Agencies which have ultimately proved so interesting in Greece, Turkey, and other parts of the East...."

56th Report, 1860

Pages 78–80
Turkey [Death of Benjamin Barker]

The close of the mortal career of Mr. Benjamin Barker, for thirty-nine years an Agent in the Levant, has deprived the Society of the services of one whose life has been devoted to the dissemination of the Scriptures ...

In 1824 another journey was undertaken to Aleppo: thence he proceeded to Damascus, Tiberias, Nazareth, and Jerusalem, returning along the coast to Beyrout; the transit to that place from Acre being accomplished in an open boat of the country, in consequence of a firman issued against him as a disseminator of the Scriptures.

Having crossed Mount Lebanon, and passed through Hens and Human, on the skirts of the Desert, he escaped the many dangers which daily threatened his life, and reached Aleppo in safety. After a period of most serious sickness, induced by anxiety, fatigue and exposure, Mr. Barker started for Smyrna, and encountered "perils on the sea" which again placed his life in jeopardy. Many evidences of the effects produced by the perusal of the Scriptures were incidentally revealed during the next few years, which were spent in visiting Macedonia, Thrace, Albania, Thessalonica, Seres, Adrianople, and other places of importance. ...

Mr. Barker's hand scattered more widely than any other the seed of Scripture truth. By his labours in the dissemination of the Scriptures "he, being dead, yet speaketh" to many sinners, of the only Saviour. Mr. Barker died on the 20th of September, 1859, calmly relying upon that 'Lamb of God, which taketh away the sin of the world.'"

57th Report, 1861

Page 108

Turkey [Appointment of Alexander Thomson]

Last year your Committee announced the decease of Mr. B. Barker, who had for a long period directed the operations of the Society in Turkey. ...The Committee have now the satisfaction of believing, that they have been guided to the selection of an individual well competent to assume the responsible position of your representative at Constantinople. The Rev. A. Thomson, who has entered upon the duties of that office, has resided for seventeen years in the Turkish capital, as a Missionary of the Free Church of Scotland to the Jews, and during that period has had ample opportunities of becoming intimately acquainted with the operations of your Society in the East. When the Constantinople Auxiliary Bible Society was formed, he was unanimously chosen to be the Secretary, and entered very zealously into plans for Scripture distribution in Stamboul and Pera. A proposed change on the part of the Free Church of Scotland, with regard to the Jewish Mission at Constantinople, led to a correspondence between your Committee and Mr. Thomson, which resulted in the transfer of his services, with the entire concurrence of his Committee at Edinburgh, to the British and Foreign Bible Society. The Committee are thankful that they have been enabled to secure an Agent for Turkey whose qualifications command their confidence. Mr. Thomson, by his knowledge of the languages, the habits, and the religious systems of the various nationalities comprised in the Turkish empire, brings to his new work advantages and facilities for the discharge of its duties to which considerable importance must be attached.

Page 120
Turkey [Report by Alexander Thomson]

If we now turn to European Turkey, the waste land is equally great. Bosnia, Herzegovina, Montenegro, Albania, and I may almost add Servia and Macedonia, and perhaps Thessaly too, have been but rarely visited, and are most of them without any regular Agency for the dissemination of the word of Life... In regard to some of these provinces, formidable difficulties lie before us. We as yet have not the word of God to offer them in their own language, or at least only a small part of it; and of course the preparation of it will involve much care, labour and expense, and much time. ... Still the cause of Bible circulation is so identified with the glory of God, and the best interests of man, that the object is worthy of all the exertions that can be made for its accomplishment; and I trust the Society will feel that no time should be lost in seeking to establish outposts in all these different localities. We shall not have the kind aid and valuable superintendence of missionaries in the regions to which I refer; but by sending thither the humble Colporteur, we shall ourselves make the best possible preparation, as repeated experience has shown, for the occupation of all these regions by the Missions of the Christian churches. "Pray ye, therefore, the Lord of the harvest, that he will send forth labourers into his harvest."

58th Report, 1862

Page 88
Turkey [O'Flaherty's Journal]

A few extracts from the journal of Mr. Philip O'Flaherty, of the Free Church of Scotland's Turkish Missions, will aid in forming some estimate of the effect of the Scriptures upon the minds of this people— ...

> Two years ago, I presented a copy of the New Testament to a certain well-disposed Pasha, who has such a love for the 'Blessed Book,' that he has furnished the grown-up members of his family with a copy each, and has even more than once requested me to visit that part of the country—Macedonia—and explain the book.

59th Report, 1863

Pages 122–123
Turkey [Death of Sultan Abdülmecid I]

Since your last Report, Divine Providence has removed the late Sovereign of the Turkish Empire. Through his liberal policy, facilities had been secured for promoting the work in which your Society has taken so large a share; while the concession which permitted a Mussulman to renounce his ancestral faith for the profession of Christianity, without injury to his person or loss of liberty, introduced a period in Turkish government which has tended materially to mitigate the intense prejudices that prevailed against the Gospel, and to dispose thoughtful Mohammedans to investigate the claims and character of the Bible. Some fears were entertained lest the present Sultan should wish to restrict, or even reverse, the religious toleration granted by his predecessor; but, to the present time, few, if any, indications of a reactionary policy are perceptible, and it is fervently hoped that in the future rule of this great Empire, no attempt may be made to return to principles so long enforced in the past administration of Turkey, and which were alike cruel persecuting and inexpedient.

60th Report, 1864

Page 104
Turkey – Circulation of Scriptures

The Greek issues exhibit a gratifying increase of 609 copies, among which are 27 with the Albanian language.

Page 115
Bosnia and Albania

One of the most interesting features of Dr. Thomson's Agency during the past year is a tour which he undertook through the provinces of Bosnia and Albania, with the view of ascertaining the spiritual condition of the inhabitants, and of judging for himself of the probable results of any efforts which your Society might make for the circulation of the Scriptures in these countries. Frequent letters were received by your Committee during Dr. Thomson's absence from Constantinople, all of which were full of interesting details, and led to the conviction that your enterprising Agent had been the means, under God, of opening a wide and effectual door for the entrance of the truth into a land hitherto shrouded in spiritual darkness, of which your Committee were most anxious to avail themselves. But he has, when furnishing his annual Report, gathered up the results of his journey in a manner so concise and satisfactory, not only as regards the geography and history of the country and the character of the people, but as regards the hopefulness of the field to be cultivated by the Lord's husbandmen, that it is felt to be best to allow him to record his own impressions in his own words. The perusal of the following details cannot fail of awakening Christian sympathy on behalf of these people in the minds of all who long for the extension of the Redeemer's kingdom, and pray from the heart, "Thy kingdom come."

Pages 115–119

A Report by Alexander Thomson

The Committee are aware that, on the very first survey of the important sphere to which I was called, when entrusted with my present office, I directed their attention to the provinces of Bosnia, Herzegovina, North and South Albania, and Thessaly amongst others, as urgently in need of the labours of the Society. In these extensive districts, embracing an area at least equal to that of all England and Wales, and a population of some three millions of souls, there is no missionary whatever, nor till last summer was there any Agent of the Society permanently resident. Even visits for evangelistic purposes had been few and far between, owing to the want of European conveniences, the wild character which still adheres in several districts to the general population, and especially their habit of going about fully armed, at least in Northern and Central Albania. Still Joannina had been visited once or twice by missionaries of various denominations, and especially by the Society's Agent for so many years for Malta and the coast of the Mediterranean, the Rev. Isaac Lowndes, whose zeal and energetic labours are too well known to require any eulogium from me. For Bosnia, Herzegovina, and Northern Albania, and I may add, Montenegro, nothing, so far as I was aware, had been done towards the introduction of the Word of God in the vernacular dialects, though inquiries made during my tour have elicited the

interesting facts—first, that the large distribution of
Turkish Scriptures to the soldiers during the Crimean war,
has resulted in the pretty wide-spread dissemination of
the New Testament over those districts from which the
regular troops were principally drafted, viz., Northern
and Central Albania; and second, that two eminent
ladies of literary distinction [Georgina Mackenzie and
Paulina Irby], who have for some time been cultivating an
acquaintance with those provinces, had distributed a good
many New Testaments in several towns of Servia, Bosnia,
Herzegovina and Montenegro. Still nothing has been done
in the least degree commensurate with the necessities of
such large and populous provinces, and as it was next to
impossible to find any one at Constantinople who could
afford the least reliable information about those districts—
their whole commercial relations being with Austria, either
by the coast of the Adriatic, or along the course of the Save
and the Danube—I felt it was indispensably necessary that
I should myself traverse these provinces, and endeavour to
open such communications as would lead to the diffusion
of the word of life among their interesting but untutored
population. I was thankful to find the Committee enter
at once and so heartily into my views, and grant me
permission to traverse these north-western provinces, as
far as my time would permit, or as I might find otherwise
practicable. I accordingly set out on this errand on the
28th of April, from Bucharest, and after spending a few
days at Belgrade, in making the necessary preparations, I
proceeded up the Save as far as Old Gradisca, then crossed
to the Turkish fortress of Berber, on the opposite bank,
and then by way of Banyalooka, Travnik, Seraievo, Mostar
and Gabella, traversed the Turkish provinces in the north
west, and arrived at the interesting old city of Ragusa. I

then proceeded by steamer to Bar or Antivari, the port of the important city of Scutari, the capital of northern Albania, with 60,000 inhabitants, where I spent a week, and then returning to Antivari, proceeded to Corfu, from whence I made an excursion to Joannina, where I also spent a week, returning to Corfu by way of Zitza, Argyro Castro and Delvino, and thence back to Constantinople. Of this tour I have already furnished the Committee with pretty copious accounts, which I need not here repeat, but a few general remarks on the history and topography of these provinces, as well as the recent reforms introduced by the Turkish Government, may not be unacceptable, especially as the whole region in question is, or has been till lately, a "terra incognita" to the rest of Europe.

The population of Bosnia, Austrian and Turkish Croatia, Herzegovina, Dalmatia, and Montenegro, belongs to the same sub-division of the great Slavonic family, as the Servians, whose dialect is for the Turkish provinces at least, including Montenegro, the literary language. Nor does it differ very greatly from the Bulgarian, Slovak, Bohemian, Polish, and Russian, all these dialects being but variations of the old Slavonic language. These tribes were converted to Christianity through the labours of Methodius and Cyrillus (obit. 822 AD) who, contrary to the course pursued by Xavier, but anticipating the labours of modern and Protestant missions and Bible Societies, conferred on those half savage nations the inestimable blessing of a valuable translation of the whole Bible. This put these tribes in immediate contact with the fountain-head of Truth, and we doubtless trace its effects in the resistance which those provinces which adhered to the Eastern Church, steadily offered to the pretensions of the emperors of Constantinople, and in the fact that the

Bohemians and the Moravians, and other Slavonic tribes in Hungary who had joined the Western Church, received so readily in the 15th century the doctrines of Revelation as preached by Huss, and by Waldensian refugees, and embodied in the writings of our own Wickliffe. The fact that the Church of the United Brethren, founded in those days, still subsists, and that a large portion of these tribes still profess Protestantism, notwithstanding the long and exhausting persecutions to which they have been exposed, is also a proof of the incorruptible nature of God's Word, and entitles them to our special interest and sympathy.

In AD 1357, when the Turks first landed in Europe, at the invitation of John Cantacuzenus, to aid him in seizing the throne of Constantinople, Albania, Dalmatia, Herzegovina, Montenegro, Bosnia, and Servia were united under the sceptre of Stephen Dushan, the most brilliant of the Slavonian kings in the Eastern Empire. On his death, however, the various provinces resumed their independence of each other, and only confederated themselves, from time to time, for resistance to the common foe. Nor was the evil day far off. Finding a rich country, and a divided population, ruled by a feeble and corrupt government, the Turks soon perceived the inviting field for conquest which Europe presented, and transferred their seat of government from Broosa to Adrianople in 1361. The Slavonic tribes, as well as the Hungarians, and Europe generally, perceived the danger, and attempted to arrest its progress, but in vain; and in spite of the efforts of Huniades and the armies of the West, and the appeals of the Eastern Church to her Western sister, the frontier tribes were broken in a series of terrible defeats at Kossovo, Nicopolis, Varna, and again at Kossovo, till they were compelled to submit at discretion to the Moslem conqueror. The whole territory was parcelled out among the chiefs of the Moslem army, exactly in the same way as was England after the battle of Hastings; and the same struggle arose in Turkey between the power of the Sultan and these feudal chiefs, whether janissaries, timariots, or spahis, as ensued in every country of Europe between the crown and the nobles. This struggle was formally and openly initiated under Selim III., contemporaneously with the French revolution; but though its movements were quickened by that great convulsion, it would have occurred in all its wide-spread influences independently of any external appliances. In Servia, which seems from the first to have enjoyed a higher degree of civilisation and education than any of the other provinces south of the Save, these feudal chiefs were all Mohammedans of Turkish descent, and speaking that language. In Bosnia, and most of Albania, and Herzegovina, as well as in Bulgaria, the original proprietors of the soil had purchased the retention of their estates, and their admission to the honours and emoluments of office, and in one word freedom, by the sacrifice of the Christian faith. This, however, brought no alleviation to the sufferings of the mass of the population; on the contrary, these renegade chiefs tyrannised over their wretched countrymen who remained faithful to their creed, with the most relentless cruelty, and nowhere were the miseries of the Moslem yoke, and especially the inhuman tax of every tenth child to recruit the ranks of the janissaries, perpetuated longer than in Bosnia. No one can travel through that romantic province at this day without seeing abundant proofs in the manners of the people of the hard bondage under which their fathers pined. By the campaign of 1832, however, the power of these chiefs was entirely broken, and thus by a remarkable coincidence, almost at the very time that the Servians, after a long and glorious struggle achieved their semi-independence, the Sultan established liberal, and to a certain extent, representative institutions in Bosnia and Herzegovina, as he had already done in other provinces. The Hungarian war produced a ferment throughout these provinces in 1849 and 1850, and there have been various disturbances from time to time, and chief of all, the late Montenegrin war; but comparative peace and liberty and order now prevail, and under the enlightened and energetic government of Osman Pasha, the present vizir of Bosnia, we believe these provinces have made progress in the construction of roads, and in other internal reforms, such as few other portions of the empire can exhibit.

Education has for some time been fostered by the Government with laudable diligence, and in most of the towns of importance there are Rushdi Mektebs, or Academies, in which instruction is given to the Moslems in Turkish, Arabic and Persian, reading and writing, geography, and a little history and astronomy, and in some cases the attendance is large, and might be indefinitely increased. Thus at Scutari, in north Albania, there were 130 or 140 pupils in attendance when I visited the school, and the teacher informed me, that with larger accommodation and twice as many teachers, they could easily have 300 pupils. There are also primary schools connected with every mosque, but these are very often inefficient. Among the Christian population, education is but beginning to be attended to, and schools worthy of the name are to be found only in the principal towns. Female education is almost entirely unknown among both Christians and Moslems, but a feeble female school exists at Seraievo, and a much more prosperous one at Mostar, the capital of Herzegovina. Small colonies of Spanish Jews are also found at the principal towns, which present the same painful, yet interesting features, as the larger communities of their co-religionists at Constantinople, Salonica, and Smyrna. May we not confidently anticipate, as the people do themselves, that the diffusion of the Word of God will powerfully promote education, and both encourage the Christian population by a substantial proof of Christian sympathy in supplying their wants, and, by its unavoidable tendency in the hands of the Spirit, elevate and purify their conceptions of Divine truth?

A large number of Bosnians, though I shall not venture to guess how many, sought refuge from their oppression in the bosom of the Romish Church, which is under the protection of the Austrian and French authorities. These Christians employ the Latin characters, and I rejoice to hope that in a few months we shall be able to supply them also with the Word of Life, in such a form as they can easily make use of.

Pages 119–120
Actions of the Committee

Your Committee have already taken steps for supplying some of the wants which Dr. Thomson has thus vividly depicted. In the early part of last year, when at Bucharest, he met with a suitable Agent, to whom he proposed that the work of Colportage in Bosnia should be entrusted, and, with the sanction of your Committee, Mr. Tabory has been appointed to superintend the work in this province, and has taken up his abode at Seraievo. Dr. Thomson states that the success which he has met with, and the sales which he has effected, bear testimony, not only to his diligence in the prosecution of his labours, but to the readiness of the people to receive the Word of God.

At a more recent date, another Agent, Mr. Constantine, whose work will be of a similar kind, has had a district, which embraces Epirus, Thessaly, and South Macedonia, assigned to him. It is proposed to station him at Joannina, and every hope is entertained that, under the efficient control of Dr. Thomson, he may prove a valuable helper in the work.

A third centre has also been chosen, whence the Light of God's Truth may radiate. In one of his last letters Dr. Thomson states that Mr. Riedel was on the point of setting out for Scutari, with a view of establishing himself in that locality, and labouring in the cause of God for a wider circulation of His truth. God grant that the instrumentality of man thus set in motion may be accompanied by the grace and teaching of the Holy Spirit, and that wherever the light of divine truth shines, the warmth of divine love may be felt, kindling emotions in many hearts which have never yet been realised, and developing principles which have God's Word as their true source, and God's Glory as their highest aim!

61st Report, 1865

Page 139
Scriptures issued from European Turkey
Greek with Albanian — 39

Pages 144–145
Macedonia and Thessaly – Joannina

The province of Macedonia has been repeatedly traversed with the Scriptures; Thessaly and South Epirus rarely; but regular and permanent labours are desired, rather than occasional efforts at distant intervals. Your Committee have concluded an arrangement which will, in some measure, provide for Thessaly and South Albania. A sub-Agent will be placed at Joannina, who will have charge of a Depot, and devote much of his time to Colportage journeys. For this position they have secured the services of Mr. Davidson, of Edinburgh, whom, they believe, will prove himself well fitted for the work. He has already reached Constantinople, and will proceed to his destination as soon as the necessary plans are completed. In the absence of an eligible Colporteur, the Rev. S. Constantine, of Athens, representative of the American and Foreign Christian Union, made a recent excursion to Albania, with a special view to the circulation of the Scriptures. Referring to this excursion, Dr. Thomson states:

> Landing at Volo, where lie experienced much kindness, as well as valuable assistance, from Henry Suter, Esq., Her Majesty's Vice-Consul, Mr. Constantine proceeded to Larissa, Tricala, and Joannina. I am sorry to have to report that the Bishops of the Greek Church threw every possible obstacle in his way, and did what they could to prejudice the minds of the Turkish Authorities against him, and the Holy Scriptures which he offered for sale. Indeed, so much so, that, unless Mr. Suter, had become personally responsible for the good conduct of Mr. Constantine, he would not have been permitted to withdraw his books from the Custom-house. The total sales by Mr. Constantine in this region amounted to

300 copies; and he reports a most encouraging desire among all classes to possess the Word of God. The remaining 91 which are put down as sold by him were disposed of in Greece. The following classification of his sales is interesting, as attesting the desire of the people to possess the Scriptures, especially when it is remembered that the practice of sales, as opposed to gratuitous distribution, was rigidly adhered to:—

Greek, Ancient and Modern, 151; Turkish, 43; French, 33; Hebrew, 22; Judaeo-Spanish, 13; Italian, 20; Albanian Testaments with Greek, 20.

Pages 146–147
Joannina – extracts from Mr. Constantine's report

[After visiting Volo and Larissa,] I next went to Joannina. Here I spent ten days: my intercourse with the people was pleasant, and the students especially were interested.

I learned by letter from parties that the Khaujees (keepers of caravanserais) with whom I put up, were thrown into prison at the instigation of the bishop, on the pretence that they did not inform the governor of my presence, although I had a crier engaged to advertise my arrival. Unfortunately, I could get no redress for these poor men, on whom I had thus unintentionally been the means of entailing loss and inconvenience.

Page 147
North Albania, Scutari

After Dr. Thomson had completed his long tour of observation in 1863, he requested the Committee to sanction the establishment of a Depot and Colporteur at Scutari, the capital of North Albania, and containing 60,000 inhabitants representing very mixed creeds. This spot forms a very convenient centre from which to reach Montenegro, Macedonia and Dalmatia, as well as the various towns of Northern and Central Albania. The proposal having been agreed to, Dr. Thomson placed Mr. Riedel at Scutari, with instructions to open a Depot and travel with the Scriptures as frequently as circumstances would permit. Referring to the importance and claims of this position, it is remarked, that, owing to the low state of education and the hostility of the Romish clergy, large sales cannot be anticipated. Mr. Riedel has been actively employed, as appears from the following statement:—

> During the past summer and autumn, Mr. Riedel visited many towns of Albania, including Durazzo, on the west coast; Monastir eastward, in Macedonia, with most of the towns on the land route to both places; and as South Albania was still unoccupied, continued his tour as far as Joannina and Prevesa, from whence he returned by sea. I regret to say that in most of the towns he visited, with only the exception indeed of Monastir, Joannina and Prevesa, he was prevented by the Turkish Authorities from colporting his books. He also suffered much from fever, which he experienced again and again in journeys through these beautiful, but often pestilential, districts.

Pages 147–148

Alexander Thomson's Report on Riedel's First Experiences in Shkodra

After mentioning that immediately on his arrival, both Catholics and Greeks had been forbidden by their respective clergy to purchase Scriptures from him, but that many promised notwithstanding to visit the Depot, and stating that he found most but not all of the Italians friendly, he adds:

Most of the Romanists are able to read a little Italian, but-not enough to comprehend fully what they read, and many inquire earnestly for the Bible in Albanian with Latin letters, as they do not understand the Greek letters, and besides regard the Greek Church with great antipathy. But many also are deterred from purchasing by the prohibition against reading any book in their own houses instead of coming to church to pray.

From May 9th to June 15th, I sold only 15 books, but even of these 8 were returned to me, and for peace' sake I returned the money. The people are exceedingly timid as well as fanatical, and most of them have not the most distant conception what sort of a book the Bible is. In general, however, I rejoice to say, that great reverence prevails for the Word of God. Often while I visit the bazaar, four or six persons will be reading the books for a considerable time; and when at length they return them to me with a most respectful silence, and I ask them why they will not purchase a copy, they reply, 'We do not know what all this means.'

On his extensive tour, although from the causes already mentioned his sales were few, he found a remarkable spirit of inquiry almost everywhere, and his room was generally full of visitors, who came both to read and converse. I must add, that among these inquirers the Turkish soldiers were pre-eminent,—a fact full of encouragement, and corresponding entirely with my own observation.

62nd Report, 1866

Page 129

Dr. Thomson also furnishes a geographical index, showing the different stations from which the Scriptures were distributed, and the agency employed for their circulation. It will be observed from this, that your Committee have sanctioned the opening of a new Depot at Ioannina, in South Albania, and that the missionaries of various Societies, both in England and America, are efficient helpers in the important work of circulating the Word of God.

Sales at Ioannina and in South Albania, 487.

Sales at Scutari, in North Albania and Montenegro, 340.

Pages 132–138

The Scriptures are also being provided, for the first time, for another interesting people, the inhabitants of North Albania. Dr. Thomson was fortunate in meeting with Mr. Constantine Christophorides, who had translated the whole of the New Testament in the dialect of Northern Albania, and who was most anxious for the evangelisation of his countrymen. This translation has been carefully revised, with the assistance of an educated native, and the Gospels and Acts are now being printed according to the system of orthography proposed by Professor Lepsius. Should this edition prove successful, the Old Testament will be proceeded with in due course.

Albania

There are many circumstances which have combined almost to shut out this province from the rest of the civilised world. Not only have the fanaticism of its people and the despotism of its rulers rendered travelling in it insecure, but its separation by a high range of mountains from the rest of European Turkey remove it from the highway between Vienna and Constantinople, and its wild and mountainous character, connected with the absence of roads, and the scarcity of its internal productions, presented but few attractions for commercial enterprise.

Latterly, however, the country has become better known and the spiritual welfare of its people is exciting the attention and drawing out the sympathies of those whose kindly feeling will result in ready help. With reference to your own more immediate work, Dr. Thomson observes:—

> It is pleasing to think that your Society had its attention directed at an early period to the wants of Albania, and that under the superintendence, and largely at the cost of the Corfu Auxiliary, the Greek and Albanian Testament was published in 1828, while the Gospel of Matthew, also in Greek and Albanian, but in a different style of orthography, had been published in 1824. A second edition of the Testament was published by your Society at Athens in 1858, the greater part of which is still on hand. It is painful to report that, while we would hope there may be good doing, and done by the volumes thus put into circulation, there is little outward evidence of it; and so far as I am aware, there is no school in which reading in the Albanian language is taught in all Greek Albania. Among the Romanist Albanians, it may be taught to a very limited degree, but the only literature in existence is, as I have already mentioned, a catechism and one or two devotional manuals. This clearly indicates the steps that are necessary in order to make the treasures of the Sacred Word provided by your Society accessible to the general community; and I am happy to say that the attention of benevolent parties is being directed to the urgent need of action in this matter.

Ioannina

Your Committee were enabled to announce in their last Report that Mr. Davidson had been appointed to this station, and had reached Constantinople in his way thither. He has now entered upon his work with much zeal, and since the middle of May, 1865, the Depot has been in active operation. He has been much indebted to her Majesty's Consul, Major Stuart, for the generous hospitality which he extended to him upon his first arrival, as well as for the official support which he has invariably received. For more than a month the Depot was crowded with visitors from morning till evening, eager to purchase or to read the Scriptures, and during that period about 200 copies were sold. Since then the monthly sales have sunk to a much lower figure, but it could not be expected that the eagerness connected with a first supply would be long maintained. Mr. Davidson has at intervals visited the surrounding country, but without any very marked success. Dr. Thomson thus alludes to these excursions:

> Mr, Davidson's acquaintance with Greek soon enabled him to undertake a few tours, the first of which was to Metzovo, a small town situated in the range of Pindus, on the borders between Albania and Thessaly, and inhabited by an ancient colony of Wallachians, who retain their own language to this day, and have most of the carrying trade between the two provinces in their hands. He was received with the utmost kindness, but such was the fear the people had of their priests, or their own timidity, that though he stayed about a week he sold only five volumes. The people all read and speak Greek; but though they speak Wallachian in their own families, they have no books in that language, and

can make no use of our Wallachian Scriptures either in
the Cyrillian or the Roman characters.

Another journey of much greater extent Mr. Davidson
undertook on September 19th, proceeding first to Arta,
thence to Prevesa, Parga, Margariti and Paramythia.
'At Arta there came one evening to the Khan,' says
Mr. Davidson, 'two tailors, who after labouring in
vain for some time to get me to believe in their creed,
and adopt their customs, bought two Greek Bibles.
One of them was a rather intelligent young man,
but the other could scarcely read at all, although I
saw him in his shop afterwards spelling diligently and
trying to learn what the Book contained. The Jews
of Arta also purchased a few copies of the Hebrew
Scriptures, but appeared to be utterly ignorant of
the New Testament.' He next proceeded to Prevesa,
where he found things very much worse. 'I have tried
Colportage,' he writes, 'but none will scarcely look
at the books, much less buy them.' At Parga he could
sell only two copies, but he met with a more friendly
reception, and had no doubt that his want of success
was owing to priestly influence. A ride of three hours
through a most romantic country brought him to
Margariti early in the morning of October 12th, but
though he went through and through the bazaar for
a considerable time, no one would make his stock of
books any lighter. There is no school in Margariti, and
but few of the Greek population can read, while those
who were in the bazaar from the hamlets were utterly
unlearned, few of them being so much as able to speak
modern Greek, their own tongue being Albanian.

His next visit was to Paramythia. 'I had scarcely
arrived,' writes Mr. D., 'when a Dervish brought coffee
to me, and after he went to his shop, he told a number

of the people that I was in the Khan with the books, and kindly offered me a part of his shop to expose them to view. In the evening I had a walk with the doctor of the place and one of the chief merchants, and I afterwards brought them to the Khan, but they could not see the books well with the light of the lamp, and promised to come next day. They did not, however, make their appearance. I stayed till Monday forenoon, but could effect no sales, although I found the people more kindly disposed to myself than in any of the other places I had visited.'

Later still Mr. Davidson visited Zitza, and returned the following day. 'I saw several small villages scattered among the mountains, none of which, however, I visited, as the weather looked rather threatening, and these villages are almost deserted of male population. Indeed, in most of the villages it is but few men who can be seen, for they leave as soon as they grow up, leaving their young wives behind them, whom they had married when mere lads. They go to seek employment in distant cities, and often do not return for fifteen or twenty years, or even longer. Such I found to be the case in Zitza, the women ploughing and doing other field work; while at Zagora (supposed to be the site of the oracle of Dodona) there are only the women, old men and children. It was sunset when I got to Zitza, so I could do nothing that night. There were two muleteers in the khan with me, however, that night, with whom I read out of the New Testament some truths of which they evidently heard for the first time. The few men in the village having learned of my arrival with the Scriptures, I stayed in expectation of a visit, but only two came, to one of whom I sold an Albanian Matthew. I then went out; scarcely a man was to be seen, and of those with whom I could speak,

none but two could read, and they had purchased from
the Depot at Ioannina. There is a good school-house
erected at Zitza, capable of containing comfortably
200 pupils. About 70 are in actual attendance, both
boys and girls.'

The effect of these excursions, though they have
not resulted in much success, has been to quicken Mr.
Davidson's interest in the people among whom he labours,
and he has resolved to revisit the same localities this
spring. In Ioannina itself four of the Greek priests have
shown themselves friendly to his efforts, and his sales have
amounted to 487 copies.

Scutari

Mr. Riedel, whose appointment in connection with
the Depot opened in this important town was noticed in
last year's Report, has been discharging the duties of his
office with much diligence, and the results are such as to
afford ample ground of encouragement. During the first
eight months, with all the advantage of the attraction of
novelty in his favour, he only sold 119 copies, whereas last
year his sales have amounted to 340. It is gratifying to find
that in this district also the efforts of your Committee to
obtain a free circulation for the Word of God have not
been in vain. The Turkish Government has sent orders
to the Pasha of Scutari, directing that all obstructions to
Mr. Riedel's labours should be removed, and the order has
been faithfully carried out. Dr. Thomson, in referring to a
visit paid by Mr. Riedel to Montenegro, says:

His reception was cordial, and these brave
mountaineers exhibited a desire for the Word of God
which was most encouraging. True, their poverty was
very great, and education was confined to a few, while

schools were often wanting in their villages; but there was a bearing about them which encouraged the hope that they would open their minds to the reception of the Truth. Much of the success which Mr. Riedel met with was also to be ascribed to the decided friendship of Mr. Vaslik, the Secretary to the Prince, who assured all parties that Mr. R.'s books were altogether safe and excellent. Mr. Riedel accomplished three visits to Montenegro, returning across the narrow strip of Dalmatia which intervenes between it and the Adriatic, and effecting a few sales in the Austrian towns of Ragusa, Cattaro, Budua, &c.

Besides these visits to Montenegro, Mr. Riedel accomplished also a visit to Berat and Avlona, taking Elbassan and other important towns in his way. His success here, among the adherents of the Greek Church, was very encouraging, notwithstanding the hostility of the Bishop of Elbassan, who made him take back 19 copies, which had been purchased the year before. His principal success was at Tyranna, where he sold 12 copies, and found a very decided spirit of inquiry among the Moslems, and at Berat, where he sold 35 copies, and found the clergy favourable. It was at Berat, too, that he sold a Turkish Bible to a party of villagers from the valley of the Lom.

I cannot but here advert to the marked friendship and kind assistance which Her Majesty's Consul, Richard Reade, Esq., has uniformly shown towards Mr. Riedel, and to the interest which he takes in the promotion of education and of Scriptural knowledge among the people. I have further to observe, that though the sales in the town of Scutari are exceedingly small at present, the chief cause appears to be the want of the Scriptures in the Albanian language and Roman letter, and Mr.

Riedel anticipates that matters will alter considerably on the publication of the North Albanian Gospels and Acts, now in the press. Mr. Riedel is further of opinion that among both Moslems and Romanists, but especially the former, there is a considerable amount of religious inquiry. This entirely corresponds with my own observations in 1863; and I quite concur with his opinion, that were Divine service opened in the Turkish and Italian languages, many would be found anxious to hear the Truth.

Mr. Riedel mentions various indications which encourage the hope that the Spirit of God is moving upon the hearts of the people. He likewise reports that, just as I found matters on my visit in 1863, the Popish priests are hated, but the people are not sufficiently acquainted with Divine Truth to take up a consistent and bold position against them. In such circumstances, we can only say that it is the duty and privilege of the Society to labour on in faith, and with earnest prayer for the blessing.

Page 143

Dr. Thomson adds,

These people ... groan under the burden of innumerable feast days, in which the people can take no interest; of long, burdensome, and unnecessary fasts; of an ignorant, profligate, and careless clergy; while they are willing at the same time that a proper remuneration be provided for the clergy, if they will diligently discharge their duty. Such opinions have been strongly expressed by teachers, merchants and clergy in Moldavia, Wallachia, Bosnia and Albania; and I trust are the forerunners of a work of wide and effectual reformation within the Eastern Church. In particular, there is a strong desire in many quarters for systematic preaching, which is at present all but unknown, and for the congregational singing of hymns."

63rd Report, 1867

Pages 157–158

No complete Bible exists in the Wallachian, or Servian, or Albanian languages, although a considerable portion of each has been issued ...

Modern Greek and Tosk Albanian, 337...

The issues in Greek, which include our sales in the Kingdom of Greece, are very encouraging. The issues indeed in Graeco-Turkish, are considerably below those of the previous year; but the diminution is more than compensated by the unusual number of 337 copies sold among the Tosks of South Albania. This latter issue is deeply interesting to those who have inquired into the condition of the Albanian people—a people estimated to amount to a million and a half of souls; but who may almost be said to remain to this day without any written literature, except in so far as your Society has supplied the want. These sales took place both in Greece and Macedonia, as well as in Albania.

Pages 162–170

Albania and Montenegro

Amongst the races embraced within the limits of European Turkey, none have been doomed to such utter neglect as the Albanians. They have been left without any education worthy of the name, and, as may be expected, the reign of ignorance prevails. Only a small portion of the people are able to read, and scarcely any efforts have been made for their moral and spiritual elevation. There is a mixture of creeds in the country, Greeks, Romanists, and Moslems being intermingled. Dr. Thomson has been very desirous of doing something for the Albanians, who, with much that is degrading, combine some fine traits of character. During the past year, a translation of the four Gospels and the Acts of the Apostles in the Gheg dialect of the Albanian language has been printed by your Society, in Constantinople, and is now in course of gradual circulation. The translation has been prepared by Mr. C. Christoforides, who is a native of the country, and much esteemed for his Christian character. His qualifications for the work, as a scholar, were satisfactory, and in the final correction of the text he had, as an additional safeguard, the assistance of an educated Albanian, from Scutari. So far as opinion is at present available, the translation is pronounced to be good and intelligible. Other parts of the text are in readiness for the press, and when there is further confirmation of the accuracy of the portion now issued, the remainder of the New Testament will be printed. As this is the first attempt that has been made to produce the Scriptures in the Northern Albanian dialect, it was naturally expected that much curiosity would be aroused, and that strong opposition to its introduction amongst the people would be manifested, especially as the inhabitants of this part of Albania are under Romish domination. Part of the edition was sent to Scutari for the use of your Depot, established in that large city. The news of its approach had gone before, and the note of alarm had been sounded in no very suppressed tones. Dr. Thomson describes the circumstances that occurred:

The Committee are aware that the great majority of the Gheg Albanians are Romanists, and hence it was to be expected that the clergy would exhibit the usual hostility of their church to the Word of God. Mr. Riedel, the Society's former depositary at Scutari, had made no secret that the books were in course of preparation, and an Albanian priest in this city, who had been at first consulted in the preparation of the work, contrived to ascertain when the books were despatched, and immediately gave notice to the clergy at Scutari. The arrival of the books was delayed for a week or two, so that ample time was afforded for the obstructive efforts of the priests. What these were, I shall leave Mr. Von Laer, the Society's representative at Scutari, to describe. Writing under date, February 12th, he says: 'I have no expectation of selling any from mere human motives on the part of the buyers; but I repose all my confidence on the yea and amen of a prayer-hearing God. The obstacles in the way are such as God only can surmount. You will be surprised to hear, that the Sunday before last, in the large Catholic Church here, the officiating priest informed his audience, from the altar, that an Albanian in Constantinople, had written and caused to be printed, in the Albanian language, books subversive of the faith of God and of His Christ. He then declared that, when these books were offered for sale in Scutari, every one who purchased them sinned against the Holy Ghost, and was cursed of the same; and, likewise, that if any one spoke to the person who should offer such books for sale, or answered him when he addressed him, he was subjected to the same curse. It was only to-day I was told of this by a person who was present in the church, and heard all. Until today, I was blissfully unconscious of the anathemas under which I and my occupation were laid; but for some days past I had observed a coldness towards me on the part of many who formerly were very friendly, and a sort of smothered fire of bigotry displayed itself in their conversation.'

Writing a week later, Mr. Von Laer describes the actual reception of the books thus: 'I was not without hopes that a good many copies would be taken, in spite of the priests; consequently, after commending the matter to the Lord, I filled my bag with copies, and proceeded to the bazaar, and opened my budget among the principal merchants in the main street. I offered them first to a man who had often previously enquired for them. He took one in his hands with a peculiar air of restraint, looked at it a moment, and then handed it back to me, remarking that he had no money. At the next shop, instead of the usual invitation to sit down and speak for a little, I was received with «Haidy» (begone), and a wave of the hand; at the next door with a «Non credo» and a wave of the hand; and after this manner they all spoke. I went through the greater part of the bazaar without being able to dispose of a single copy. As I proceeded from stall to stall, a sort of triumphant self-righteous titter ran along, which repeated the sense of what I am so often told in words; «We are faithful Christians.» A very few expressed their readiness to purchase the books, «But,» said they, «what will it avail us? We shall be reported to the priests, who will take them away; and so we shall only get into brawls.»' Such procedure does not, of course, surprise either the Committee or myself; but, to Mr. Von Laer, it was a new experience of colportage operations, and he was somewhat discouraged. He very wisely, however, took the opportunity of paying a visit to Durazzo, where he disposed of a few of the new books, as well as of Scriptures in other languages. He has since returned to Scutari, and I hope to hear shortly that some have ventured to purchase in defiance of the anathema. Before dismissing my notice of this new publication, I may observe that, though there are but few Ghegs in Constantinople, some twelve copies have been sold in town by an Albanian newsboy, who has also sold more than that number of Tosk or South Albanian Testaments in the same time."

Respecting the actual circulation of Scriptures in this portion of his agency, Dr. Thomson makes some remarks:

The issues in Albania and Montenegro are very satisfactory, being 924 copies, or ninety-seven above those of the previous year. Considering the small number of persons able to read, one might not have been surprised to find the issues stationary, or even slightly retrograde; that it is otherwise, is therefore very encouraging; and still more so, that the increase should have occurred wholly in North Albania and among the Montenegrins.

To give a fair opportunity of obtaining the Scriptures, Colportage is indispensable. By no other means are the people to be reached. Mr. Riedel, who until recently acted as your Depositary at Scutari, made four tours during the year, and carried the Divine Book into localities which had never been previously visited on a similar errand. From the account given of these journeys, it will be seen that "perils by robbers" must be classed amongst the trials to which the Colporteur is exposed, in the faithful discharge of his duty:

During the past year, Mr. Riedel performed four important colportage tours; viz. one to Ipek, by way of Prisrend; one southward to Berat, and two to

Montenegro. The first of these tours occupied three weeks, and being we believe the first occasion on which those remote and neglected districts had ever been visited by any Missionary or Bible Agent, it was one of much interest. Mr. Riedel left Scutari, Jan 23d, for Prisrend, situated in the midst of a magnificent Alpine country. Here, owing probably, in no small degree, to the kind offices of Richard Reade, Esq., Her Majesty's Consul at Scutari, Mr. Riedel found a very friendly reception among the adherents of the Greek Church. On visiting the Episcopal school, he found 192 boys divided into three classes, and was welcomed by the teachers, who bought 20 copies from him. There is also a girl's school. Among the Romanists he could sell nothing; but it must be added that, as the Albanian Gospels were not then published, he had nothing to offer them but Italian Scriptures, which very few, if any of them, could read with intelligence. He sold in Prisrend 84 copies. Mr. Riedel then turned northward, up the magnificent but sequestered valley of the White Drin. The first town of importance he visited was Jakova, chiefly inhabited by Moslems, and bearing the stamp of great poverty and barbarism. He found a Greek Christian school, however, with about 40 pupils, and sold 20 copies of the Scriptures, but few were able to read. He next reached Detshany by a very dangerous road, where he sold 18 copies; after leaving which, on his way to Ipek, he was attacked by a robber, who presented a musket to his breast, and demanded his money. Mr. Riedel at once threw down his purse, but the guard who attended him on this dangerous journey, presented in turn his pistol at the robber, and ordered him to restore the money. He did so, and immediately disappeared in the forest, and happily nothing further resulted from this alarming incident. On arriving at

Ipek, the ancient ecclesiastical capital of the Servian nation, he received a very cordial welcome from the patriarch, who gave him a plan of the celebrated church and monastery, built by Stephen Dushan, the great king of Servia, whose kingdom reached to the Adriatic. Mr. Riedel found a good school, but depressed by the extreme poverty of the people, yet he sold 45 copies at Ipek. He continued his route to Plava and Gasinye; at both of which places he found matters a little better, the latter having a school of 40 pupils; and then returned on foot, by a five days' journey over the mountains to Scutari, which he reached February 13th. His total sales on this tour, amounted to 210 copies of Servian Scriptures, for which he received 605 piastres, a very large sum indeed, when the poverty of the people and the scarcity of money in those remote regions are duly considered. Mr. Riedel bears hearty testimony to the friendly disposition of the people, and their thirst for the Word of God; and it must be gratifying to the friends of the Society, that this important but perilous journey was accomplished in safety. On his journeys to Montenegro, the one in July, the other in September, Mr. Riedel found the same cordial welcome as on former occasions and the same desire for the Word of God; and though from the scarcity that then pressed heavily on the people, he feared he would sell but few books, he met with even greater success than before; disposing in his first tour of 75 copies, and in his second of 92. He explains this success by intimating the institution of one or two new schools, for which the Scriptures were required as text-books, and holds out the prospect of an increasing circulation, keeping pace both with the augmented number of readers, and the additional portions of the Old Testament which may be published.

Mr. Riedel, having retired from your service, is succeeded by Mr. Von Laer, who has entered upon his work with much zeal and interest.

South Albania, Ioannina.

The Depot here continues under the charge of Mr. Davidson, who has proved himself diligent in all things, and is cultivating a difficult field with prudence and energy. The sales have been less by 121 copies than in the preceding year—a circumstance to be regretted, but not at all surprising, as the mass of the people are grossly illiterate, and large sales were effected when Mr. Davidson commenced his labours. The district which is attached to the Ioannina Depot is extensive, and can only be explored gradually by personal visitation. There are many towns and villages which will come within the range of Mr. Davidson's journeys, where the readers may be few, and fewer still those who are inclined to purchase the Scriptures, but where, nevertheless, efforts should be made to impress the people with a sense of the value of the Bible, and the duty of having their religious faith and practice governed by it. It may be that for some time the sales effected in these excursions will be small, but a foundation is being laid for future work, and some rays of Heavenly Light are thrown upon the thick darkness around. Dr. Thomson describes pretty fully the labours of Mr. Davidson during the year. After referring to notorious scandals amongst the clergy of the Greek Church, which create disgust for a time, and raise a clamorous demand for reformation, he observes:

> Even such scandals, however, maybe overruled for good, especially now that so many of the people have the Word of God in their hands; and Mr. Davidson

mentions that some of his most intelligent friends, who had formerly been staunch defenders of the honour and authority of their church, had been obliged to admit its corruptions, and almost to despair of its reformation. Such causes as these have led elsewhere to the most blessed results, as at Unieh, of which I have already given some account; and we would fain see some earnest movement for better things at Ioannina also.

As in some degree a counterpart to all this, I must notice that Mr. Davidson mentions, with great satisfaction, the sale of two Greek Bibles to two village priests, who were brought to the Depot by one of the priests of the cathedral. On another occasion, too, he experienced the friendly services of one of the clergy; for, being at Philates, the people looked on his books with suspicion, and were especially offended that he had but one price for them, from which he would make no abatement. It seemed as if not a single book was to be sold. But just then, the hegoumen of the Monastery of St. George, near Ioannina, came up, who assured the people that the books were perfectly good and orthodox, and that the prices asked were the true prices, adding that he knew Mr. Davidson to be an excellent person, and that such was his way of dealing. The result was that a considerable number of copies were sold there.

Three important tours were taken by Mr. Davidson; one was northward to Argyrocastro, and then north-west to Avlona, etc. Particulars of this journey have already appeared in the pages of the "Monthly Reporter." Another journey was to the fair of Grevena, where some of his neighbours, who were present, boldly vindicated his books and work when they came under attack or suspicion.

The most extensive tour was to the province of Thessaly, a district in which your Agent had long desired to do something to get the Bible amongst the people. The route was long and fatiguing; and from the very low state of education and the absurd superstition of the inhabitants, large sales of the Scriptures were neither expected nor attainable....

Larissa was visited, but Mr. Davidson only succeeded, after great trouble, in selling twelve copies; and he was assured that, as soon as he departed, the purchasers would be compelled by ecclesiastical authority to surrender them. The town of Servia was then reached, where the Scriptures were exposed for sale at a great fair, but success again was very limited, the people suspecting the character of the books. After further efforts, through an entire day, to sell some copies, Mr. Davidson goes on to say:

> ... On Monday, the market was not much crowded; and the merchants and others, not being busy, had time to come to my stall; and a few of them possessed themselves of copies. A teacher from Kozan assisted me considerably, for he read the Turkish Testament to the Turks, urging them to purchase a copy and read for themselves at home; telling them they could not say whether their own vineyard was better than their neighbour's till they had seen both. He also brought two or three of his acquaintances, and prevailed on them to purchase copies. On Monday I thus sold eighteen copies, of which six were Turkish and two Albanian.

64th Report, 1868

Pages 139–144

Turkey

Your Agent, Dr. Thomson, who has been watching every opportunity of usefulness with much anxiety, and employing what means were at his disposal with patience and perseverance, acknowledges with thankfulness the measure of success which has attended his labours. The issues of the past year have amounted to 18,955 volumes, and though these numbers show a slight decrease when compared with those of the preceding year, yet when the fact is taken into account that Eastern Bulgaria and Macedonia were, from causes which your Agent could not control, left without Depot or Colporteur during seven months of the year, the deficiency is easily explained.

It is right, however, to state that 4,960 copies have been sold to the American Bible Society, and 522 copies to the National Bible Society of Scotland, so that strictly speaking, the exact number circulated through the agency of your Society, amounts to 13,473 volumes, for which the sum of £702 12s. 4d. has been received. And when it is remembered that it is from the peasantry of the country that this money has chiefly been drawn, and that comparatively few of them are able to read, your Committee feel that they have much reason to thank God, for the comparatively large number of Scriptures that have been circulated.

Classified according to their languages, the issues have been as follows:—

Albanian Gheg	300
Tosk, with Modern Greek	116

...

This table cannot but be very interesting, as showing the rapid progress of Gospel light, the increased facilities which are gradually being afforded for the study of God's Word in all languages, and the readiness with which, as regards some of them at least, the people give themselves to the study of the Scriptures, and search therein as for hid treasure. The Gheg Albanian is a language which appears for the first time in the list, and when the facts are taken into consideration that its orthography was altogether new to the people, and that a short time ago there was not a single school in which Albanian reading was taught, the issue of 300 volumes in the course of the year is most encouraging. ...

The following are expected to be sent to press at once, and, with perhaps one exception, to be finished in the present year:

Tosk Albanian Psalms	2,000
Gheg Albanian Psalms	2,000

...

I shall only further notice here the Tosk Albanian Psalms, which have already been sent to the press. The versions into the Tosk and Gheg Albanian dialects are entirely new, and were executed by Mr. Christoforides, the translator of the Gheg Gospels and Acts, with the most efficient assistance that could be procured from the Tosk and Gheg Communities in this city. The Tosk phonetic system is the same as that adopted in the Gheg Gospels and Acts, with the exception of the mark of nasalisation, which is not required. The letters employed, however, are the Greek, not the Roman, with the addition of the Slavonic b and Roman D and J. A primer has already been published in this style of orthography by the Religious Tract Society, and is rapidly gaining favour. This we hope will greatly help the circulation of the Psalms when they are published.

Constantinople

Dr. Thomson is unable to furnish any facts illustrative of the progress of Divine truth in this city. Various schools, some maintained by the Established and Free Churches of Scotland, and others by private individuals, still continue their labours; and in this manner the minds of the young are to a certain extent influenced by the precepts of the Gospel. ... The sales from this centre have amounted to 2,762 volumes, which have partly been sold at the Depot, but to a much larger extent by Colporteurs. One of these especially was most successful, and in the autumn when but little could be done in the town, he undertook a tour into the country, about fifty-two miles west of Constantinople. ...

On the subject of the Gheg Albanian, Mr. Thomson observes:—

Almost the whole circulation of the Gheg Albanian Gospels and Acts was effected in this city by an Albanian Colporteur. Constantinople, like all large cities, has a representation within its walls of the population of all the provinces. The Albanians in this city are estimated by some of themselves as high as 20,000, manifestly an important field for evangelisation, and still more so for being a medium of communication with their native province. Notwithstanding considerable effort, I am unable to ascertain what proportion of the copies sold here remain in town and how many are sent to Albania, especially about Dibra. In those regions, though the people are Albanians, the language employed in their schools and churches is the Slavonic, or rather the

Servian; and it is said that both the clergy and the people are hailing with pleasure the publication of the Holy Scriptures and of school books in their vernacular language. These people are Ghegs, and belong to the Greek Church, and are mostly very poor; but just so much greater is the delight with which we find them purchasing the Scriptures, and eager to learn the art of reading their own native tongue.

Pages 146–150
Albania and Montenegro

These are provinces which for a long time have been enveloped in the gloom of the darkest night, and the best interests of whose inhabitants have been altogether neglected. Some attention is now being directed to their spiritual necessities, and the circulation of the Bible is not only progressing satisfactorily, though amidst many impediments, but producing a marked effect. The issues have amounted to 709 volumes; 212 having been sold by Mr. Davidson at Joannina, 412 by Mr. Von Laer at Scutari, and 85 by Dr. Thomson and Dr. Koelle during their tour through this District, an account of which has already appeared in the "Monthly Reporter." Some interesting incidents occur in an account of a journey undertaken by Mr. Davidson, which are thus recorded:—

> Mr. Davidson visited in the spring the towns of Philates, Plushovitza, Paramythia, Margariti, Parga, and Prevesa. The only place where he had decided success was Philates, where he sold 17 copies, and he notes, as affording the probable explanation, that no priest resides there. In most of the other towns many came and read his books, but few bought. Such things, as I know from experience, are trying to a zealous Colporteur, but they lay a good foundation for future

success. At Paramythia he sold nine copies, and found a favourable reception. Five other copies taken away for inspection were returned, the parties saying they had been warned against such dangerous books. The ridicule, however, which their compliance with such warnings brought on them will, I trust, deter any in future from acting in this way. Mr. Davidson met here with some opposition from the Moodir, who had but recently been appointed to the post, and so had not seen him on his former visits.

At Parga he sold only three copies, but met with proof that the simple reading of the Turkish Scriptures was admitted to have changed the religious character of several Moslems, who were beyond the suspicion of having been bribed. He also was enabled to explain the nature of Bible Christianity to a large audience in the khans, on the occasion of a Greek saying, "that if Mr. Davidson and he could agree as to the sum to be given him, he was ready to become a Protestant, and to eat cheese, meat, and everything else, all the year round." The incident was not unwelcome, and Mr. Davidson seems to have used it to good effect.

Mr. Davidson's second tour occupied him from September 30th to December 6th, and was an exceedingly interesting one, not only from the very encouraging sales effected, but also because much of it was in districts which he had never before visited, and where, for the first time almost, he came into full contact with both the Albanian and the Wallachian population; for I have mentioned before, that there is a large and very ancient colony of Rumans in those regions, who have nearly the whole carrying trade in their hands. The first town he visited was Metzovo, where he sold ten copies. The doctor, who bought a

Testament, said he was once induced to burn a few of the Society's copies; and the chief teacher who was present, said he too was once as foolish, but looked upon it now as a heavy crime. He wished me much success during my journey, saying that the world at large was under great obligations to the Society, which is doing a great and a good work. He deplored also the folly of the Eastern monks in opposing the Society's operations. Mr. Davidson found all the teachers favourable, and was much interested in the schools, which were efficiently taught and well attended in the boys' and infant departments, but not equally so in that of the girls'. The next important town he visited was Castoria, situated on both sides of an isthmus that leads to a peninsula in the lake of Castoria. He found the people exceedingly bigoted, and could sell nothing; and two doctors, a merchant, and three Jews, were all that came near him. Turkish is the language of trade, but the majority of the people are Greeks, with a good many Spanish Jews, and a few Bulgarians. He next crossed the lake to Mavrovo, the fair of which it was one of his chief objects to attend. Nor was he disappointed. His sales indeed were not very numerous, but he had much valuable intercourse with the people of all classes. Amongst others, he found a Greek in delicate health, who had once been a teacher in the town of Klissura. This person told him that he had purchased from a minister who passed that way in 1848 upwards of 1,000 piastres (£9 1s. 10d.) worth of Scriptures, with a view to introduce them into his school, and among his neighbours. Orders, however, soon arrived from the Patriarchate, that all who possessed such books should deliver them up, or commit them to the flames. Refusing to do this, he retained the books, and gradually disposed of them, but lost his situation, and was excommunicated. Mr. Davidson had many visitors on this occasion, some of whom, especially Moslems of all ranks, read largely from the New Testament, and doubtless got new and important ideas, though but a few bought copies. The number of Greek Reference Bibles disposed of was very encouraging. The next town of importance he visited was Koritza, where Albanian is the spoken language, and where he found a flourishing elementary boys' school in a spacious building, attended by some 300 pupils in summer, and 500 in winter, when the shepherds descend into the plains. This school was erected and endowed by a native of the town. There is also a higher boys' school, and a girls' school, for which last a teacher had recently been got from Athens. Here he sold twenty-three copies in Graeco and Tosk Albanian, and quite exhausted that department of his stock.

The season was far advanced, but as the weather was favourable, Mr. Davidson resolved to visit Berat, the northernmost boundary of his District. Changes of weather, however, in mountain districts, are proverbially sudden; and I shall give you, in Mr. Davidson's own words, an account of his journey: "All night snow had been falling heavily, and when we set out in the morning at daybreak, it was no cheering prospect with six or seven inches of snow on the ground, more falling, and twelve hours before us over a path in nowise good in summer. About thirty of a caravan started, every one armed to the teeth with guns, pistols, and yataghans. No murders or robberies have occurred for about three years, but the road has such a bad name, that even a mounted policeman will not go alone. We had indeed a bad day of it, sometimes trudging on foot up to the knees in snow; at other times riding, with a cold wind driving the snow in our faces.

So cold were the muleteers, accustomed as they are to such work, that instead of going forward to the Khan, they halted after nine hours' journey at the village of Duschari. My hair was frozen to my hat, and I had to sit for a while before I could take it off, when a roaring fire thawed the frost upon our clothes. The village is small and entirely Mohammedan, though of recent conversion from Christianity, possessing a church, but not a single professor of the Christian name." Next day the severity of the weather was somewhat abated, and after a ride of thirteen hours on the snowy sides of Mount Tomoros, they safely reached Berat, two hours after sunset. As I had visited Berat, and spent five days there in the end of May last, it was not to be expected that Mr. Davidson could sell much. Still he sold a few copies, and met with a very friendly reception.

The next and last town of importance on this route was Konitza, where he sold but one or two copies, but as before, had the satisfaction of beginning the good work in a new locality. He found, however, a warm and intelligent friend of the Society in a Greek merchant, who had purchased a Bible from him two years ago at Joannina. He assured him that he took it with him in his journeys, and found it an unfailing source of comfort. He had frequently been urged to give it up, but steadily refused, and openly expressed his admiration of the efforts of the Society, whilst he characterised the monks as lazy, ignorant, and too often worthless fellows. A son of this merchant was teacher of the higher department of the public schools, and Mr. Davidson had much pleasure in observing the thorough way in which he conducted his classes. Some hopes are entertained that the New Testament may be introduced as a school-book there.

Of Mr. Von Laer's exertions in North Albania and Montenegro Dr. Thomson speaks in the highest terms. Though he dwells at Scutari, among a population fanatical and ignorant, and blindly attached to the errors of the Papacy, he has yet been enabled to avoid any unpleasant collision with them, whilst at the same time he has been bold in his testimony for the Truth. Mr. Von Laer has during the year undertaken five separate journeys with a view of exploring the country and diffusing the light of the Gospel among its inhabitants. It is still the day of small things among the Montenegrins, who nevertheless seem to have a great regard for the Scriptures, and some of them showed him the books which they had purchased from his predecessor, bearing evident marks of having been diligently read. Of one of these tours Dr. Thomson thus speaks:—

His journey to Prisrend was one of great success. He found the schools there in a very flourishing condition, and the people disposed, in a degree he had never before witnessed in Albania, to purchase the Scriptures. It was the 20th of October before he could set out on his tour. One box of Scriptures was emptied, and another which had been sent for was also disposed of, and, but for the lateness of the season, which made him apprehensive he might be compelled to winter in those Alpine regions, Mr. Von Laer would have sent for still further supplies, which he was confident he might have disposed of. I should mention that the people of Prisrend are Albanians, but unlike those of Scutari and of the Matt country, are members of the Greek Church. They use in their churches and schools the Servian language, just as the Montenegrins do, and the books sold to them were the Servian Scriptures. Mr. Von Laer is full of zeal in his work, and greatly desires

to visit again the valley of the Drin, where he found so
cordial a reception for the Word of God.

65th Report, 1869

Pages 184–188

The Rev. Dr. Thomson reports a period of great
diligence and labour in all parts of the wide field assigned
to his supervision. He observes that no stations have been
unoccupied, and no province, excepting Montenegro,
unvisited. The Colporteurs have zealously fulfilled their
duties, sometimes amidst circumstances of provocation
and insult, yet always with courageous hearts. A greater
disposition has been manifested to receive the Scriptures, as
may be legitimately inferred from an increased circulation,
as compared with the previous year. ...

The peculiarity of Dr. Thomson's agency is that the
Scriptures are required in so great a diversity of languages.
It may be readily supposed that the expense and literary
labour involved in preparing so many translations for the
population of Turkey must have been enormous. Nor is
the work yet complete. Several versions are in progress, or
undergoing such revision as may more thoroughly adapt
them to their purpose. It is interesting to note in what
proportions, as to vernaculars, the Scriptures have gone
forth:—

Albanian, Gheg	280
Albanian, Tosk	105
Albanian, Tosk and Greek	147
Total	**552**

Dr. Thomson considers the above enumeration as
furnishing a fair clue to the progress of education and the

love of the Scriptures amongst the various classes of the population. His own deductions are quoted:—

> The Albanian issues show an increase of 116 copies, which is wholly in the Tosk editions, and is a gratifying recompense for the special efforts that have been made, during the past year, on behalf of this people. ...

The Servian presents the very large decrease of 713 copies. This is partly owing to Montenegro having been unvisited during the past year, ...

The works enumerated below are now in the course of printing. ...

Gheg-Albanian New Testament   2,000

Pages 190–192

Reference has been made on former occasions to the Albanian translations which have been made at the expense of your Society, both in the Tosk and Gheg dialects. Dr. Thomson attaches great importance to the appearance of these works, and believes that they will have a valuable Christian and educational influence on both sections of the Albanian race. There has been a considerable demand for these Scriptures, and some interesting circumstances are cited in connection with the inquiries made at your Depot.

> As falling under the issues from the capital, I may here notice the Tosk and Gheg Albanian Psalms. I have already informed the Committee that there is a large Albanian population in this city, who mostly retain their own language, and maintain an intercourse more or less intimate with their native province. On the publication of the Psalms in these dialects, there was from the first a considerable demand for them, though latterly, perhaps in consequence of the excitement

produced by the threatened rupture with Greece,
there have been very few sales. One very interesting
circumstance, however, is, that Moslems from both the
Tosk and Gheg tribes have come to purchase Scriptures,
and to be taught to read in the system of orthography
adopted in our publications. In one instance these
parties were of high rank; and not only were cadis
and muderrises (preachers) delighted to purchase
the books, but promised to use all their influence to
promote their circulation, and indeed themselves
returned the following day for a further supply. These
parties were Tosks; but equally encouraging things
have occurred among the Ghegs. I may here mention,
that having observed from the public prints that there
was an intention on the part of influential individuals
at Scutari to publish there a newspaper in Turkish and
Albanian, which should be partly of an official nature,
I took the liberty of requesting the kind aid of Her
Majesty's Ambassador to bring under the notice of
the Government the Books published recently by the
Society, and the system of orthography employed in
them. This His Excellency did, and the gentleman
who is expected to be the editor of the journal has
called and purchased copies of the Gheg Gospels
and Psalms, and we have considerable confidence,
that should such a publication really be issued, the
Albanian portion will be printed in Lepsius' Latin
orthography. The importance of this for promoting
the circulation of the Scriptures can hardly be over-
rated; but like many other things in this land, its actual
realisation may be postponed for an indefinite period.
Among such a people as the Albanians, so long utterly
neglected, predatory and semi-independent in their
habits, progress must necessarily be slow; and, indeed,

what has already been done gives ground for abundant thankfulness." ...

Dr. Thomson mentions, however, one circumstance connected with the large territory of Rumelia, which may afford an opportunity ultimately for getting the Scriptures into the possession of many, to whom at present the character in which they are printed is unintelligible:—

There is one circumstance regarding Macedonia (Western Rumelia) which I think worthy of notice. There has existed for some centuries a Wallachian colony, occupying the mountainous regions of Central Albania and the lofty range of Pindus, and its northern continuation, that separate Albania on the West from Thessaly and Macedonia on the East. I had met with some of these people on my visits to Albania, and on Mr. Davidson's settling at Joannina, Wallachian Scriptures were sent for their use both in the Cyrillian and the Roman letters. But we found that no use could be made of these books, as the alphabetical characters were unknown to the people, and there was nobody among them to teach them the art of reading them, or explain words which might be unintelligible. How to meet this case was very perplexing. For to print Wallachian books in the Greek character for South Albania was not to be thought of; yet I had no prospect of schools being opened in which books printed at Bucharest or Jassy might be used as text books, and any differences of dialect be explained. Yet, without this, it seemed impossible to evangelise that people, as the Wallachian is their family language, and, I presume, the only one which the generality of the females understand. Singular to say, I had noted this very matter as one for early and careful examination, when I received communications from Mr. Von Laer, of Scutari, and Charles J. Calvert, Esq., Her Majesty's Consul at Monastir, from whom Mr. Von Laer received much kindness on his visit there, to the effect that teachers had lately been introduced from Rumania, and had begun to teach the Wallachian language in schools, in at least two towns. The origin of this movement is said to have been, to some extent, discontent under ecclesiastical rule, and a desire for reform, aided by the patriotic feelings of their brethren beyond the Danube. Be that as it may, and in whatever light the mere politician may regard it, I cannot but rejoice at the prospect of the Scriptures being ere long made available for a people that otherwise may remain, no one can tell how long, strangers to the message of salvation.

Bulgaria

The great want of Bulgaria is education. Books, even the Bible, will not operate as a charm upon those who can make no intelligent use of them, and till the capacity to read is imparted to the people more freely than at present, there cannot be a large demand for books of any description, even that best and holiest of Books which it is the function of your Society to disseminate. But amongst the reading classes of the Bulgarians there has ever been manifested a considerable desire to possess the Word of God in their own language. In many cases the priests of the Greek Church have not proved themselves inimical to the diffusion of the Scriptures, and have even shown interest in the work. The sales throughout the province have amounted to 1,772 copies; a proportion of these were in other languages, so that, probably, 1,500 copies may be considered as the number of Bulgarian Scriptures circulated. In addition to these, 900 copies were supplied to the sister Societies of America and Scotland, for their operations in Thrace and Macedonia.

Pages 195–198

Albania and Montenegro

The Albanian race enjoys the reputation of being distinguished by many noble qualities, but both generous and heroic as they may be, there is scarcely a nationality in the whole Turkish dominions so low down in the scale of culture and intelligence. To the present day they remain without any written vernacular literature. Dr. Thomson states that this has probably arisen from "the circumstance that their ancient language was not of importance beyond their own nationality, that their numbers were much fewer than those of the other races of the Empire, and that, consisting of Moslems, Romanists, Greeks using the Greek liturgy, and Greeks using the Slavic liturgy, the people were broken up into fragments, and seem never to have been able to adopt any common method of writing." Reference has been already made to the efforts in which your Society is now engaged, to prepare the Scriptures in both divisions of the Albanian, and according to a system of writing and orthography simple in its nature and easy of acquisition. In this province, which is about three hundred miles in length and sixty in breadth, your Society has two important Depots—one at Ioannina, in the south, under the superintendence of Mr. Davidson, and the other at Scutari, in the north, of which Mr. Von Laer has the charge. Both spheres of labour are trying, and hard to cultivate, demanding no ordinary faith and perseverance on the part of those who, to serve the great object of the Society, have willingly placed themselves in positions where many privileges have to be foregone, and

much is daily witnessed that cannot fail to be depressing
in its influence on the Christian's heart. Considering the
extremely illiterate condition of the Albanians, it cannot
be expected that there should be a large circulation of
Scriptures amongst them; and so it has proved during the
past year, 465 copies only having been sold in connection
with both Depots. Looking at this limited result in view of
the heavy outlay by which it has been attained, your Agent
remarks:—

It is well that the friends of the Bible should look at such
facts in their simplicity, and ask, Is such a circulation
worth the cost? We unhesitatingly reply that it is. For if
ever Albania is to rise from her degradation—if ever the
incessant turbulence of her tribes is to be exchanged
for peace and good-will—if ever her divisions are to be
healed, and the enterprise and energy of her people to
be turned into any other channel that that of war—it
must be through the agency and power of the Word
of God, written and preached. The sooner, then, this
sovereign means of restoration, under the blessing
of God, is brought into contact with the people,
and pressed on their attention, the better; and if we
cannot preach the Gospel, let us at least supply the
Volume containing it, and commend its doctrines as
we may. In this respect the operations of the Society
in Bosnia, Albania, Thessaly, Rumania, and other parts
of this country, where there are no Missionaries, are
of the very highest spiritual and educational value,
and I have no doubt are laying the foundation for
glorious progress in days to come; but, like all other
foundations, it is hidden from the careless observer.
The whole condition of Albania is so analogous to
that of the Highlands of Scotland, as they were two
centuries ago, even down to minute particulars, that I

am sanguine of the very best results, if only the same all-powerful instrumentality be employed—the Gospel of the grace of God. Let us do what we can.

To accomplish such results as have been described, great labour, long journeys, protracted discussions, much argument and earnest persuasion were necessary. Mr. Von Laer, of Scutari, performed three tours in his division of Albania—one to Trebigne, in Herzegovina, a part of which is allotted to him; a second to Prisrend and Pristina, in the east; and a third to Durazzo and Monastir. At Trebigne, which had never been visited before by any one of behalf of the Society, the sales were not large. In Durazzo there was more encouragement, and at Monastir copies were purchased by the people. At Prisrend and Pristina hope was disappointed, but some seed was sown.

Mr. Davidson, at Ioannina, has been unremitting in his efforts to disseminate the Scriptures; and if success has not proved greater, it is to be ascribed to causes which he cannot control, such as the unsettled political state of the province, and the poverty, bigotry, indifference and immorality of the people. During the year, Mr. Davidson accomplished four important and extensive journeys. These journeys Dr. Thomson fully explains, and reference to any map will enable the reader of these pages to trace Mr. Davidson's movements:—

One tour was to the south to Arta, Prevesa, Parga, Margariti, Paramythia, and Philates; a second to Delvino, and along the romantically situated villages on the Chimara coast, northwards, to Avlona, and then back to Ioannina by way of Tepelen and Argyrocastro; a third to Greveno Fair; and the fourth and most extensive, to Metzovo, Greveno, Kozan, Schatista, Castoria, and so to the fair of Mavroro, and back by way of Koryza. On this last tour, he visited two places of considerable size, Selitza and Bogatziko, for the first time, and certainly met with a few tokens of progress and encouragement; but he had to encounter much severe exposure to the weather, and reception, on the whole, very trying to the feelings. Fanaticism and priestly hostility on the one hand, and utter indifference on the other, were fitted severely to try faith and patience, yet his reports contain one or two incidents, which I shall mention. At Arta, a young man who had purchased a modern Greek Bible from Mr. Davidson, two years and a-half before, was so taken with the reference edition, that he exerted himself to get a purchaser for his old copy, that he might buy a reference one. He strongly recommended the Scriptures, and induced two to purchase. In Prevesa, a young merchant of rank told Mr. Davidson that he had procured one of the Society's Testaments before, but that a priest entering one day, and seeing it, threw it into the fire. He added that he believed the book was perfectly correct, but that he could not oppose the priests.

66th Report, 1870

Pages 158–159
Number of copies distributed:

Albanian, Tosk	142
Albania, Gheg	101

The sinking of the Albanian also to less than one-half of last year's issues arises from the departure of our Colporteur and our inability to procure another in his place, with the further fact that the Albanian colony in the

Capital is now pretty well supplied, while no Agency has been provided in Albania itself with special reference to the native language of the people.

Page 161

The completion of the Gheg-Albanian New Testament affords Dr. Thomson an occasion of devout thankfulness. For some time indeed it was feared that the plans of the Government for the promotion of education might interfere with its free circulation. A Commission, which was appointed for Albania, sought to introduce an entirely new alphabet, whose characters should be neither Turkish nor Greek, Roman nor Slavonic. This proposal was eventually rejected, and they then agreed to recommend the adoption of the Roman alphabet, but with new characters, to represent those sounds which, in the system of Lepsius, in which the Gheg-Albanian Testament is printed, are produced by various marks placed over the Roman letters. The scheme, however, being accompanied with a plan for building schools and supporting schoolmasters, the Government pleaded their inability to meet the expense, and no further action was taken in the matter. It was more than suspected that the Greek and Romish Churches, terrified at the prospect of so much light being introduced among the people, brought an adverse influence to bear upon the proposal. If so, their opposition may tend rather to the furtherance of the Gospel, as no impediment will now exist to the use of the editions printed by the Society.

Page 165

In Silistria [Colporteur Krzossa] again encountered some trouble at the customs, but sold in six days fifty-six copies, and found a colony of Albanians for whom he regretted he had not with him a larger supply of their vernacular Scriptures. It is pleasing to know that this town, so long forbidden ground to the Society's efforts, was thus found accessible.

Pages 170–172
Albania and Montenegro

The two centres of operation in this province, one at Joannina in the south, and the other at Scutari in the north, remain the same as they were last year. A change has, however, taken place in the superintendence of the latter. Mr. Von Laer has resigned his Agency, and Dr. Thomson has it in prospect to remove Mr. Davidson from Joannina to Candia, it being his wish to secure the services of a Colporteur for the former of these places who thoroughly understands the Albanian language. It is always to be regretted when those who have made some acquaintance with the district in which they labour are obliged to relinquish it. The knowledge of the country and of the habits of the people which they gain during a single tour is a great advantage to them, and very much facilitates their work when they visit them a second time. This is one, though only one, of the difficulties which in such a country as Turkey your Agent has to contend with. It is not easy, in the first place, to find Christian men suited to his purpose; when found, they have often to learn the language of the people to whom they are sent, and then there are all the contingencies connected with health and adaptation to the particular circumstances in which they are placed, bad roads, hard fare, but little sympathy or encouragement, and not infrequently opposition and persecution. Dr. Thomson has met with a hopeful successor to Mr. Von Laer in Mr. Michael Treiber, a German by birth, but a colonist in Bessarabia, who for some time studied in the College at St. Chrischona, and afterwards had some experience of Missionary work in Nubia. He occupied his new post in July last, and besides giving himself diligently to the study of the Turkish and Albanian languages, he has paid a visit to Cettigne, the capital of Montenegro, with a view of making arrangements for the supply of the National Schools of that province with the Word of God. Very advantageous terms were proposed, but for some unexplained reason they were not accepted. Otherwise Mr. Treiber's visit was successful. His experience of Scutari itself corresponds entirely with that of his predecessors. He speaks of the bulk of the population, who are members of the Church of Rome, as the subjects of gross ignorance and bigotry, and kept in degrading bondage by an unprincipled and corrupt priesthood. The following is the report of Colportage furnished by Dr. Thomson:—

> I should mention that, encouraged by his success at Prisrend in the autumn of 1868, Mr. Von Laer returned there in the spring of 1869 with a large supply of books. He had much conversation with the people, and was generally well received, but the weather was severe in the Alpine regions, and greatly impeded his operations. At Jakova, on the banks of the White Drin, he mentions having had a discussion with a Moslem hodja (teacher) as to the person of the Lord Jesus Christ. The Moslems sympathise with our simplicity of worship, but stoutly refuse to admit the Divine Sonship of the Saviour.

> Passing now to Epirus, it is but simple justice to Mr. Davidson to state that nobody could have been more diligent in visiting every part of his wide territory than he has been during the past year. This is all the more

to be valued because, while Mr. Davidson never at any time enjoys robust health, he has this year suffered more than usual debility from the heat. He performed three journeys—the first to Prevesa, and thence northward by way of Parga, Paramythia, Philates, Delvino, ArgyroCastro to Avlona, Fieri, and Berat, his northern limit, and then returning up the vale of the Viosa by Premedi and Kionitza, having performed a circuit of above 320 miles. His other two tours were much shorter—one to Arta, and thence to various towns in the vale of the Aspropotamos, or ancient Achelous; the other by way of Metzovo to Greveno, Kozan, Shatista, Klissura, Castoria, and Mavrovo. Upon the whole, the sales were equal to the average of former years, and in some towns, such as Philates, Delvino, Fieri, Arta, and Mavrovo, they exceeded it considerably; but other places, such as Prevesa, Parga, Margariti, Paramythia, Argyro-Castro, and Avlona, by the indifference, and even hostility and mockery with which they treated the Word of God, were a great trial to faith and patience. At Parga the people were not so much afraid of the books being bad, as that the priests would demand them and burn them. Where was the use then of buying? One friendly resident there told Mr. Davidson he trusted in Christ alone; yet he was as diligent in picture-worship as his neighbours. At Margariti he had to bear much bitterness and rudeness from the youth, but many Moslems came and read the Books, while no Christian took any notice of them. At Paramythia the bishop had been summoned to the capital to answer for high misdemeanours, and his example had deteriorated as well as alienated his flock. In Delvino the bishop bought a reference Bible, and enquired about our churches in Scotland. At Argyro-Castro, amid much infidelity and indifference, Mr.

Davidson witnessed the interesting spectacle of the ordination of a priest for the Albanian colonies in the south of Italy, which date at least from, the time of Scanderbeg—400 years ago. In Fieri, just as when I visited the place with Dr. Koelle in 1867, the teacher seemed unable to determine whether to approve of the books, which were perfectly good, as he knew, or to condemn them, as he was commanded by the bishop; but in both instances his better sense and feelings prevailed. In Premedi, though he was there during two feast days, he could sell nothing. In his other tours he came in contact with the Wallachian colony in Mount Pindus, and visited many flourishing towns, in some of which he had formerly sold well; but except at Arta and Mavrovo, his sales were on this occasion very discouraging.

Pages 176–177
Greece

Mr. Dewar has a companion in his Colportage work in Mr. Coulouriotis, a Greek Albanian, who has now for two years devoted himself to the faithful service of the Society, with special reference to his own countrymen.

Page 344
Progress in Translation and Revision of the Scriptures

Albanian – The whole New Testament has been completed in the Gheg or North Albanian dialect. It has been printed in the Roman character, according to Lepsius' system, under the superintendence of Mr. Christoforides, the translator. A new system of orthography has been proposed by the Literary Commission lately appointed by the Government, but has not been accepted by it.

67th Report, 1871

Pages 187–189

Turkey

There is no part of Europe which contains such masses of illiterate and uneducated people as Turkey, and it is only by little and little that the Word of God can be introduced amongst them. If the field of labour is hard to cultivate now, it was much harder twenty or thirty years ago, and what has been effected in the meanwhile, if collected in an array of statistics, would form a striking chapter in the history of modern Christianity, and furnish innumerable proofs of the triumph of steady, patient, prayerful efforts over obstacles of surprising number and magnitude. ...

One consequence of the war has been to suspend several lines of steam communication worked by French companies, and thereby to paralyse all the trade activities with which they were identified, and which necessarily depended on their continued regularity. Distress has become severe and wide spread, and not only the western seaboard of Asia Minor, with Smyrna as its capital, but Thessaly, Macedonia, Greece, and even Bulgaria and Roumania, have all suffered from the gigantic struggle which brought the two great military powers of Europe into mortal combat. ...

Dr. Thomson also mentions the deplorable act of brigandage in Greece, which excited so much attention at the time, and issued in the massacre of a party of Englishmen, observing that the prevalence of this evil has proved a serious hindrance to the development of your work in many parts both of Turkey and Greece. Some tours projected in the latter country had to be abandoned in consequence of the general sense of insecurity and alarm to which the lamentable event near Marathon gave rise. The whole of continental Greece, Thessaly, and South Epirus, are regions in which it is most desirable to make vigorous efforts for the dissemination of the Scriptures, but they cannot be penetrated without great personal risk, and into some parts it would be quite impracticable to enter.

Page 196

Bulgaria

This country, stretching from the Balkan range to the Danube, and from the Black Sea to Mount Pindus, has been diligently cultivated by the agency of your Society, but not to the full compass of its requirements. There is yet much land to be possessed on which Dr. Thomson is anxious to enter, and arrangements now agreed upon hold out the prospect of an early fulfilment of his wishes. Hitherto your operations have been very much restricted to the eastern parts of Bulgaria as being most accessible, and containing the great centres of population. But action has not been carried so far west as to include Old Servia, a district lying between the southern limits of modern Servia and the Turkish provinces of Bosnia, Albania, Macedonia and Bulgaria, forming a semicircle of territory about one hundred miles wide at the broadest, thinly peopled, cut off from sea and river navigation, and traversed by lofty ranges of mountains. The population possesses little culture or means of education, and its inland position deprives it of many advantages. Dr. Thomson has been desirous of sending a colporteur into these regions, and the Committee have sanctioned his proposal, as little or nothing has ever been attempted for the circulation of the Scriptures amongst the ignorant and neglected natives. Providentially a very eligible and well qualified person has offered for the work, and has been accepted. He is familiar with the people and their vernacular, and being possessed of much courage and zeal, seems fitted to become a useful pioneer in the sphere of his future labours. He has already entered upon his duties, and after some experience in the country, he will fix upon a place of residence most convenient for carrying out his tours of visitation.

Pages 202–205
Albania and Montenegro

Your agent states that these provinces have received a fare amount of attention during the year, but the results do not bring into prominence any features of strong encouragement. The peculiarity of the population must be taken into account in attempting to form an opinion as to the amount of good effected. Little and much are relative terms, whose significance must be determined by circumstances; and it is needful to bear this in mind if we are to be fortified against positive discouragement when cultivating difficult fields of labour. The depositary at Scutari, Mr. Treiber, finds himself in the midst of a people, few of whom cherish an atom of sympathy for the object which has taken him thither. They are composed mostly of bigoted Romanists and fanatical Moslems, and the mission of the Book meets with no favour from the one party or the other. The opinion is expressed that there is not another city in Europe where Popery is more strongly entrenched in the ignorance and superstition of the people, and where the priests, as a body, are more corrupt and tyrannical. From such a scene of labour it is not surprising to hear that the circulation of the Bible is small; but even that is not to be despised. If a few grains of the incorruptible seed drop effectually into the heart and germinate there, under the quickening energy of the Holy Spirit, they may lead to such a living testimony for Christ and His Truth as shall sway the convictions of many and win them to the obedience of the Gospel. Mr. Treiber made several tours through Dalmatia into Herzegovina, and to Prisrend and Montenegro, but sales were trifling. Sickness in his family prevented such extensive operations as he had contemplated. The new year is entered upon with more hopeful prospects, and better results are anticipated.

In central Albania the success has been very marked. In compliance with the request of Dr. Thomson, the Committee sanctioned the employment of Mr. Christoforides, the translator of the Scriptures into the Gheg Albanian, as a colporteur, for a limited period. It may be instructive to record here some observations of your agent on the issues in the Gheg dialect and the character of the translation:—

The Gheg issues present, however, a most interesting fact, being nothing less than, as we trust we may say without fear, the addition of one more to the written languages of Europe. So long as the orthography, in which the Society had published parts of the Holy Scriptures in Gheg, was accepted by, and intelligible to, a small circle only, fear might reasonably be entertained that the system would never be adopted generally by the nation. Such fears, we trust, are now to a large extent removed. The Gheg sales have been effected almost entirely in Albania itself, by the Society's translator, and such large numbers in the chief towns of central Albania have bought copies, and learned the art of reading, that we may venture to hope the use of Albanian books, in this form, will be considered henceforth a necessity of social and national life. To how many minds and to how many family circles access may now be had through this medium, may be understood from the fact, that there are probably a million of Ghegs, male and female, unable to speak, except in the most imperfect manner, any other language than their own, and wholly without books or education of any kind.

The tour of Mr. Christoforides was the first attempt that had been made to circulate the Gheg Scriptures in Albania itself, and the hearty acceptance they found in the country opens a door of hope for the entrance of educational and religious agencies:—

His reception for once quite belied the proverb that a prophet is not without honour, save in his own country, for, after having made the tour of several neighbouring towns, and instructed his countrymen in the value and mode of reading the new orthography, his return to Elbassan, his native town, was rather a triumphal procession than the return of a peaceful literary man to his humble home. He is hopeful that our Scriptures in Gheg, along with the preparatory publications by the Religious Tract Society, without which the introduction of the Scriptures would have been far more arduous, may soon be introduced universally into the principal schools, and many new schools be established.

As it appeared unnecessary to have three colporteurs in Albania, it was resolved by Dr. Thomson to transfer Mr. Davidson from Joannina to Crete, where for some time he has desired to station a representative of the Society. Mr. Davidson took a final tour through some parts of Albania, visiting Arta, Prevesa, Parga, Margariti and Paramythia, and then, turning north, proceeded to Philates, Delvino, and Argyrocastro. Little in the way of sales of Scriptures was effected. The people admitted that the Bible was good, but evidently cherished the suspicion that some sinister design was hid behind these efforts for its circulation. With a strong passion for gambling and intoxicating spirits, they were not disposed to give much heed to anything that condemned their favourite practices. At Philates and Delvino a few copies were purchased, and when Mr. Davidson was at Paramythia, Bishop Anthimios evinced a friendly spirit towards him, and urged the people to embrace the opportunity of providing themselves with the Scriptures. On the whole, the journey was not very fruitful in cheering results.

The entire circulation in Albania was 590 copies, a large number, when it is recollected that the province is not thickly populated, and education at a miserably low level.

Page 212

[Mr. Dewar's] second tour was one of still greater importance, attended with no small danger and rewarded by abundant success. It was undertaken in August, and had for its object continental Greece, a country both difficult to travel in at any time, from its mountainous character and the want of roads, and notoriously unsafe from the numerous brigands that infest almost every part of it. Mr. Dewar felt that to these regions also he was a debtor, and, notwithstanding the fears and remonstrances of his friends, he set out. His first destination was Chalcis, in the island of Euboea, where he sold eight copies, and then proceeded to Thebes, now a mean village entirely inhabited by Albanians, for whose instruction in their native tongue the Greek Government, intent on Hellenizing all its subjects, will make no provision. Here he sold six copies, then proceeded to Thespias. ...

Page 404

Progress in the Work of Translation and Revision of the Scriptures

Albanian – Satisfactory testimonies have been received concerning the acceptableness of the Gheg or Northern Albanian New Testament and Psalms, prepared by Mr. Christoforides; and the Committee are proposing to purchase a translation of two Books of the Pentateuch made by the same hand. Mr. Christoforides was Gheg instructor to Dr. Hahn, the author of the standard work on the Albanian language.

Page 89 of the Appendix

Donations to the Library

From H.I.H. Prince L. L. Bonaparte:

The Gospel of St. Matthew, in the Calabrian-Albanian Dialect of Frascineto, London, 1869.

The Gospel of St. Matthew, in the Gheg-Albanian Dialect of Scutari, London, 1870.

68th Report, 1872

Page 147

Italy

Calabria is occupied by one of your colporteurs, who states that readers of the Bible are to be found in all the small towns. ...

Mr. Bruce further states that there are ten or twelve Albanian villages, all the inhabitants of which are well disposed towards the Truth, and that at San Demetrio there is a college with about 200 students, among whom the colporteur always finds some customers, in addition to receiving board and lodging free of expense. There is but little of that scepticism so common in other parts of Italy prevalent here.

Pages 152–153
Turkey

The retirement from the service of the Society of Mr. Treiber, of Scutari, [left] the vast Province of Albania for some months without superintendence. ...

That a considerable increase would be exhibited in the issues of the past year was to be expected. The addition to them of the Scriptures sold in Egypt, the opening of a Depot in Alexandria, and the employment of a larger staff of colporteurs, one of whom has been stationed in Old Servia, one in Lower Egypt, and another in the Lebanon, all tended to the enlargement of your circulation, and helped to give a fresh impulse to your work.

Pages 156–157

The following are some of [Alexander Thomson's] thoughts upon the languages and nationalities referred to in the preceding table:—

> First in order, and on many accounts entitled to a large share of our sympathies, stand the Albanian issues, in which the extensive circulation effected in recent years presents a striking contrast to the insignificant numbers of former times, and leads to the hope that the Albanian people have at last resolved to introduce the use of their own vernacular as the medium of education. The Gheg circulation is less indeed by 122 than it was in 1870, but when it is added, that, literally, every copy of every book that could be spared has been sold off, the limited circulation need be no discouragement. On the other hand, the Tosk circulation of 711, exhibits, in

contrast with the 60 of 1870, the difference between the new and the old rate of sales, and encourages us to expect, that as the Tosk dialect is spoken by a larger population than the Gheg, which is better supplied with schools and foreign literature, so when once the demand for Albanian literature shall have taken root, a large supply will be required in that dialect. How needful Christian education is for the Albanian nation, the troubles of the past year but too conclusively show.

Pages 169–171

Albania and Montenegro

Dr. Thomson states that during the past year Joannina, which had for some time been the residence of Mr. Davidson, has been unoccupied, and that, consequently, there has been no distribution of the Scriptures in South Albania. A small Depot has, however, been entrusted to a merchant, and Mr. Zabanski paid a visit to the city which was fairly successful. In Central Albania, Mr. Christophorides distributed 1,019 copies, whilst he earnestly pressed upon the people the need of studying the Scriptures in their own language. After selling all the books that he had in the Gheg dialect, he purposed returning to Constantinople to prepare new editions for the press, but he was so urged to visit Berat, and commence a similar work among the Tosks to that which he had done among the Ghegs, that he could not resist. At Berat a surprise awaited him. He found that a female teacher had already mastered the new system of orthography, and had taught the three elder classes of her pupils to read it with ease. Before he left the country lie had put into circulation 600 Testaments and Psalms. Some of these were printed in the old and defective system, but were still sufficient to convey knowledge to the ignorant and light to the blind. Of those printed in the new system your Agent observes—

> Mr. Christophorides assures me that they are introduced into all the six boys' schools and both the girls' schools at Berat, whilst the Albanian Psalms are used in the church there, and at Elbassan the Society's Psalms are for the most part read, and the lessons invariably taken from the New Testament. That seems satisfactory testimony to their correctness and intelligibility. It was on every ground to be anticipated that the Albanian Scriptures would be received by the adherents of the Greek Church sooner than by Romanists, of whom there are many in North Albania, or by Moslems. But it is pleasing to find that many Romanists in Durazzo and Tyranna, as also a few at Avlona, have received the Society's books, some of which have found their way even into Scutari. Mr. Christophorides mentions particularly the case of a poor tinker from Scutari, who, though a Romanist, bought and read the Scriptures with the utmost diligence, studying them, and asking for explanations, and even teaching others to read. Not a few Moslems also, in all the towns of Central Albania have learned to read, and the more enlightened of them recognise in a national literature the only means of securing national unity and progress. I should further mention that our Scriptures are affirmed to be in use in the schools of Dibra, in a wild sequestered valley, so unsafe for travellers that Mr. Christophorides did not venture to visit it. The Bishop, however, is favourably-disposed towards our work. Mr. Christophorides visited the Matt country—a wild region wholly independent of the Sultan—and has collected much interesting information respecting the Matts and the Mirdites, which is well fitted to deepen the interest of Christians in these people, but for which I have no

room here. One thing is certain, that if anything is to be done, schools and books of varied information are necessary. Schools may be established by the people themselves, but for books they must look to friends without.

Mr. Treiber, who lately represented your Society at Scutari, has felt it necessary to resign his post. The difficulties which he had to contend with were very great, and the state of the country, both political and social, was most unfavourable. Still had he been of a more hopeful disposition his other qualifications might have been turned to good account. Dr. Thomson thus refers to his work before he left the Society:—

In the early part of the year Mr. Treiber performed three tours, one to Dulcigno on the sea coast, and back by Antivari and Spezzia; another to Budua, Cattaro, and Ragusa; and a third to Cettigne, the capital of Montenegro; his sales in all amounted to 139 copies. In Dulcigno he found the Slavonic priest (an armourer by trade), but he was favourable to the sale of the Scriptures, and bought six New Testaments. In Cattaro and Ragusa rationalism and infidelity were rampant, and even blasphemy not unfrequent, and Renan in high repute. In Scutari itself the people were ignorant, bigoted, suspicious, crouching beneath the tyranny of Rome, yet here and there raising a rigorous protest against her usurpations. In Montenegro alone he found a state of things the reverse of all this. Ignorant though they were, and, therefore, to some extent superstitious, these indomitable mountaineers seemed to be animated by a powerful thirst for knowledge, as well as love and reverence for the Word of God. On being assured by their priests that the books were correct, they bought in a short time 50 copies, and were so anxious each of them to possess a portion, that thousands of copies would have been thankfully received by the vast throng, and would have been valued. Experience, however, forbids such a mode of distribution, except on rare occasions of an exceptional kind.

Thessaly

Mr. Zabanski, to whose faithfulness and zeal Dr. Thomson bears his willing testimony, has succeeded in selling 278 copies of the Scriptures, being sixty- one more than in 1870. ... Mr. Zabanski's work is thus referred to by your Agent:

> ... In addition to visiting every part of his proper province of Thessaly, Mr. Zabanski went last year to Joannina, the capital of Epirus, formerly occupied by Mr. Davidson. The journey was every way as successful as could have been anticipated, but being made in early summer, across the lofty range of Pindus, it was attended with no small danger from extreme cold and roads broken up by torrents. Mr. Zabanski mentions the high appreciation in which Mr. Davidson was held in Joannina by both Jews and Greeks, who made many kind inquiries for him....

Pages 177–179
Greece

The kingdom of Greece has not proved so favourable a soil for cultivation by your Society as was at one time expected. ... Great difficulty has also been experienced in providing a suitable agent for the prosecution of colportage, which has been proved to be by far the most successful method of diffusing among the Greeks a knowledge of

Divine Truth. Mr. Koulouriotis, who superintends the Depot at Athens, has in vain sought after a man on whom dependence could be placed for such a purpose, and failing to meet with one, has himself under taken the work, as far as his time and circumstances would permit. ... Mr. Koulouriotis has been enabled twice to engage in the work of colportage, and Dr. Thomson has furnished the following account of his tours:—

> At Achouria he very unexpectedly succeeded in selling nine copies, and at Doliana, on the brow of a steep but fertile hill, he sold six. Here he met with an Albanian, eighty years of age, who had served in the British fleet against Napoleon, and who, after the lapse of fifty years, could still speak English. This old veteran was superstitious and tenacious of old rites, and had left the British service on religious grounds.

69th Report, 1873

Pages 200–203

The report of your Agent, the Rev. Dr. Thomson, is, as usual, very copious, and enters largely into all the questions and interests which affect the Society's operations. operations. After stating that his uniform purpose is to secure godly men for the duties of colportage, or the superintendence of Depots in the sub-divisions of his agency, he observes that though some advance has been made in the circulation. of the Scriptures, it is much less than he had desired or anticipated. In explanation Dr. Thomson remarks that there were various untoward circumstances which tended to defeat his wishes and plans, whereby a check was given to the work in several directions. Mr. Christophorides, the Albanian translator, was detained in Constantinople for editorial purposes longer than had been expected, and this circumstance postponed the resumption by him of colportage operations in Albania. ....

Three of the colporteurs were interfered with by actual violence, viz., Mr. Koulouriotis at Corfu, Mr. Pilo at Samos, and Mr. Misaelides at Kalymnos, all of whom had to endure rough and unjust treatment. ....

Dr. Thomson sent a colporteur to occupy an altogether new region, comprising the northern part of Macedonia and the western part of Old Servia, with Uscup for his residence. But disappointment followed this plan, for the colporteur and his whole family were smitten with malignant fever, and after burying two of his children he was so much enfeebled in health that he could do very little to realise the hopes of Dr. Thomson before the close of the year.

During the year there have been printed 23,000 copies in Arabic, Ruman, Bulgarian, and Albanian. ...

The issues are classified by Dr. Thomson according to language:

Albanian, Tosk and Gheg – 117 issues.

The decrease as compared with last year of 975 copies in the Albanian issues, is so far satisfactorily explained by the total exhaustion of the Gheg editions, and the absence of any one in Albania to prosecute the circulation of Tosk Scriptures there.

Page 204

In regard to the Albanian—both Tosk and Gheg dialects—it was deemed desirable that further translation and printing should not be proceeded with until more ample and satisfactory testimony was available as to the acceptability by the people of the new system of orthography adopted.

Page 215
Old Servia, Albania, and Montenegro

On these divisions of his Agency Dr. Thomson has little to report. His plans for Old Servia were defeated, as has been already stated, by the protracted and dangerous illness of the colporteur who was sent to Uscup, and at the close of the year operations had scarcely commenced, but some few sales had been effected, and Mr. Klundt had access to Albanians, Servians, Bulgarians, Jews, Greeks, and Moslems, amongst whom he hopes to find ample opportunities for useful labour.

On his return from Bosnia Dr. Thomson had entertained the design of passing through Central Albania, to collect on the spot testimony concerning the new editions of the Albanian Scriptures issued by the Society, but he could not command the necessary facilities, and had very reluctantly to forego the fulfilment of his wishes. There was no colportage in Albania last year, Mr. Christophorides having been withdrawn temporarily, that he might superintend the printing of a revised edition of the Gheg Albanian Testament and Psalms. This work being finished by the middle of November, he was enabled to take his departure from Constantinople, and commenced sales immediately on his arrival in Albania, of which country he is a native. Concerning Mr. Christophorides the subjoined observations occur:

Under date January 23, 1873, he reports the following sales in Durazzo, Kavaya, and Tiranna:

Gheg Testaments with Psalms	30
Gheg Testaments	44

Gheg Gospels and Acts	58
Gheg Psalms	72
Tosk Psalms	25
Tosk and Modern Greek Testaments	13
Tosk and Modern Greek Epistles	20
— 262 copies total	

In a still later communication, dated February 28, he reports that in Durazzo, Kavaya, Tiranna, and especially at Elbassan, where he then was, the Gospels and Epistles, and still more generally the Psalms, were read from the Society's editions in the churches, after their perusal in the original Greek, and what is perhaps quite as interesting, that in many families in these towns the evening was spent in hearing the Word of God, and certain publications of the Religious Tract Society, read in the presence of the whole family, the females particularly being much interested in them, and urging and entreating the reader to continue, when he was inclined to desist. One merchant, Anastasius Goga, of Durazzo, reports that he read thus to the household at the direction of his mother, and another, named Nova, mentions that he made his son read aloud every night the Albanian Scriptures to the household. Mr. Christophorides mentions also, that in several cases he had heard of the Lord's Day having been spent in this way.

Your Depot at Scutari being at the present without a colporteur, the Principality of Montenegro has not been recently visited. As a line of railway now in course of construction is expected to be continued northwards in the vicinity of the Montenegrin frontier, it may be hoped that the district will eventually become far more accessible than it has hitherto been.

Page 410

Progress in the Work of Translation and Revision, 1872-3.

Albanian (Gheg) – A revised edition of the New Testament and Psalms in the Gheg or Northern Albanian Dialect has been printed, under the superintendence of Mr. Christoforides, the translator.

70th Report, 1874

Pages 126–127

[Alexander Thomson] writes, "The Albanian language again appears in respectable numbers, and in both dialects, in consequence of the labours of Mr. Christophorides, the translator, among his own people. Let us hope that the Gospel in their own tongue may thus reach many a family, and especially the females, who have hitherto been strangers to it."

Pages 135–137

Albania

Dr. Thomson states that there is no province of Turkey which is more entitled to the sympathy and aid of Christian nations than that which is formed by the tract of country extending along the shore of the Adriatic for a distance of 260 miles, between Dalmatia and Montenegro on the north, and the Gulf of Arta and the Greek frontier on the south. There is good reason to believe that its inhabitants received the Gospel from the great Apostle of the Gentiles, but as they had no part of the Word of God translated into their own language, it is very doubtful whether Christianity ever prevailed to any extent. As yet they have no vernacular literature, and their personal courage and independence, which has prompted them to set all authority at defiance, has at the same time tended to perpetuate a condition of ignorance and barbarism which has left them far behind the other nationalities of the empire. The Religious Tract Society has published some elementary books both in the Gheg and Tosk Albanian, and these it is hoped will pave the way for the wider circulation of the New Testament in the former dialect, and of the Psalms in the latter, both of which your Society has published. These have been translated by Mr. Christophorides, who has spent the whole of the past year in the endeavour to introduce them to the people. He began his work in Central Albania, where the Gheg dialect is spoken in its greatest purity, and where the number of readers is proportionately large, and he succeeded in selling 1,049 copies, of which 905 were Albanian. He next proceeded to North Albania, and visited Antivari and Scutari, but here he found the people sunk in the most abject superstition, and in entire bondage to the Romish priests, whose bishops are sent from Rome. Still, his visit has done good, and a beginning has been made which it is hoped may be the harbinger of fight to its long neglected population. In the south, where the Tosk is spoken, he met with a cordial reception, and found the people awaking to the necessity of cultivating their own vernacular. As the medium of instruction and literature, Dr. Thomson evidently feels a deep interest in the progress of this work, and expresses an earnest hope that the subject may be taken up by some Christian Mission, through which the intelligence of the people may be developed and the standard of their literature fixed.

Old Servia and Macedonia

With a view of circulating the Scriptures in the district known as Old Servia, which encircles the modern principality of that name, Colporteur Klundt has been stationed at Uscup, which, being a station on the Great Northern Railway from Salonica, enjoys many advantages. It is, however, somewhat unhealthy, and both Klundt and his family have suffered from sickness. During the ten and a-half months that he has been enabled to work, he has sold 509 copies, and has manifested much zeal and faithfulness in the discharge of his duties. He was, however, as has been already mentioned, suspected of being a Russian spy when visiting Scutari with a view of getting possession of a stock of books which had been left there, and thrown into prison. He was thence sent under a military escort to Prisrend and Uscup, where, though he had resided in the town for a twelvemonth, he was required by the Caimakam to find a surety for his good conduct, and was forbidden to sell any books, or to quit the town. Nor was this embargo removed until Dr. Thomson had enlisted the services of Her Majesty's ambassador at Constantinople. Even then, however, no pecuniary redress could be obtained for the losses which he had sustained. The colportage which is carried on in Macedonia is through the instrumentality of the National Bible Society of Scotland, under the direction of the Rev. P. Crosbie, to whom your Committee are indebted for his kind interposition on behalf of Mr. Klundt, having at Dr. Thomson's request gone to Uscup, and done all in his power to sympathise with him in his distress, and to remove from the mind of the Caimakam all suspicion concerning the occupation in which he was engaged.

Thessaly

Mr. Zabanski is reported to have discharged his duties in this province with his usual perseverance and with some success, having sold 386 copies, which, though fewer than last year, is above the average. Dr. Thomson thus reviews his work: "Besides visiting Thessaly Mr. Zabanski also performed three distinct tours, the first to the Jewish colony at Chalcis, in the island of Euboea, the second to Joannina and Arta in Epirus, and the third to the island of Thasos, ..."

Pages 139–141

Greece

As illustrative of the work done in Greece, Dr. Thomson has furnished an outline of a tour in the Ionian Islands, taken in the autumn by Mr. Koulouriotis:

> Mr. Koulouriotis started from Athens just after the currant vintage, and reached Zante, his first station, August 17. ... [After visiting Zante, Cephalonia, Lixuri, Ithaca, and Leucadia], he next attempted to proceed to Corfu, but found his way barred by the quarantine regulations, which had been enforced immediately on the appearance of cholera. He, therefore, proceeded to Prevesa, in South Albania, but could effect only a very few sales, owing to the opposition he met with from the Greek priest of the town, who used every exertion to get him banished from the place. He had afterwards to proceed by boat to Missolonghi.

71st Report, 1875

Page 116

Turkey

Local interruptions must be looked for every year; but of late months they seem to have been unusually numerous. Thus Crete has been left entirely unprovided for through the death of the depositary, Mr. Davidson; Albania in like manner was vacant for nearly six months; colporteurs Pilo in Mitylene, and Risk Butros on the Lebanon, were laid aside for several weeks each; Mr. Koulouriotis could make only one tour in Greece instead of two ...

Page 118

A recent utterance of M. Musurus, the Ottoman Minister in London, has appeared disclaiming all desire on the part of his Government to prohibit the printing of the Scriptures, and asserting that it seeks only to prevent "colportage and gratuitous distribution in the open streets of the capital of an Empire the inhabitants of which are, in a great majority, Mussulmans." To this it is sufficient to reply (1) that the Society does not distribute gratuitously, save in rare and urgent cases; and (2) that colportage of all kinds has gone on for nearly twenty years in the various quarters of the city without single instance of popular disturbance. The seizure of Mr. Klundt's Scriptures in Upper Albania, and their detention in spite of all remonstrance, help to shew that the Turkish Government is feeling a decided dread of a Volume whose power is beginning to be felt in the land. Certainly no act could be more inconsistent than to promise to its subjects freedom of religious choice, and yet debar them access to the very books which could alone be brought into comparison with the Koran. Your Society has always been anxious to avoid a proselytising spirit in its Turkish work. It desires to respect the authorities that be, and will rest content if permitted to lay freely before the people, and in their own tongue, the Book upon which each man is called to judge for himself.

Pages 120–123

Two faithful colporteurs have died during the year. One was Mr. Davidson, a Scotchman whom your Agent sent ten years ago into Epirus. He laboured there with diligence and success, but his services being required for Crete, he was transferred thither in 1870. The same zeal and fidelity were displayed in his new sphere, in which he secured the respect, amongst others, of Her Majesty's Consul at Canea. In the summer of 1873, while crossing the lofty Sphakian range, he was seized with pleurisy, which compelled his return to Scotland. He died this winter at Edinburgh, at the early age of 38. The other case was that of Mr. Constantinides, who had laboured in Greece for about three years. In the autumn he returned to his family in enfeebled health, and sank after four months' suffering, borne with great patience....

The issues are classified according to languages, thus:

Albanian, Gheg   ...   463
Albanian, Tosk...   303

The decrease in Albanian is due to the suspension of colportage since last summer... Bulgarian shows a gross increase of 608, attributable to Klundt's labours in Old Servia and the opening of an American Mission in Western Macedonia.

Pages 127–128, based on reports from Alexander Thomson
Albania and Montenegro

Of these countries, which are so often a cause of alarm and anxiety to their neighbours, there is less to report than there was last year, as colportage has been interrupted since August. Mr. Christophorides, in whom full confidence had been placed, pursued his work up to that date, distributing 1,019 copies, two thirds of which were in Tosk or Gheg Albanian, and the rest mostly Greek. His reception, whilst journeying in Central Albania, was cordial, and even in the north he found several of the Roman Catholic clergy and laity willing to encourage his labours. This colporteur is no longer in the Society's service. After prolonged search, another man, who seems to possess the requisite qualifications, has been sent to this district, of which it may be said that it would be absolutely unprovided for, were not your efforts on its behalf continued.

Old Servia

No part of Dr. Thomson's extensive Agency has been cultivated with greater diligence and success than this province, which is under the care of Mr. Klundt. It has been the scene of ferment, the Bulgarians standing out staunchly against the authority of the Greek Patriarch, which the Greeks and Servians are not less resolute in upholding. The former seem likely to win the day and spread their love of liberty. At present—

Education is advancing, the schools being in every instance erected and supported by the people themselves; while the languages to be taught, the salary to be allotted, the introduction or exclusion of the Scriptures, the mode of instruction to be pursued, and such like, are topics discussed with warm interest in every town.

Your Agent paid a visit in April last to Uscup, using the new railway which has been carried along the valley of the Vardar from Salonica. There he had a satisfactory interview with Klundt, whose sale of 833 copies in 1874 bears witness to his activity. The latter made recently two journeys to Prisrend, Ipek and Jakovo in the north-western extremity of his district, and was more successful than he had anticipated in those strongholds of ecclesiastical authority. On each of his tours he was attacked by brigands, being saved on one occasion only by the heroic courage of his muleteer. It was on his return from the later tour that his Turkish Scriptures were seized by the Governor of Prisrend, who has not since returned them.

Thessaly

A letter was received by your Committee some weeks ago, stating that brigandage had, for the first time in the memory of man, been stamped out in Thessaly. If this news be true, it is a matter for sincere congratulation; but it is a fact that Mr. Zabanski, who superintends the Society's work in Thessaly, has been compelled by fear of personal danger to limit his journeys to certain parts of the country. ...

The visit which Dr. Thomson paid last spring to Greece gave him an opportunity of renewing acquaintance with the work in Thessaly:

> I did not reach Volo till the morning of the 10th. It was obvious at a glance that the last five years had been rich in material prosperity to Thessaly, for the merchants of Volo had erected so many elegant private mansions as to give the place quite a new aspect. The beautiful scenery of the straits through which we had passed, and the grand amphitheatre of mountains with which

we now seemed to be encompassed on the shore of
a lovely gulf, suggested to the mind thoughts of the
grandeur and beneficence of the great Creator, who
had provided such a dwelling-place for his creatures. But
as we reached the pier, the stolid, degrading ignorance
of the porters and others who crowded forward, made
one suddenly and painfully realise the terrible ravages
that sin has brought on this fair world. These people
were mostly Albanians—an active, independent
race, with great capabilities of improvement, but
remaining hitherto utterly unapproached by Gospel
agency. Saddening as was the impression they made
upon the spectator, Mr. Zabanski assured me that the
general aspect of the peasantry in the interior is far
more painful—the sad result of long decades, if not
centuries, of brigandage and neglect. On the morning
of the 11th, however, Mr. Z. and I walked a couple
of miles to attend one of the fairs, which almost
invariably accompany the great festivals of the Greek
Church. I was anxious to take copies of the Scriptures
with us and attempt sales; but Mr. Z. knew better on
the whole than I the character of these gatherings,
and said it was needless. Certainly the scene of bustle
which we witnessed explained to me, better than any
words could have done, the poor results that attend
the efforts of our colporteurs everywhere to dispose
of the Scriptures at such gatherings. The Society's
work in Thessaly must be one of steady, unwearied
perseverance, in the full assurance that, done in faith
and for His name's sake, the Lord will not, cannot
permit it to be in vain.

72nd Report, 1876

Pages 98–99

Old Servia and Upper Macedonia

In no part of the agency are there to be found more distinct evidences of the power of Divine Truth than in this district, a result which Dr. Thomson ascribes largely to the faithful zeal and blameless character of colporteur Klundt. It comprises a fairly representative population— Bulgarians and Servians, Turks, Greeks, Jews, and Circassians, and Gheg and Tosk Albanians. The Greeks are the most advanced of these in point of education, having trained teachers and schools for both boys and girls. They, however, almost uniformly oppose the circulation of the Scriptures, which is the more to be regretted as it is said to arise from ecclesiastical differences among themselves. ...

At Prishtina [Klundt] received an invitation to the house of a Bulgarian shopkeeper to whom he had sold a Bible two years before. This man had read it through three times, and had received all the cardinal doctrines of the Gospel, and amidst much opposition confessed the name of Jesus. In two other towns, Djeeb and Kratovo, he met with much encouragement, finding in the first a lady of some wealth, who was also rich in good works and anxiously seeking after the Truth, and in the second a disciple wholly on the Lord's side, and who has such delight in reading the Scriptures, that he is not ashamed to face hatred and opposition in his confession of Christ. The sales of Klundt have amounted to 562 copies.

Albania and Montenegro

The extensive province of Albania is perhaps, all things considered, the most backward in the empire as regards civilisation and religious instruction. Sunk in deep ignorance and addicted to plunder and violence, the people have not even a written language, and are so disunited among themselves that they have no disposition for self-help. At the same time the publication of the New Testament and Psalms in Gheg and Tosk Albanian has not been without its influence, and Dr. Thomson has been most anxious to find a suitable colporteur who by his life and conversation would commend the Gospel which he offered for acceptance. His efforts have at length been crowned with success, but Fischer, who is the man chosen for this purpose, has had to endure heavy affliction in the shape of personal and family sickness. His wife and daughter have both been stricken with fever, the latter twice, so as to have been brought to the brink of the grave. He has, however, been raised up again and enabled to undertake two tours, during the first of which he sold 70 copies, and during the second 96. In South Albania a few schools have been opened, which is a satisfactory evidence of progress, and may be traced to the action of your late colporteur, Mr. Davidson, at Joannina. For Montenegro nothing has been done during the past year. With every desire to meet the wants of this people, it has not been possible to send anyone to their distant and almost inaccessible eyrie.

73rd Report, 1877

Pages 130–131
Turkey

The long-expected, long-delayed crisis at last has come. The Powers of Europe have exhausted all the resources of counsel and persuasion with a view to obtain from the

Sultan some guarantee for the better government of his Christian subjects, but to no purpose; and now he is left to make his account with the nation which borders on his own and is most closely related to the oppressed race. But while it is the object of others to stand aloof and avoid entanglement in a war which is terrible in the religious antipathy of the combatants and the means of destruction at their command, it is the duty of a Christian Society such as this to press forward with the soothing influence of the Divine Word and the exhibition of brotherly kindness on the part of its Agents. It is easier to do this on the Russian side than on the Turkish, since the Moslems identify everything Christian with their present enemy; but their sick and wounded may yield to the approach of the colporteur ...

Pages 138–139
Albania and Montenegro

The condition of these two countries during the past year has been very dissimilar, Montenegro being engaged in a not unsuccessful war, while Albania has been far less agitated than the warlike character of its people and its proximity to the scene of conflict might have led one to expect. For the former absolutely nothing could be done from the Turkish side. Whenever peace is concluded and free navigation opened up the river Boyana and the lake of Scutari, your Agent will at once avail himself of this mode of access to the brave and intelligent subjects of Prince Nikita. Colporteur Fischer continues to reside at Berat as the most populous town of Central Albania, though like all the neighbouring towns it suffers from the lack of drainage and the presence of malaria. Your Committee having determined on fresh arrangements at Janina, Dr. Thomson only awaits a settlement of political affairs to assign to Fischer a suitable and more healthy position in the north. With continual sickness in his family this colporteur has done well in selling 339 volumes. His sales were effected along the line—an imaginary line unfortunately, not one of railway communication—between Durazzo, Avlona, Premed, and Janina.

In Berat a rich merchant, who was at first very hostile, afterwards had many interesting conversations with Fischer as to the Bible and the operations of your Society, which he greatly praised, finally buying as many as 29 volumes. Still more interesting is the case of a young man, also of Berat, who had bought a Bible, and who assured Fischer that he read two chapters of it every night on his knees before retiring to rest, and then went to the pictures of the saints and crossed himself; which was the only way in which, like most members of the Oriental as well as the Romish Churches, he was wont to express prayer and adoration to God. Fischer urged him to continue the diligent and devout reading of the Scriptures, but endeavoured to give him more adequate conceptions of the nature of prayer. He mentions this young man again, and with continued approbation. Fischer describes, what I myself have seen in Albania, the deep poverty in which the people are ever becoming more involved, as the natural consequence of having to support a dominant, rapacious section of the population, who add little comparatively to the productive power of the community. It is, doubtless, largely in consequence of this that the female school, which till within two years ago existed in Berat, has been discontinued. The teacher claimed no less than 30 liras of arrears of salary, and finding no prospect of recovering the debt, she withdrew to Durazzo. Such an event no one can regard without the deepest regret; for it is not merely stagnation but retrogression. And, in keeping with this, Fischer reports that, cheap as our books are, many are unable from sheer poverty to buy them, as their earnings amount only to about 4 ½ d. a day. Such is Turkish rule, producing, as its invariable consequences, depopulation, desolation, and impoverishment.

Old Servia

This part of European Turkey attracted the closest attention of the Constantinople Relief Committee, inasmuch as it was found that, though not so many lives had been sacrificed in it as in the region of Philippopolis and Tatar Bazardjik, incredible wrongs had been done by the lawless bands of Circassians to the wretched peasantry, especially in the villages on the great plain of Kossovo. The Society's colporteur Klundt has rendered invaluable service in reporting on the destitution and dispensing the funds entrusted to his care. The railway from Salonica now extends to Mitrovitza, and the company conveyed free of charge all blankets and articles of clothing which were destined for the suffering district. Prior to the declaration of war Klundt was able to leave Uscup on short tours, one of which was to Monastir in the south, where terms of harmonious action were arranged with the American missionaries.

74th Report, 1878

Page 103
Turkey

A revised edition of the New Testament in Tosk Albanian, which is the vernacular of a people numbering about four millions, is also in course of preparation, and when complete will be published in alternate columns with the Modern Greek. The system of Lepsius, which had been previously used with success in the Gheg Albanian, has been adopted also in this; and Dr. Thomson looks forward with no small satisfaction to the speedy conclusion of a work in which he has taken much interest, and on which he hopes for the blessing of God.

Pages 107–109
Albania and Montenegro

It has been quite impossible to do anything in Montenegro during the past year, but Dr. Thomson waits, in anxious expectation, the return of peace, and looks forward with no small pleasure to the introduction of the Word of God among these brave mountaineers, who have for centuries maintained so noble a struggle for political freedom. On the other hand, the greater part of Albania has enjoyed an exceptional freedom from disturbance, and there Colporteur Fischer has been able to prosecute his labours with encouraging success, having sold within the year 739 copies. When Dr. Thomson visited Albania one of his objects was to make acquaintance with this colporteur, and he was glad to ascertain that he occupied a good position, and was highly respected. At Berat, where he lived, and where Dr. Thomson spent the best part of four days under his roof, he found his house frequented by earnest enquirers after Truth, his own interview with one of whom he thus describes:

One intelligent young man, who visited Fischer on Sunday, shortly after midday, and who spoke Greek freely, particularly interested your Agent. He was anxious to learn what were the religious views of the Protestants, and enquired into the orthodoxy of your Agent on all the articles of the Nicene Creed. After satisfying him on these points, your Agent became in turn the examiner, and asked the young Albanian what answer he would give to one who asked the all-important question, 'What must I do to be saved?' His answer brought out the indistinct teachings of the Greek Church, for he insisted on instruction, faith, prayer, good works, the Sacraments, the intercession of the saints, and various other things. He was not a little surprised when your Agent insisted on faith in the Son of God as the one essential requisite, and represented all good works and graces as the fruits of a living faith. The conversation now assumed a more practical turn, and continued till the shades of evening gathered around us.

Fischer visited during the year most of the towns in central Albania, and went as far south as Ioannina. He reports that in most cases the teachers of schools encouraged their pupils to buy; but in one instance, in which the master threw his influence into the opposite scale, his opposition produced a contrary effect to what he intended, for the pupils bought 57 copies. At Konitza he found a most earnest spirit of enquiry after Truth, and one young man especially interested him by the eagerness with which he sought instruction on questions of faith and practice.

Old Servia and Macedonia

It is useless to repeat the causes which rendered it impossible to carry on the Society's work in Old Servia. Colporteur Klundt was chiefly employed in the distribution of corn and clothing to the famishing and destitute population. In Macedonia the country was less disturbed, and the Rev. P. Crosbie, of Salonica, was enabled to effect a few sales, which, with those sold by Colporteur Klundt at Uscup, made a total of 113 copies. Dr. Thomson expresses his high sense of the services rendered by Mr. Crosbie during the past year, not only to the cause of religion, but of humanity. The encouragement which he gave to the Society's colporteur was most valuable, and the influence which he has obtained through his high character and long experience at Salonica rendered his efforts for the circulation of the Scriptures and the relief of the needy most effectual. Klundt disposed of the 80 copies, which he sold chiefly at Uscup, and during the month of September. He resides at Mitrovitza, and it was there that Dr. Thomson visited him last year on his way to Albania. He could only stay with him one day on account of the arrangement of the trains; but he saw enough of him to be convinced that he was well qualified for the work, and that the fruit of his labour would one day appear.

Pages 113–114

Greece

The ground occupied by the several colporteurs and some of the incidents of their travels are thus described by Dr. Thomson:

> The territory that your colporteurs had this year to occupy was the Peloponnesus and the Ionian Islands.

Accordingly Colporteur Gadjos was sent out in the spring to Cerigo or Cythera, whence he passed on to Zante, Cephalonia, Ithaca, Paxos, Leucadia, and Corfu. Both at Paxos and Ithaca he found people who had bought Scriptures from Mr. Dewar, your former Agent, and sent warm salutations, which, alas, he was never to receive. All along his tour, with few exceptions, he was exposed to great enmity and petty persecution, as well as to the violence of which we have already given some instances.

From Corfu, he passed over by special permission to Albania, to pay a short visit to Argyrocastro, his native place, taking with him a few books. On landing, he and his books were regarded with suspicion, and he was conducted first to Delvino, and afterwards to Argyrocastro. At the former town an Albanian Moslem was greatly interested on hearing your colporteur read the New Testament, but especially the Psalms, in Tosk-Albanian, wondering that the language had at last been committed to writing, and repeatedly exclaimed— *Adjaeeb! Adjaeeb!* (Well done! Well done!) which, as Mr. Koulouriotis observes, may well be translated to mean, like the Macedonian cry, 'Come over to Albania and help us.' Gadjos met with a good deal of difficulty, but chiefly from the Greek clergy; he succeeded, however, in selling a number of copies, and then returned to Corfu. Landing on the coast of the Peloponnesus, opposite Zante, he followed the northern coast quite round till he reached the Isthmus of Corinth, having visited in all about ninety villages ...

Lastly, Colporteur Zaros was sent to Nauplia, and directed to visit the central regions of the Peloponnesus. As the whole country, from Megara westward to the plain of Argos, and by Charvati, near the ruins of Mycenae, which have lately revealed their golden treasures, is largely inhabited by Albanians, as are also the islands of Spezzia and Poros, for whom the Greek Government has provided no instruction whatever in their own tongue, it is no wonder that he found there a large amount of stolid ignorance, and could sell very little.

Page 222

Progress in the Work of Translation and Revision

Albanian Tosk – M. Christoforides is engaged at Berat in revising the Tosk-Albanian New Testament. By the help of a native assistant he is expected to complete the work in about seven months, when it will be published at Constantinople, in parallel columns with Modern Greek. Dr. Thomson is very anxious to have portions of the Old Testament also prepared in the Tosk-Albanian, which is spoken by a people numbering about four millions.

75th Report, 1879

Page 111

In turning to the general work of the Turkish Agency, it will surprise no one that the year has been one of restricted opportunity. The provinces superintended by Dr. Thomson were those in which the colporteurs found travelling next to impossible, and where their lives were exposed to constant peril. For example, around Volo the brigand troops became so bold in carrying off people and holding them to ransom, that the very children attending the public schools had to be guarded in going to and from their homes. The colporteur in Macedonia had his house swept away by an inundation of the river Vardar, leaving him barely time to escape with his family and rescue his furniture and books.

Pages 113–114

Editions printed in 1878:

Bulgarian New Testaments, 32mo.	5,000
Turkish Gospels and Acts for separate circulation	5,000
Turkish Bible, 8vo.	1,500
Tosk Albanian & Modern Greek Matthew	1,000
	12,500

The Tosk St. Matthew is an instalment of the New Testament, which is being prepared at Constantinople by Mr. Christoforides, assisted by a native named Coleas. It is a curious fact that the Albanians exhibit a strong contempt for their own language, though it is the only one which the vast majority of the people understand. When the Society's colporteur Pilo arrived at Berat he found how strong was the Hellenizing, denationalising policy at work:

> With characteristic energy and acuteness he immediately began to urge upon the most influential Christians of Berat the necessity of cultivating their own language, and pressed to the utmost the circulation of the Albanian Scriptures, representing that till their worship was conducted in Albanian, and till the Albanian Scriptures were found in every family, there could be no intelligent profession of Christianity among them.

It is hoped that the publication of the historical books of the New Testament separately may give an impulse to the work in this neglected land of Albania, and meet the touching desire expressed by the women to know something of the life of the Saviour. Your Agent says:

> Fischer and his wife read to the women of the adjoining families, and Pilo to the female members of the family under whose roof he lodged, various portions of the Scriptures in Albanian, and were much interested to find a strong desire for instruction among them all, as well as a painful consciousness of their ignorance and helplessness. A more necessitous field for the labours of Christian women could not be found.

Pages 115–117

Macedonia

The sales in this province have been 409 as against 113 in the previous year. The Rev. P. Crosbie continues kindly to superintend the depot at Salonica, whence 227 copies have been sold. Colporteur Klundt remained at Mitrovitza until the crowd of refugees, who had poured into Uscup, made his return thither desirable. Here his house was swept away by the flood, as already described, and it was some time before he was able to get to work again.

It was with heartfelt pleasure that Klundt resumed colportage, feeling it quickened both himself and others to be occupied directly with the Word of God. Many he found crushed down without redress or hope, but all were pleased to meet again one who had been the instrument of ministering so liberally to their relief. With a respectable merchant of Uscup he had a long discussion, which turned practically on the point whether the decrees of the great ecclesiastical Councils were to be put on a level with the Holy Scriptures.

On the other hand he found some persons openly avowing atheism, with the one compensating circumstance that they bought several copies of the New Testament, because, as they said, they were no longer afraid to read such books.

Bosnia, Herzegovina and Montenegro

The position of [Colporteur Franz] Tabory at Seraievo was, for many months, one of much anxiety; and when an obstinate resistance was offered to the Austrian occupation, and fighting took place in the streets of the city, the lives of himself and his family were in great jeopardy. They were however mercifully preserved, and as soon as he could procure a supply of German Scriptures, he set to work among the Austrian troops, and had the satisfaction of ministering to the men in the hospital. His sales numbered 300 copies.

Albania

From the semi-barbourous condition of a large part of this province, it has always been found difficult to provide colporteurs for it; yet for this very reason your Agent has been specially anxious not to leave it unprovided. Fischer has laboured faithfully from Berat as a centre, until, owing to the unhealthiness of the town and the sickness of his wife and child, he was compelled to leave. Pilo, who was summoned from Crete to take his place, found a serious obstacle to his work in the person of the Bishop, who took his stand upon the Septuagint and forbade the people to purchase anything else:

> All reasoning was of no avail; and after spending several hours on two or three occasions, in earnest discussion with the Bishop, Pilo had to desist. The only concession the Bishop made was in these words: 'We are no enemies to the circulation of the Holy Scriptures, and

we acknowledge the object of your Society to be holy and excellent; but you must get more learned men, and men sanctioned by the Greek Church [that is the Patriarch and his Council] to prepare the translations.' We know by long experience what this means. It is too thin a veil to conceal the enmity to the enlightenment of the people, which lurks below. The Bishop spoke more truly when he said: 'It would be very hard indeed for the Church to authorise the reading of the Scriptures by the people in any other language than the ancient Greek originals.

If Pilo did not prevail on the Bishop to sanction the circulation of the Society's editions, the news of his long and ardent discussions soon spread, and the arguments on both sides were revived in all the Christian cafes of the town, it may be hoped, to the advantage of the Truth. Among the Jewish colony at Berat, Pilo found a more cordial reception of the Gospel than usual. His sales, with those of Fischer, amounted to 293 copies.

Crete

The circulation here has been even smaller. When Pilo left for Albania, in the summer, he had been able to sell only twenty-nine copies, so merciless was the strife between Moslems and Christians.

Pages 120–122

Greece

Greece is at present the only country in Europe, with the exception of Austria, in which the authorities throw deliberate obstacles in the way of the free circulation of the Word of God in the vernacular tongue. The Government and the Holy Synod continue to oppose the spread of the

Scriptures in Modern Greek, and, in pursuance of this object, do not scruple to misrepresent and traduce the Society's translations. ...

[Colporteur] Gadjos, who is himself an Albanian, took an interest in some Albanians who had recently renounced Islam and been baptised into the Orthodox Church; like Aquila and Priscilla, he expounded unto them the way of God more perfectly:

> On inquiring what instruction they had received, and what promises they had made, he found that the principal points were that they promised to abstain from certain meats during the fasts appointed by the Church, to observe the feasts, to reverence the pictures of Mary and the Angels and Saints, to make to sign of the cross, and so forth. He astonished them by observing that there was no authority for these things in Scripture, while some of them were strictly forbidden; and told them that a true Christian was one who trusted in the perfect righteousness and the atoning death of Jesus Christ, the Son of God, and kept His commandments. The poor fellows replied that they had been driven to the step by the hardships they had suffered in the Turkish Army, and that if there was anything wrong in what they had done, the blame lay with the priest who had misled them.

All sorts of objections were raised against the Scriptures in the places which this colporteur visited.

Page 235

Progress in Translation and Revision, 1878-1879

Albanian-Tosk – Mr. Christoforides, assisted by Mr. Coleas, having completed the revision of the New Testament at Berat, proceeded to Constantinople to carry the edition through the press under the superintendence of Dr. Thomson. The printing is now proceeding satisfactorily, and the Committee have authorised separate Gospels to be bound up and circulated as portions. The Albanian is printed in parallel columns with Modern Greek.

76th Report, 1880

Pages 123–125
Turkey

It might have been expected that in this Empire, so smitten, so shaken, so devastated, so nationally hopeless, the report of your Agent would tell of lessened labours, smaller issues, shrivelled results. On the contrary, Dr. Thompson's report is amongst those where the issues are in excess of the number reached in the previous year; and the work of the colporteurs, performed amidst unusual perils, has been marked, not in one place but in many places, not in one language but in many languages, by features of more than average encouragement.

Part of this improvement in the present and better hope for the future is no doubt due to the changes brought about by the late war. The two strongest enemies with which our work in the Turkish Empire has to contend are the fanaticism of the Mahommedan rulers and the hostility of the Greek Church, specially in Greece itself. But since the war a large area of the Turkish Empire has ceased to be under the direct rule of the Porte, and has passed permanently from the Crescent to the Cross. And then as to the Greek Church, especially in the Greek kingdom, though it has not repented of its hostility to the circulation of the Vernacular Greek Scriptures, it has consented to permit the use of the New Testament in the sacred language itself in all the schools of the land; and if the prosperous and educated Greeks at home and abroad would exert their influence, your Agent thinks it would go far to wipe away from Christian Greeks the reproach which cannot be laid to the charge even of the Turks, that they deny to their own children the sacred book of their religion in the speech understanded of the people.

Your Agent desires to see the boundary question between Turkey and Greece settled speedily, that the minds and the resources of both nations may be free to engage in peaceful pursuits; but he deprecates any such division of territory as would overlook the claims of the Albanians to a distinct national existence, for the recognition of which there is a growing desire amongst them.

It is interesting to notice that the solitary version added to the list in previous use in the whole length and breadth of the Turkish Empire is an edition of a diglot New Testament in Tosk-Albanian and modern Greek, together with separate Gospels and the Acts of the Apostles similarly arranged.

Dr. Thomson's description of the conditions amidst which the work was carried on includes a terrible variety of evils: Bulgarians flying from Turks, Turks flying from Bulgarians, agriculture suspended, commerce paralysed, taxation grinding, money scarce, coinage debased, brigands numerous and daring, and famine and pestilence just held at bay by the money and the energy and the Christian devotion of the country which sends forth the Scriptures. ...

The Albanian Tosk shows symptoms of activity amongst that division of the people which has been most touched by educational influences. The Ghegs give no such signs. Ignorance and bigotry are stout foes to the colporteurs.

Pages 130–132
Albania

After an interval of twelve years your Agent revisited this part of his field during the summer. Joannina had risen from the ashes of the great fire an European city. Here he found education advancing and widening, here also the upward movement was shared to the full by the Jews. Dr. Thomson speaks of the Jewish school-rooms as 'crowded.' He had more intercourse with them than with any others, 'scarcely a day passing without some one coming to pay a friendly visit or to propose a hard question.'

Colportage had been unintermittent, although the men had been changed. Pilo laboured during the first half year, Sevastides during the last. A third colporteur had been tried and found wanting.

> Sales by Pilo, at Berat and Joannina, 660
> Sales by Sevastides, in Central Albania, 311
> Sales by Jura, 173
> Total, 1,144

Both Pilo and Sevastides are men of most valuable qualities, admirably adapted for their work.

At Berat Pilo maintained with success a friendly argument with the Greek Archbishop, who attempted to prove from the case of Philip and the Eunuch that the Bible alone was insufficient. It is interesting to find a Greek prelate now urging the same objection that an English prelate thought so strong in the Bible Society's early days; but it is a proof either of the strength of the colporteur or the weakness of the argument that he did in a single sentence what it once was thought to need a whole pamphlet to set out, viz., that the reading of the Scriptures predisposes men to receive the teaching of the Church when that teaching provides the true answers to the anxiety which leads men now, as it led them of old, to search the Scriptures.

The sales of Sevastides, although only half of those of Pilo, are a more correct index of the general condition of Albania, for they were effected, not in large numbers in large towns like Joannina, but piecemeal all over the district.

His impression was that the people were living in the deepest spiritual ignorance, blind followers of the blind. The cry, so difficult to understand, but so common from Greece to Persia, 'Far-masoon' (Free-mason), was raised against him. Howbeit some nobler souls clave to him, and cheered and helped him. Sometimes his enemies suffered notable defeat, as at Giorcha:

Shortly before Sevastides left Giorcha it was known that the Governor was to visit the market-place, and some considered this a good opportunity to inform him of your colporteur's doings, and have him sent off. Accordingly, after the Governor had taken his seat with some ceremony in the public square, these men went up to him and said, 'Your Excellency is not perhaps aware that a man has recently come to the town who sells various books in different languages, Turkish among the rest, at merely nominal prices, and seems very anxious to have them disposed of. We think your Excellency should look after him.' 'Let him be sent for at once,' said the Governor. Accordingly, Sevastides and his books were led by an officer through the eager crowd to the Governor's presence. On looking over the books, however, the features of the

Governor at once relaxed. He desired your colporteur to sit down and talked familiarly with him, saying he had a Bible already, otherwise he would have bought one.

Thessaly

Your Agent truly speaks of this as an 'unhappy province,'... Colportage has been impracticable, and the only sales effected were from the depot in the charge of Mr. Zabanski, and amounted to 207 copies. But even this handful is three times as much as last year's still more feeble results. Here in the autumn are to be found numbers of Albanian Ghegs. Mr. Zabanski endeavoured to find amongst them some who could read, but without success. Your Agent is much concerned for these poor children of darkness.

Page 245

Progress in Translation and Revision, 1879–1880

Albanian-Tosk – The Revised New Testament has been issued from the press at Constantinople under the editorship of Mr. Christophorides, the reviser. The Albanian is accompanied by the Modern Greek text. The increased demand for the new edition has encouraged the Committee, at the request of Dr. Thomson, to have Genesis and Exodus transcribed from the Gheg dialect into the Tosk, and printed. They have also authorised Christophorides to proceed with the translation of the books of Isaiah and Proverbs.

77th Report, 1881

Pages 103–106
Turkey

The soil is not so barren as many suppose. Your Agent, the Rev. Dr. Thomson, who is ably supported by Mr. W. Sellar, says of Bulgaria that there are in it a large number of high-minded men intent on the elevation of the people and the reform of abuses; while in comparing the attitude of various parts of the population around Constantinople, he says, "Every one who knows the Turkish people must admit that they are sedate and thoughtful. No small interest in Divine Truth seems now to be diffused among them. The colporteurs report that of all classes the Turks are at present the most ready to listen to the claims of the Bible, and that while others will only talk and dispute, the Turks buy."

Hence, although parts of the country are in a deplorable state, as for example Upper Macedonia, where it is supposed that a colporteur was murdered last autumn, the returns of the Agency show "a moderate but decided interest, both in all the provinces to which the Society's direct labours extend and, with few exceptions, in all the more important languages spoken within it."…

It is always of interest to observe the proportions taken by each of the many languages spoken in this Agency.

> *Albanian, Gheg,* 17
> *Albanian Tosk,* 704

Albanian shows a very gratifying increase, which is all the more to be valued as most of the copies were sold to the Albanians of the capital, there having been no colporteur in Albania proper for half the year.

The very marked increase in Bulgarian is due to the enlightened policy, adopted both in Bulgaria and Eastern Roumelia, of vigorously promoting education, in connexion with which there has also been a very large demand for Slavic New Testaments. ...

The Albanian population of Constantinople is largely composed of men who have left their families in order to seek a livelihood. The agitation made by their northern chiefs has aroused their national feeling, and the remarkably clear and cheap Gospels in Greek and Tosk which the society has published have fostered their desire for a literature of their own.

Pages 109–111

Macedonia

The colporteur just referred to [Klundt] spent a part of last year in this province, where brigandage has been so rife that travelling has been attended with great risk: ....

> At Mitrovitza he was beset for help by many to whom he had formerly distributed the charity of British Christians; while at Liplyan the enlightened teacher bought a Servian Bible for himself, and urged his pupils to buy, so that eighteen copies were soon disposed of. At Djeeb the teachers were very friendly, and bought a large bible for the use of a union for reading, which they had established among themselves.

When, at this own request, Klundt was transferred to Bulgaria, the people of Uscup were loud in expressions of esteem for him, and a company of the most respectable citizens went with him some distance out of the town to bid him God-speed. His successor, C. Sosnovski, was an elderly man of simple faith, who appears to have suspected no evil. In an unguarded hour he ventured across the mountains into a dangerous district, and all trace of him was lost at Prisrend. Whether he was killed for small sum of money he had with him, or shot as a spy by the Albanian League, or beguiled into a monastery, is not known. Although your Agent proceeded to Uscup, and active inquiries were made by the Rev. P. Crosbie and the British Consul at Salonica, J. E. Blunt, Esq., no clue whatever could be gained to the sad mystery ...

Before quitting the subject, a single extract from the journal of this colporteur will show the desperate condition of the country. Dr. Thomson says:---

Albania

This province of Turkey, with a population craving after national unity, yet hopelessly divided in itself, has attracted, during the past year, the attention of Europe. Partly through persistent and intelligent colportage, and in part from the merit of the Albanian Portions thus far published by the Society, the sales show an increase amounting in all to 1,320 copies. Steps have been taken for opening a depot at Jannina, to be held jointly by the American Presbyterian Mission and your Society, under the direction of the Rev. Mr. Michaelides.

Landing at Avlona, Colporteur Sevastides made a successful journey by Argyrocastro and Delvino to Jannina. At Paramythia the bishop sent round a deacon to announce his coming and encourage the people to buy; the result was the sale of nearly 100 copies. In general Sevastides reports a spirit of inquiry to be rising up, especially at the capital.

Colporteur Pilo, a man of long experience, made a journey last May over classic ground. He was detained a month at Prevesa by the objections of the authorities,

which were only removed through the kind interposition
of Sir A. H. Layard:

> Yet the time was not wholly lost, for the people came
> privately to his lodgings and bought some 56 copies,
> while Pilo had long discussions daily with both Jews
> and Greeks. Some seemed afraid of the books because
> they were so beautiful yet so cheap, regarding them as
> a tempting bait to allure readers to perdition. Others
> rejected them because not allowed by their Patriarch,
> nor by the Greek Church, nor sold in Greece. Some
> would not even touch them: others kept timidly aloof,
> because they had no crosses or pictures of the saints
> in them.

NO PICTURES

> Thus while Pilo was in the shop of a baker who had
> purchased three copies, a priest entered and examined
> the books, but asked why they had no pictures of the
> saints, like those sold by the Church. 'If you must have
> pictures,' said the baker, 'you can buy some and put
> them in. But of what use are such pictures? It is the
> words that profit us.' 'If there be no pictures, said the
> priest, 'what can I give a sick man to kiss?' 'Let him kiss
> the book itself,' said the baker, ' But you should visit
> the people,' added he, 'not to give them the Gospel
> to kiss, but to read and to learn the way of salvation
> from it.' The priest seemed inclined to buy a copy, but
> was dissuaded by a youth, and came no more. After
> some time, and meeting with considerable success,
> Pilo proceeded to Arta, across the Gulf of Arta or
> Ambracia, the scene of the famous battle of Actium,
> by which Octavius Caesar gained the throne of the
> Roman Empire. But the interest of the people had now
> been awakened, for on leaving Prevesa he had twice to
> undo the fastenings of his books to sell Bibles, while at

the customs at Saragosa he sold five Albanian copies. At Arta in the first two days he sold 120 copies, and found both teachers and people far superior to those of Prevesa.

Page 252
Progress in Translation and Revision, 1880-1881

Albanian-Tosk – Genesis and Exodus, transcribed into the Tosk dialect from the Gheg and revised, have been published under the care of Mr. Christophorides, who has also translated the Books of Isaiah and the Proverbs. The Committee have authorized Dr. Thomson to allow Mr. Christophorides to proceed with the translation of Deuteronomy, which is to be bound up with Genesis and Exodus as a portion.

78th Report, 1882

Page 60
Switzerland

Bible colportage in many parts of Republican Switzerland is only a counterpart of that in the mountainous wilds of Albania, and the colporteur may meet with much the same treatment. In September 1880, Sosnovski disappeared in Albania, as described in the *Monthly Reporter* for March 1881.

Page 78
Roumania

The Albanians have formed a small congregation at Bucharest, and have adopted for their school books a system, midway between our Tosk and Gheg versions.

Pages 151–153

Turkey

Of the provinces under the direct rule of the Ottoman Government your veteran Agent, Dr. Thomson, says:

> Albania, Thessaly, Macedonia, and Bithynia have been so overrun by brigands that colportage could only be prosecuted in them at the risk of life and property. Moreover the great bulk of the population in Turkey have been steeped in poverty. This has been specially observable in the capital, where many who wish to buy a Bible or Testament are compelled by poverty to purchase only a Portion, if they can purchase anything....

In Albanian the question of the alphabet to be employed is still unsettled. The use of the native language is opposed by the clergy, and by many of the people. In Gheg there is decided progress, and in the Albanian Portions unaccompanied by the Greek version.

Pages 154–155

Constantinople

This great city, drawing people from America and every part of Europe, as well as from every province of the Empire, is an important field for Bible dissemination. In its crowded streets one can reach not only Turks and Greeks, but Albanians, Montenegrins, Servians, Bulgarians, Armenians, Jews, Arabs, Persians, Syrians, Copts, and exiles from the recesses of Africa ...

All the colporteurs report an inclination among the Turks to buy the Scriptures, but the inability of many of them to do so from poverty ...

The difficulties at which some persons [do not buy Scriptures] are many and varied. An Albanian objects that the colporteurs do dot cross themselves; a Greek that they have no pictures in their churches; and a Turkish Imam, that their books do not begin "In the name of God and his Prophet."

Pages 158–159

Macedonia

Seefried was appointed to Uscup at the beginning of the year in succession to Clement Sosnovaki, whose untimely fate was recorded ago, though the particulars of it are still unknown. Colportage at Prisrend to the north-west, where Sosnovski disappeared, was impracticable while it was the seat of the Albanian League, and Seefried made tours to Kumanova in the east and to Kuprili in the south. When the measures of Dervish Pasha appeared to have restored order, Seefried started to the stations along the line of railway north of Uscup. Reaching Pristina, the seat of the Vali of Kossova, he went to the house of a Protestant. Next day (Saturday) he sold ten copies.

On Monday he sold seven more. While he was at supper an officer came with six policemen, and took him to the government house. He was there questioned as to whence he came and who gave him leave to sell. His boxes were nailed up till they could be examined. "But," said they, "if you have nothing but the Bible, you may sell."

Next day the books were carefully examined, and were found to be nothing but Scriptures. He got leave to sell, and sold that day fifteen copies, of which seven were complete Bibles. The day after, he could only sell one copy, so he resolved to leave. Having engaged a muleteer, he went to the court for a passport. He was told that he moat not leave, because he sold books. "But you gave me leave to do to," said Seefried. "Yea," said they, "but it is at an end. You sell Christian books in the Turkish language in Arabic letters. If we allow this to go on, the Muslim faith will soon disappear." They agreed to consult the Vali. Seefried was directed to come again in an hour.

On his return he was told to bring a surety, or he would be put under arrest. He got a friend to become surety, and two days passed. He was then summoned to the court and questioned. All his answers were recorded. He wrote to his wife, who was not well, not to be alarmed if officers came to examine his books, but before his letter reached her, an officer and six policemen came after she had gone to rest and greatly alarmed her. They confined her to one room, searched the house, and sealed up the books and papers.

Seefried was kept at Pristina twenty-four days, and was then sent under guard to Uscup, and lodged among the worst characters in prison. He was kept there six days and five nights. His friends applied for his release in vain, till Mr. Veith, a German residing in Salonica, and employed on the railway, procured it by producing two sureties. Soon after, the seals were removed from Seefried's room. All his books were taken to the court, and he and his family were banished from Uscup.

Seefried is a German, born in Russia, but his passport was in perfect order, and described him as a Turkish subject and a bookseller. Still, even Christians in many places cannot believe that the Scriptures are circulated out of pure benevolence, much less can Muslims, though the residence of Klundt in Uscup for ten years and his abundant labours ought to have made the people there familiar with the character of your Society. The original charge was that Seefried sold Christian books in the Turkish language and Arabic character. This is done daily in the capital and elsewhere, and to admit it as a valid ground for prohibiting colportage would be to sacrifice work everywhere.

Pages 160–161
Albania

The copies sold have been:
By the colporteur at Berat, Central Albania,
        8 months, 238
From the Depot of Janina, 7 months, 370
To a correspondent, 514
Total copies, 1,122

The decrease of 198 copies, as compared with 1880, is explained by the disturbed state of the country, and other hindrances both to depot sales and to colportage. Your Agent feels a deep interest in Albania, and is anxiously seeking efficient labourers for it.

The town of Janina (or Joannina), probably a Greek colony originally, has long been distinguished for its excellent Greek "Gymnasium," and a high state of education. It is the natural centre of South Albania, and hence Turkey and Greece equally wish to hold it. Hence, too, the importance of your depot and of the American Presbyterian Mission in such a place. Without the Gospel, secular education leads to unbelief. The Rev. Mr. Michaelides enlarges on the important influence of the depot. He has employed a young colporteur in the streets with some success.

Colporteur Sevastides has visited the towns and villages on the sea-board from Argyrocastro to Schodra, or Scutari, but has found it impracticable to penetrate into the interior. He is received much more cordially than at first. In Berat, where he resides, a school for females has been opened under Greek auspices. His reports are not without interest.

At first he was regarded with much suspicion, but inquiries gave him an opportunity of explaining the Society's work, and in several towns he found people who defended his views. The Albanians do not curse, or swear, and they are very pure in morals; but they are easily provoked, and care is necessary in addressing them. Premet contains many educated persons who have graduated at eminent schools abroad. They emphatically condemn the ignorance and superstition of both clergy and people. In some towns both Christians and Muslims were suddenly afflicted with an irresistible desire to spit as Sevastides passed by, but beyond hard names he met no opposition. He was questioned whether he attended Divine service on St. Demetrius' Day.

As he passed a group of Muslim officers, one asked what books he was selling, and after some conversation bought a Turkish Bible. The rest said that the Government ought not to allow Christian doctrines to be publicly avowed. Many crowded round, and Sevastides read aloud several passages of Scripture. On one occasion the army-surgeon of a battalion of Circassians, a devout Greek, joined Sevastides and a few friends in Bible-reading and prayer on the Lord's Day.

In North Albania there are a good many Roman Catholics, priests and people, who have raised discussions. In Scodra they petitioned the governor to banish the colporteur, and he complied, but he has since admitted to Her Majesty's Consul that he had acted too hastily.

Page 369

Progress in Translation and Revision, 1881–1882

Albanian-Tosk – The translation of the Book of Deuteronomy, authorized by the Committee, has been completed, and an edition of 1,500 copies has been published under the care of Mr. Christophorides, the translator, who is now carrying through the press, for the Committee, a similar edition of Proverbs and Isaiah. This work has been superintended throughout by the Rev. Dr. Thomson.

79th Report, 1883

Pages 118–119

Turkey

From all parts of this Agency come reports of maltreatment, persecution, and even imprisonment, endured by your colporteurs. That men like Seefried in Roumelia, Sevastides in Albania, Yanelli at Mitylene, and Moschobakes at Rhodes, have been able to persevere in their work at all is due, under the blessing of Him who defends His servants, partly to earnestness and patience in the men themselves, and partly to the stand made on their behalf by Her Majesty's Consuls or Vice-Consuls, acting under instructions from the British Embassy at Constantinople.

Page 122

The diminution to less than one-half of the parts in Tosk Albanian is entirely owing to the obstinate refusal of the Porte to allow the publication in mixed Greek and Roman letters of certain books of the Old Testament, lest Moslems able to read Greek should read them and embrace Christianity.

There is a decrease of 5,056 copies in Modern Greek … [Among the many reasons, this is due to] the restrictions on the labour of our colporteurs, in Albania and the Islands and on the coasts of Ionia, by the Turkish authorities …

Pages 124–126
Rumelia

The issues from the Salonica depot have been 103 copies, and by Colporteur Seefried 232. This extensive region is occupied by agreement, Thrace by the American Bible Society, and Macedonia partly by that Society and the National Bible Society of Scotland.

Your Agent thus describes the tyranny of which Seefried has been the victim:

After having been expelled arbitrarily from Uscup, as mentioned in the last Report, he was permitted to return from his exile to Salonica, and settle at Koprili, the nearest important railway station to Uscup. But here he was annoyed by frequent and most untimely examinations of his books, which he was at first required to transport to the Government House, but which afterwards, as a 'special favour,' were allowed to be examined in his own house. He suffered also from the fanaticism of the Turks of Koprili, one of them having, without the least provocation, struck him a severe blow on the back with a copper vessel, from the effects of which he did not recover for some time. The fanatic collected some dozen others like minded with himself armed with sticks, and attempted further violence, but was prevented by the innkeeper. It is right to add that on this occasion the Caimakam endeavoured to discover the offender, and gave Seefried a policeman for his protection. His sales in the region of Koprili were not very successful, partly on account of the poverty of the people, but principally because the territory had been well worked by the American Mission from Monastir.

At length when his exile had been sufficiently prolonged to preserve official dignity, he was permitted, though the kind offices of J.E. Blunt, Esq., C.B. (H.M. Consul-General at Salonica) to return to Uscup, this result being also favoured by the appointment of a new Governor to Uscup. It was thought advisable on his return, that our kind friend the Rev. Mr. Crosbie, who was personally known to the new Governor of Uscup, should introduce Seefried to him, and do all in his power to establish a kindly relation between them: and he succeeded.

Rearrested

Nevertheless, on the night of his return to Uscup with his family by special permit, Seefried was arrested as soon as he left the railway carriage, and hurried off for examination as a dangerous person. This turned out to be due to the officiousness of an under official at Koprili, who regarded Seefried as a suspicious person, and ignorant that official permission had been given for his return to Uscup, had telegraphed to the authorities there to look after him. The Governor of Uscup was much annoyed at the incident, but the alarm and discouragement which it produced on Seefried and his family were far from trifling. Since then he has worked quietly in about half of his former field, being still restricted by the Vali of Kossova from visiting the northern part of it.

Seefried's last letters speak of a hopeful religious movement at Uscup, the people searching the Scriptures and listening to the reasoning of the Protestants. He says that a Greek, alarmed at this, went to the Caimakam and asked what was to be done, as everyone was turning Protestant. 'If so,' replied the other, 'I shall be very glad, for no class gives me less trouble than the Protestants.'

Albania

The experience of colporteur Sevastides in North Albania has been not less trying that that of his comrade just named. He was arrested on the mere suspicion of the Commissary of the Police and expelled from the city, and made to walk on foot over an inundated country behind a mounted policeman, till after thirteen days he returned to Berat, his lodgings at night having been the prisons on the way. At Berat he was recognised as a quiet decent man, and was released without further ado. It is difficult to say whether his treatment was the result of the mere wanton exercise of arbitrary power, or of the intrigues of the Jesuits, or of general orders issued by the Government, or of enmity to Britain and antipathy to the truth. Be that as it may, poor Sevastides reached home utterly exhausted, and was confined to bed for some weeks. But not a word of resentment did he utter. It is but justice to add that W. Kirby Green, Esq. (H.M. Consul at Scutari) did everything in his power for Sevastides, and exposed the false pretences which the Vali of Scutari offered for his conduct, but he was unable to procure any redress.

The people at Berat are described as sunk in ignorance; but it must be admitted that they have among them a bold witness for the truth. Sevastides meets the denunciations of the Bishop by reading the Scriptures to the people in the cafés, that they may hear and judge for themselves. "Why haven't you the Koran?" asked the Moslem teacher. "Because it came afterwards," replied the colporteur, "and the Gospel has no need of its help. The Gospel does not seek to advance by the sword; it is itself the sword of the Spirit." Besides the 368 copies which Sevastides has sold, 131 have been issued from the Jannina depot, eleven have been sold by colporteur Michael and fifty copies given. As to Jannina, your Agent says:

> The capital of South Albania was occupied, as the Society are aware, for several years by Mr. Davidson, whose memory is fragrant there, and but for the impossibility of finding really suitable Greek colporteurs it would have continued to be occupied regularly and not merely occasionally. As it is, your Agent rejoices that now not only the depot continues its unobtrusive but valuable influence on the community, but a colporteur, Michael, has been engaged, who knows the vernacular languages of Albania, including Albanian and Wallachian, as well as Turkish and Greek, if not also Bulgarian, and who by his quiet Christian demeanour contributed not a little to subdue the suspicions and alarm which his arrival with his books created among the magistrates of the villages he visited, some of whom resorted to measures of great severity.

80th Report, 1884

Pages 141–143

Turkey

The Porte still refuses to allow the publication of certain portions of the Old Testament in Tosk Albanian, or to admit into Albania the Tosk and Greek New Testament, which was published with the express sanction of the Ministry of Instruction. But in time these difficulties may be removed.

Linguistic Table

Albanian – The Gheg copies old were only six. The Tosk sales are very encouraging, and prove the importance of work in the capital. ...

Ruman – For Wallachian colonies in Bulgaria, Albania, and Thessaly.

Pages 145–148

Rumelia

From political causes Macedonia is still in a very unsettled condition. Colporteur Seefried has made some important tours, and has sold 307 books, an increase of 75 on his sales in 1882. He is highly spoken of by the missionaries who have met him as a spiritually-minded and faithful man. Since the cruel treatment narrated in the last report, he has been permitted to reside at Uscup as his headquarters, but the place is very unhealthy, and he and his family constantly suffer there from fever.

Albania

In this important province the circulation of the Word of God in the vernacular is encompassed with great difficulties, owing to the prohibitions and restrictions enforced by the Government for above a year. Moreover, Colporteur Sevastides was obliged to quit Albania in August, owing to the dangerous illness of his wife. Under these circumstances it is satisfactory to be able to report that the issues of all kinds have been 1,087 or nearly double those of the previous year. Of these only 34 were free gifts.

The depot at Ioannina (Janina) is under the friendly superintendence of the Rev. S. Michaelides and Mr. Merourius, both of the American Presbyterian Mission to the Greeks. Your Society is also much indebted to the same friends for directing the movements of Colporteur Michael (whose sales have been 616 copies), for transmitting to him supplies, and for reporting his work to your Agent. The depot sales were 222 copies, as against 131 in 1882. Your Agent himself feels the deepest interest in the Albanian people, and thinks them deserving of more general attention than they have yet received.

For South Albania the Society has still only one colporteur. He is 56 years old, but is well fitted for the work by his quiet, humble character, as well as by his knowledge of languages. He has been several times imprisoned, but his quiet patience by degrees disarms hostility. In C. the magistrates confined him in the Khan (inn), and would not let any villager visit him. But the schoolmaster intervened on his behalf, and he was set at liberty. At G. two persons of influence diverted the people from interfering with his sales, and encouraged them to buy copies.

He was unable to meet the strong desire for Albanian Scriptures, the books being locked up in the custom-house at Prevesa under suspicion of their being dangerous to the stability of the empire.

It took some time for Colporteur Sevastides and his wife to recover from the effects of his cruel expulsion from Scutari, and his being marched under guard to his home in Berat, as recorded a year ago. Since then, notwithstanding much trouble from hostile authorities, he has travelled in Central Albania both alone and in company with the Rev. G. D. Kyrias, 215 books having been disposed of by one or other of these valued workers.

Mr. Kyrias is an Albanian preacher, born at Monastir, and educated by the American Mission in connection with their work in Bulgaria. His services being offered to your Committee, they authorised his engagement in the first instance for a tour to circulate the Scriptures amongst his own people. This was carried out very successfully.

The first part of the journey was in company with Colporteur Seefried, of Uscup. They started from Monastir, and halted for some days at Goritza, an important town. They were soon summoned before the Governor to show their credentials, but he was satisfied on being assured that every book they had bore the stamp of the Vali of Salonica. Several encouraging circumstances attended their stay at Goritza, and then they proceeded to Premet and Berat. From that place Seefried returned to Uscup through Elbassan, Struga, Ochrida, and Kessen.

From Berat Mr. Kyrias was accompanied by Sevastides. At Kavaia, the Governor finding that they had no special licence for selling the Scriptures, although their passports as booksellers were in perfect order, sent them under guard to Durazzo, eight or ten miles off. Here, although they assured the Governor that every one of their books had passed the censor and paid duty in Constantinople, they were ordered to prison unless they found security. Mr. Lazarus Theocharis nobly came forward, and became their security. But their books were not restored until an energetic appeal had been made to the Porte on their behalf by Hugh Wyndham, Esq., Her Majesty's Charge d'Affaires. The tour took in Avlona, Tirana, Elbassan, and so came back to Berat, whence Mr. Kyrias returned to Monastir. He has since been working among the Albanians in Constantinople, partly as a colporteur for your Society, and partly as an evangelist. The attachment of the people to their own tongue is evidently strong, but it would be unadvisable to enter further into details on this subject.

81st Report, 1885

Pages 124–125
Turkey

Dr. Thomson, now happily restored to health, sends, as usual, an interesting account of his work, which shows that he has been able to hold his own and to record some achievements for which it is easy to be thankful.

The plan which guides the movements of your Agent in Turkey is that every year each part of the district is visited either by himself or his principal subordinate, Mr. W. Sellar. That arrangement was interfered with to some extent by untoward circumstances, but in the end, with the exception of Bithynia, Crete, and Albania, the whole territory was visited. ...

The editions issued from the Press during the past year were:

> 3,000 Greco-Turkish Bibles
> 3,000 Greco-Turkish Genesis
> 1,500 Albanian (Tosk) Isaiah and Proverbs
> 2,500 Turkish Proverbs

Pages 127–128

Albanian exhibits an encouraging increase of 127 copies. It is plain that little impression has been made on the Ghegs, who are nearly all Muhammadans or Roman Catholics, but the sale of 135 copies in Tosk alone shows that the language is understood and valued as the medium of instruction. ...

I ought also here to repeat the diminished sales in Greek and Bulgarian to the Scottish Bible Society have been chiefly caused by the lamentable condition of Macedonia and Albania, where colportage requires heroic moral courage, and but for which increased sales might have been effected in Albanian and Turkish.

Pages 131–133

Rumelia (Macedonia)

During the past year the Society opened a new centre of circulation in the town of Monastir in Western Macedonia. The object was to advance its importance among the Albanian people; but as difficulties had arisen, which had long prevented the admission of the Albanian Scriptures directly into Albania, it was considered advisable to disseminate them in Western Macedonia, where there are many Albanians, and where Albanian Scriptures had not been prohibited. Monastir was selected both as containing about a thousand Albanian families, as being on the great highway from Albania to Salonica, and as being already a station of the Mission of the American Board to the Bulgarians, from whose missionaries we confidently looked for counsel and encouragement to the Society's agents. Accordingly, Mr. Gerasim Kyrias, a preacher of the Gospel, who had been trained in the Theological Seminary of the American Mission, was sent there to his native town, as superintendent of colportage, accompanied by Colporteur Tsiku, also an Albanian, in the month of June. They were cordially welcomed by the Revs. Messrs. Baird and Bond, who also materially aided them in commencing their work. A house was hired. Colporteur Tsiku went forth to colport, and Mr. Kyrias soon began a regular weekly Albanian service in his own house, which was attended usually by from thirty to fifty, and likewise made at least one important and successful visit to the neighbouring town of Krushevo, where he both preached the Gospel in Albanian, and sold every Albanian, and indeed every other copy of the Scriptures he had taken with him, as well as defended his liberty to preach and sell against the intrigues of the Greek Bishop and of the Turkish Governor, who was but too ready to lend himself to injustice. It was shortly after this that your Agent visited Monastir on his return from Bulgaria. He was delighted to find Mr. Kyrias vigorously at work, cheerful and hopeful, and highly esteemed by the missionaries of the Board, to whom he had long been known as a distinguished student of theology.

On November 13, while on his way to the town of Gortcha or Koritza, in Albania, and travelling in the humblest manner in a public carriage, Mr. Kyrias was seized by a band of thirty brigands, who carried him off, and have kept him for months in captivity exposed to severe hardships, and permitting him only once, on the day after his capture, to communicate to his friends the notice that he had been seized by brigands, who demanded £500 (Turkish) for his ransom. Much prayer has been offered for his release, and every possible effort made, but hitherto in vain. Now, March 3, the intelligence has just reached us that instead of £500 Turkish, the brigands demand a ransom of £2,500 Turkish. How to act in these circumstances it is difficult to decide, for to pay any ransom at all, and much more £2,500 or even £500, may endanger the safety of every colporteur in Turkey; while to withhold the money may lead to the mutilation or even the murder of the unfortunate man. Besides, it is extremely difficult to communicate with the brigands, either for the purpose of attempting to negotiate with them or to pay them the ransom,especially should they be hard pressed by the troops of the Government. During the visit to Monastir of Major Trotter, the military Attache to H.M. Embassy, the local authorities did exhibit for a time considerable activity in pursuit of the brigands, but without success.

[The Committee have heard with much satisfaction of the release of Mr. Kyrias.]

Seefried, whose sufferings and trials were described last year, has been removed by Dr. Thomson to Monastir, and his place has been taken at Uscup by a new man of considerable recommendations, moral and mental—Jovancho by name.

Albania

This important province has been less vigorously worked this year, owing to the removal of Sevastides. North Albania, with its important capital, is unoccupied, and Janina alone has had a resident colporteur. Michael has had "encouraging sales," but the accounts had not come to hand in time. The depot is still superintended by the members of the American Presbyterian Mission.

82nd Report, 1886

Pages 148–149

Turkey – Semi-jubilee review

In the list of Foreign Agents on an early page of this Report it will be seen that Rev. Dr. Thomson is the second of that noble missionary band in seniority by length of service to the Society. A previous residence of seventeen years in the Turkish capital, as a missionary of the Free Church of Scotland to the Jews, had given Dr. Thomson an intimate knowledge of the languages and characteristics of the medley of peoples to be found in the Turkish Empire before he became the Society's Agent there. A further residence of twenty-five years, ending with July 31, 1885, as the Agent of your Society, naturally leads him to reflect upon the changes which a quarter of a century has produced. Modestly throwing it into the background as an 'appendix' to his report, your Agent supplies a valuable and instructive summary of the progress to which his own active labours have, under God's blessing, so largely contributed.

The standard by which the work is tried is distinctly spiritual. The tone is humble and devout. The enormous, vexatious, and trying difficulties which obstruct and retard and overturn Bible work among the heterogeneous factors of his field of labour have a place, but a subordinate one, in Dr. Thomson's review. He has had the trying honour of seeing areas where he had been the first to break ground, and to sow the seed, and to rear the tender plant with toil and anxiety, transferred, as soon as some fruit appeared, to the charge of others. His twelve years' labour in Rumania ended in its transfer to the Austrian Agency; and his twelve years' cultivation of Syria, Palestine, and Egypt ended in their erection into a distinct Agency of their own. His plan of advance has been to select one important town as the centre of a district, and to make it the headquarters of a colporteur of piety, energy, and adequate education, whose duty it was to visit once a year all the larger places within his district. In this way Bulgaria north of the Balkan, Bosnia, Herzegovina, Albania, Thessaly, Wallachia, and Moldavia (now together forming Rumania) were occupied. Ancient Thrace was left to the American Bible Society, and South Macedonia to the National Bible Society of Scotland.

After European Turkey was thus provided for, more attention was given to Smyrna and its neighbourhood. ...

Page 151

Translations Made

Dr. Thomson also alludes to the translations more or less executed within the last twenty-five years, such as the Osmanli Turkish, the Modern Ruman, the Bulgarian, the Judaeo-Spanish, the Albanian (Tosk and Gheg), the Servian and Croatian, the Arabic, the Russ, the Modern Armenian, the Ararat-Armenian, and the Armeno-Kurdish,--assigning to each translator, reviser, or publishing society a due meed of recognition for the work accomplished. "Infinitely more blessed is it—not to say more economical—to address our fellow-men in their own language with the words of divine grace, than to view them with suspicion and hostility, and to be obliged to repel force by force."

Pages 152–153

Release of Kyrias

At the opening of the year, Mr. Kyrias, the Albanian colporteur, of Monastir, was a captive in the hands of Albanian brigands. Much prayer was offered, and many exertions were made for his release. After five months of cruel treatment, his ransom was effected, and his return home, on April 30th, changed a meeting called for prayer on his behalf into one of praise for his release. Your Committee thank God for the spared life, the preserved health, and the sustained faith of this sorely tried brother in Christ. They record also their warm gratitude to the Rev. L. Bond, of the American Mission at Monastir, for superintending the Society's work during the captivity of Mr. Kyrias, and for his unceasing and invaluable aid in the efforts for his release. The contribution of £48"5"3 towards the ransom of Mr. Kyrias, which was sent by the American missionaries of Monastir and Samokov and their colporteurs, has been heartily appreciated as an act of brotherly generosity and a token of the esteem in which the captive was held. Colporteur Tsiku continued to work in Gortcha during that trying time with courage and fidelity, but the insecurity for life and property in the region of Lake Ochrida and elsewhere, then and since, has naturally tended to lessen the results of colportage.

Official Helpers

Your Committee feel that the best thanks of the Society are due to Her Majesty's Foreign Office in London, to the Embassy in Constantinople, to J.E. Blunt, Esq., C.B., Consul-General at Salonica, and to W. Kirby Green, Esq., C.M.G., Consul-General at Scutari, in Albania, for ready and valuable assistance and advice in the case of Mr. Kyrias, and on other occasions.

Jovancho at Uscup

Seefried is one who has in the past suffered much in the faithful execution of his duty as a colporteur, and this affected the health of himself and of his family. Their removal from Uscup to Monastir made it necessary to find a new colporteur for the former, and, as mentioned in the last Report, one was appointed. His faith has been tried in the furnace:

> Jovancho Chismajief, who bore a high reputation for piety, intelligence, and zeal, was engaged for a year, from January 1885, on trial. Amid trials of no ordinary kind, he has laboured to my entire satisfaction. Two children were taken away in the summer, and the neighbours ascribed this, not to an unhealthy house, but to the anger of God, or the saints, because the parents had become Protestants.

Pages 159–161

Macedonia and Albania

Practically the Society's operations in these two provinces have been closely connected. The sales were:

From Monastir depot	132
By Colporteur Tsiku in Albania	363
By Jovancho, North Macedonia	235
By Seefried, South Macedonia	304
From Ioannina depot	549
By Colporteur Michael, South Albania	880
Total copies	**2,463**

The disappearance of the Salonica depot, so long and so kindly superintended by the Rev. Peter Crosbie, of the Church of Scotland Mission to the Jews, will be noticed. As sales were made from the depot through a colporteur superintended by Mr. Crosbie for the National Bible Society of Scotland, it has been thought the better plan to make over the depot to that society also. It has purchased the stock, and all the sales stand to its credit.

The sales by the colporteurs indicate Christian heroism of a high order. It is no wish of your Committee or your Agent to expose any colporteur to certain, and perhaps, fruitless hazard in their work. But when the men themselves, exercising all proper prudence, venture, in the cause of Christ, to incur personal risk for the extension of His kingdom, their zeal and courage are ground for thankfulness.

Besides the Society's debt to the American missionaries at Monastir during the captivity of Mr. Kyrias, to which reference has already been made, it is under no slight obligation to the Rev. Messrs. Bond, Baird, and Locke, and to their families for the privilege of Christian fellowship and counsel which the colporteurs and their families enjoy from the presence of these devoted missionaries at Monastir:

> Mr. Kyrias has sold 132 copies in and around Monastir. Though not without risk, he visited two villages at a short distance. One man from Megarovo came to him, and bought with great joy an Albanian New Testament. His services in Albanian continue to be fairly attended. He had called on the Bishop, who received him very courteously, and refused to prohibit attendance at his services, though begged to do so.

> Seefried and his family enjoy much better health at Monastir than they did at Uscup. He has laboured in Monastir itself, and has made two journeys, one north to Krushovo and the neighbourhood, and the other south-east to Vodena and elsewhere. The union of Eastern Rumelia with Bulgaria so disturbed the Turkish authorities that on the second tour he was

a good deal harassed through their suspicions and precautions.

Tsiku's work in Gortcha has already been mentioned. He was denounced as a heretic by the Bishop, but had a cordial reception among the Albanians. They asked for a preacher and for schools. On a second tour he went as far south as Delvino, and then going north he visited also Argyrocastro, Tepelen, Avlona, Tirana, Elbasan, and so back to Monastir through Struga at the top of Lake Ochrida. During his tour, which lasted over four months, he showed exemplary diligence and zeal, and unhappily suffered much from the severe weather on the lofty plateau. He returned encouraged by his experience, and more devoted than ever.

Jovancho's trials at Uscup in North Macedonia have already been mentioned. He is a Protestant Bulgarian, and seems of the right spirit. He made several important tours and sold well. At Kuprili a priest bought a Slavic Testament. Jovancho asked, 'How are the sheep?' 'They are well,' he replied; 'but we must pray that God would send us shepherds that care for the flock, and able to instruct them.' The region north of Uscup is still a great extent forbidden ground to a colporteur. At Pristina he was allowed to sell, but the people were too afraid of the Bishop to purchase. His sales and Tsiku's have only been reported in part time for this year's figures.

The large sales at the Ioannina depot bear witness to the efficiency with which the Rev. S. Michaelides of the American Presbyterian Mission to the Greeks superintends the Society's work there. The gymnasium of the city has long maintained a high standard of classical, and latterly also of scientific and general, education. Mr. Michaelides spends several hours daily at the depot, and converses with people there. The depot has been hitherto kept by Mr. Discus, but after May 31 the American contribution towards his salary will cease.

The sales of good old Colporteur Michael amply testify to his diligence amid many difficulties. He made two long and important chief tours; the first north and west among the Albanians up to Argyrocastro; the second to the east among the Greeks. In places where it is believed no colporteur ever carried the Sacred Volume before, he met all the ignorance and fanaticism of a half-civilised community. Still, on his journey he experienced many mercies, effecting good sales, and returning home in safety, though much exhausted.

On the General condition of Macedonia and Albania Dr. Thomson says:

The population of Macedonia consists of Greeks, Albanians, Wallachians, Bulgarians, Servians, and Turks. Most of these are at present seeking to secure the largest share of its soil, chiefly on the ground of the language spoken in each district. In this cause, Greeks and Bulgarians are vigorously promoting schools taught in their respective languages. The Wallachians and Turks are doing the same to benefit their own people. Your Agent prays that something may be done to provide schools for the large and utterly neglected Albanian population. They are a brave people; but brigandage is too often the form in which their misguided, half-savage energy finds expression.

83rd Report, 1887

Pages 140–146

Turkey

Dr. Thomson, by the retirement of Mr. E. Millard from Vienna, is now the Society's senior Foreign Agent....

The past year has not been a propitious one for Bible circulation. Many circumstances have been adverse to it. The stagnation of trade, with its attendant poverty, has prevailed in the east as well as the west of Europe, rendering it impossible in some districts to effect sales. There is great reason to thank God that war has not actually broken out, yet the remembrance of recent wars has left the people in a perturbed and nervous state. To quote Dr. Thomson's language – "Like the sea after a storm, the country has heaved and tossed so violently and so long," that men's minds are still too agitated to listen to a colporteur's message; while in Bulgaria, events have kept the inhabitants in a chronic expectation of war, and both Turkey and Greece have had large bodies of troops massed along their respective frontiers, in some cases within sight of each other.

Before commencing the details of the year's work, Dr. Thomson mentions two incidents which he considers worthy of prominent record. The first is the voluntary retirement from Greece of the American Bible Society. ...

The other event relates to Albania, a country in which Dr. Thomson takes a peculiar interest, believing that it will eventually prove a most remunerative field of Christian labour. If discouragements could have disheartened him he would have abandoned the effort long ago, but he has spared himself no trouble, either in correspondence or travelling, to re-establish the Society in the important town of Scutari, and he is to be congratulated on his ultimate success. His narrative is given almost entire, to afford some insight into the enormous difficulties attending Christian work in Turkey. It may render some parts of it more intelligible if it is borne in mind that Albania is divided into North and South. The language has two dialects; that spoken in the north is called Gheg, and that in the south Tosk. The southern is the more civilised portion.

Dr. Thomson writes: -

On your Agent visiting Albania for the first time in 1863, he was much interested in Ragusa, Montenegro, and North Albania, and their stirring memories; and by the kindness of the Committee, he was enabled to occupy for the first time Scutari, the capital of the Albanian Ghegs, and to disseminate from that centre the Holy Scriptures, both in North Albania and Montenegro, and in the adjacent parts of Dalmatia, through which, in fact, the colporteur had to pass, though geographically forming a portion of the Austrian Agency. Much precious seed was sown; but the locality was a trying one, and after upwards of eight years' occupation, he found it easier to attempt the evangelisation of North Albania from the central town of Berat, than from Scutari in the extreme north. This was done, and not without profit, though manifestly a most important post was sacrificed when Scutari was vacated. At length the way seemed open for reoccupying that city; and in May last your Agent proceeded thither with Colporteur Thoshe, having been preceded by Colporteur Seefried a week before. Seefried's arrival and the Agent's expected visit the following week, had inevitably announced the intention of the Society to reoccupy Scutari. The result was that the Roman Catholic clergy, who are very influential in Scutari, filled the minds of the great mass of the Christian population with alarm and jealousy; and also petitioned the Vali to forbid your Agent opening a depot, or establishing colporteurs there for the dissemination of the Word of God. The consequence was, that on his calling upon the Vali, instead of allowing him at once to open a depot, as he had a legal right to do, he decided to ask instructions from Constantinople. Your Agent was well aware of the delays that would probably intervene before this question could be settled, but in the circumstances he judged it wise to comply with the request of the Vali, and draw up a statement of what he proposed to do, to be transmitted for the consideration of the Porte; clearly, however, stating that he was only resuming a work he had previously carried on for eight years in that city, without offence to anyone. At the end of four months the Porte declined to grant your Agent's request for the sale of the Scriptures, but ordered the books to be delivered to the Society's colporteurs which till then had been detained by the Custom House. Meanwhile at Scutari the alarm of the people and of the authorities, produced by the denunciation of the Jesuit clergy, had passed away; and the colporteurs by their intelligence and friendliness, their unobtrusive demeanour, and the force with which they defended the circulation of the Scriptures, had won golden opinions for the Society, and the Vali saw that he could without danger withdrawn the prohibition; he accordingly instructed the Director of Customs to deliver up the books. The Director, however, was a Romanist, and did nothing. A second order came from Constantinople, and the Director was now peremptorily commanded to deliver them to your colporteurs, and rebuked for not having done so before. Immediately on receiving the books,

Seefried, assuming in the absence of any prohibition that they were intended to be sold, offered them for sale, both in the Government House and in the streets, and met with ready purchasers. A depot also was rented, which your Agent had seen and approved of; and thus, tacitly, permission was given for all that had been asked. The attitude of the general population, which is about equally divided between Christians and Muhammadans, has been from the first quiet and respectful.

Dr. Thomson, as mentioned in the last Report, has had from various causes successively to transfer province after province into other hands. The reoccupation of Scutari, however, restored Montenegro to his Agency, by the Committee's decision, as this principality is more readily supplied from Scutari than from any other centre.

The Scutari incident has shown the perplexities and annoyances which beset colportage in Turkey. Every local governor, or minor authority, has it in his power to paralyse a colporteur's action. An appeal to Constantinople entails heavy expense and loss of precious time, to say nothing of the trial to the temper and patience of the victim. So long as colportage is not regulated by the Government, a remedy is unattainable. From want of a law, every official does what is right in his own eyes, frequently to the confusion of the Society's work. It is, therefore, a gratification to learn, that at least an attempt is being made to place colportage on a legal basis …

The following editions have been published during the year: …

Greek and Tosk Albanian, Matthew and Luke, 10,000

The diminution in Albanian [from 687 copies sold in 1885 to 530 copies sold in 1886] is at once explained by the enforced inactivity of Colporteur Seefried. It is pleasant, however, to see a slight increase of 12 in the Gheg sales; and considering that there are only two schools for teaching the people to read their own language, the circulation is satisfactory. ...

Bulgarian shows a diminution of 205 in Slavic for the use of schools; but the large gratis distribution already referred to, raised the total issues to a figure unprecedented in that language. I regret to have to point out a decrease of no less than 3,081 in Greek, chiefly in modern, notwithstanding an increase in Greco-Turkish of 285, and a gratis circulation of 582. ... Rouman represents the sales to the Rouman colonies on the Bulgarian bank of the Danube; and Servian the circulation in North-east Albania, the north of Macedonia, and the Bulgarian frontiers of Servia, and is a proof that these districts, most of which are still unsettled, have received their due meed of attention.

Pages 150–153
Macedonia and Albania

We class, says the Agent, these two provinces together; because while anxious to impart the Word of life to all classes of the people, the National Bible Society of Scotland has for many years occupied South Macedonia; and the American Board more recently Central, with a particular view to the Bulgarians; while the special object of our Society's own Agency has been to operate on the Albanians. The sales were:

	1886	1885
From Monastir depot	278	132
Outstanding from Salonica and Serres	100	—
Colporteur Javancho at Uscup	433	235
Colp. Tsiku in Macedonia and Albania	613	363

Colporteur Seefried in Macedonia	257	304
Colporteur Thoshe in Scutari	21	—
Ioannina depot	191	549
Colporteur Michael in South Albania	564	880
Total Copies	**2,457**	**2,463**

The total circulation is thus almost identical with that of the previous year, though the items differ considerably. The great increase in the sales from Monastir depot, though kept in a room of Mr. Kyrias's own house, seems to justify his request for an open depot in the marketplace; Monastir being the channel through which the commerce of Central and Northern Albania finds its way eastward – in fact by the old Roman *Egnatian Way*. His services in Albania are continued; and some as they pass through the city hear the Gospel preached for the first time in Albanian, or indeed in any language.

Early in the year Colporteur Jovancho made a tour through the north-west of Macedonia to Monastir, in order to get instruction from Mr. Kyrias in Albanian reading, and other matters. This was very useful; but besides, his tour was the first made in that region for many years, and was both interesting and successful. He sold well to Turks, Bulgarians, Wallachians, and Albanians, and had much conversation with all these. In a subsequent tour he visited Prisrend, which probably no colporteur had visited since poor Sosnovski was murdered in returning from it in 1880. He began his sales in the market-place, and on being summoned to the Government House found there ready purchasers. He next visited the Servian school, and had a hearty reception from the teachers. Lastly he visited the Latin quarter, but met with such hostility that he could not sell a single book. In all he sold in Prisrend 44 copies, and could have sold more if he had had more Servian and Turkish Bibles. He then returned by the railway, visiting the various towns on the line, and those lying near it. He sold fairly, but found the fatal leaven of atheism diffused by schoolmasters at several places.

The Committee are very thankful to learn that Dr. Thomson has not a few colporteurs who make full proof of their ministry. In a country such as Turkey it is no small mercy to find men of undoubted piety and consecration to Christ. Tsiku is evidently one of these.

> The very satisfactory sales of Colporteur Tsiku testify to his diligence and success, both in Macedonia and Albania; though he was laid aside by fever from all work for three months, and for a considerable time had to confine his labours to the town of Monastir. I need not again enlarge on the wretched condition of Macedonia, where not a road is safe, and where both life and property outside the towns are at the mercy of lawless banditti. I shall simply observe, that for a man in delicate health to make one long and two minor tours, evinced no small courage, and was the best proof that, as he wrote, he rejoiced in his work. He mentions especially the readiness and joy with which the Muhammadans in many cases bought the Holy Scriptures.

A Turkish officer ordered a Bible of Tsiku, who obtained one for him from Ioannina. It was received and paid for with evident signs of delight. Even a repulsive-looking Fakir bought some Gospels for his sons to read. The changed disposition of the Muhammadans towards the Bible is one of the most encouraging facts recorded in the year's report. An attempt was made at Castoria by an officer of the Bishop to stop his sales, on the ground that his books had not the seal of the Patriarch. Tsiku repudiated the Patriarch's authority, and maintained that the command of Christ, and the seal of the Sultan, were all he required. He was speedily summoned to the Court of the Kaimakam, who, after examining the obnoxious Scriptures, and looking at Tsiku's papers, returned them to him, and forbade the police to interfere with his work. The Bishop was politely informed that the law courts were open to him if he wished to appeal. Much interest was excited by the trial, and the issue of it emboldened many to buy.

Colporteur Seefried's work at Scutari has been already referred to. Before going there he made an extensive tour in Macedonia, and was rejoiced to discover small communities of Christian brethren at Bafadav, Strumnitza, and Monaspitova. So demoralised is the whole country, that most of the way he had to travel with the armed escort of the Post, to escape the brigands. He witnessed at Radovitz a curious exhibition of the bitter animosity now existing between the Greeks and Bulgarians:

> A marriage had been celebrated in the Bulgarian language, and this so incensed the priest, who was a partisan of the Greeks, that he laid his staff right heartily on the heads of his flock, and sent them bleeding to the Kaimakam to seek protection from their shepherd.

Michael, a colporteur highly valued by the Agent, received most barbarous usage at Doliana, a town to the north of Ioannina. Because he declined to withdraw from the town at the command of some members of the municipality, one of their number struck him a severe blow which knocked him bleeding and unconscious to the ground, while his books were seized, and a Testament was burned on the spot. This cruel outburst of fanaticism was the result of an episcopal circular against Protestants. Michael had to find his way to his lodgings through an excited mob, and the next day he returned on foot to Ioannina. Being an old man, he suffered much from the savage assault.

Mr. Galdemus, a teacher in Ioannina who had joined an evangelical Church, and thereby forfeited his situation, has been engaged as a colporteur on probation for six months. Dr. Thomson narrates a furious struggle which grew out of Mr. Galdemus's 'apostasy,' between the champions of the Greek Church and the upholders of freedom of conscience. There is only room to notice that, while it involved Galdemus in two months' rigorous imprisonment, it happily ended in the recognition of the Protestant community in Ioannina by the Government; which for the future rescues them from the authority of the Bishop.

Dr. Thomson himself made a long journey through Albania last summer, visiting many towns mentioned in the foregoing account. As a most interesting narrative of his travels, from his own pen, was given in the November number of the *Monthly Reporter*, there is no need to do more than call the reader's attention to it.

84th Report, 1888

Pages 151–152

Turkey – Survey of the Year

Dr. Thomson's review of what he expressively calls "another year of imperfect but joyful service" is very far from being pessimistic in tone. He and his associates have had to work under a lowering political sky and in most unsettled social weather, but they have not hesitated on these accounts. Their work is one of those things which goes on, whatever tides may ebb or flow. And it always tells. The following paragraphs have—each in its own way—deep interest and importance.

Tribute to the Colporteurs. New Fields Opened.

Our chief difficulties during the past year were the prevalence of brigandage in Macedonia and Albania, entailing much anxiety on those who had the superintendence of colportage, and requiring not only high moral courage, but large Christian devotedness on the part of our colporteurs. What no mere hirelings would have ventured to do unless for high remuneration, the Society's colporteurs in many cases have done, we trust we can say, from love to Christ and the souls of men. And they have had their reward. Not only did they all return in safety, but two regions, hitherto for many years inaccessible to them, have this year been thrown open—we mean the important city of Prisrend and its surrounding territory in North-East Albania, and the region of Old Servia stretching between Uscup and Mitrovitza, and embracing the historic battle-field of Kossovo, where Sultan Murad gained his decisive victory and established Turkish power over all that region. The prudence of Colporteur Jovancho contributed much in both cases to this result …

Inundations in Thessaly and North Albania

I need only refer farther in these introductory sentences to two inundations, local and limited, yet entailing loss of both time and property, and embarrassment in our work. The one occurred at Volo, the port of Thessaly …

The other inundation occurred at Scutari in North Albania, the waters of the lake overflowing, especially the mercantile quarter, which is built upon its brink, and extending wide over the alluvial plain on which the inhabited portion of the city is situated. The Kiri, too, a mountain stream which joins the Boyana just below Scutari, overflowed its banks and committed great devastation. But both at Scutari and at Volo the greatest injury resulting from these inundations was the prevalence of malarial fevers and zymotic diseases generally, affecting all classes of the population.

Page 154
Circulation According to Languages

I would point out the encouraging feature of the Albanian issues. It is not merely the increase of 727 copies over 530, but that 79 copies of the entire New Testament were sold, the greatest number yet reached, and that the sales in Gheg and in Tosk alone have each more than doubled. This would seem to indicate that the people are beginning to appreciate the Word of God in their own language, and to escape from the singular idea that they must worship God in an unknown tongue. The Gheg sales are to be attributed partly to the Society's occupation again of Scutari, but partly also to the enthusiasm for the native tongue which has appeared at Elbasan, among both Muslims and Christians.

Pages 161–163
Albania and Macedonia

These two large and important provinces have a common centre of operations in Monastir. There, with a carefulness and diligence which Dr. Thomson is anxious to acknowledge, the Rev. G. D. Kyrias directs the Society's work. Six colporteurs have been engaged. The record and the incidents of their labours are given by Dr. Thomson with a respect and warm appreciation which is the best testimony to their devotion. Again and again they have been vexatiously hindered by the authorities, and as often they have returned to the work to which they give themselves so unreservedly. The total circulation of the year is higher than that of 1886 by over three hundred copies in a total of over two thousand seven hundred. The following extracts will tell their own story, and, while much is left out, each is complete in itself—a glimpse of the daily life of those who, eighteen hundred years after Paul, and on the very plains once familiar to him, are spreading the same old Gospel. The first refers to Mr. Kyrias and the new campaign he is planning.

GOING TO THE FRONT

There are many villages which, we fear, have never yet been visited with the Word of Life; and not only so, but there are towns which the semi-independent state of the people, the difficult nature of the country, and the prevalence of brigandage, make it extremely hazardous for ordinary people to visit. With the spirit of a strategist, Mr. Kyrias has his eye on these, and is preparing to occupy them. Not only so, but in the Scutari district there is the important, nominally Roman Catholic tribe of Mirdites,which fondly cherishes the memory of the heroic Scanderbeg, and maintains a rude semi-independence, under their own laws, to this day. By your Agent's direction, Colporteur Seefried has been gathering all possible information as to this people, and few copies of the Gheg New Testament have found their way among them; but for many more direct effort to reach them we must, at least in the first instance, employ Mr. Kyrias, who is an Albanian, and not a foreigner like Seefried. It would be wonderful, indeed, yet not without parallel in many instances, should the Gospel find admission into strongholds which the whole power of the Government has been unable to subdue. We must attempt great things for Christ in faith and hope, if we would ever accomplish anything.

The next is an incident from the journals of Colporteur Tsiku, who at the large village had been hindered by the authorities for a week, but when the embargo was removed, he made large and interesting sales:

AMONG THE MACEDONIANS

What prepared the people to purchase so freely was that on the preceding Sunday, and on a feast-day, he had read to them the Gospels and the Psalms, and, indeed, he did so every evening to many that came to his lodgings. He thus gained the respect and confidence of the people, who, though themselves unable to judge of the books, knew their priests to be as ignorant as themselves, and distrusted their newborn zeal. In Leskovitch, another large Albanian village, he stayed six days and sold seventy-one copies. Every evening he talked with the priests and others, and read the Gospels and the Psalms. He found there the Musalmans more ready to hear and to buy than the Christians, who they asked, 'Why don't you have these books which you hear read in your churches in Greek, but which this man has brought you in our own language? Why don't you love our own language?'

The next extract refers to Mr. Kyrias, whose own work—for he is not exclusively engaged in Bible circulation—is seen blending with that of the Society.

BIBLE MEETINGS AT GORTCHA

He was more than requited for any discouragement by his visit in the autumn to the town of Koritza, or Gortcha, near the south extremity of the Lake of Ochrida, and an important transit station on the old Egnatian way. The population is principally Albanian, and an Albanian school has been established there for children of both sexes, while the text-books are printed in the Roman alphabet, with the addition of certain newly devised characters to express the more numerous sounds of the Albanian language. The teacher is well known to us, and friendly to the Gospel. Mr. Kyrias's object was to preach the Gospel for a few weeks, and, if permitted, to give Bible lessons in the school, and to teach the pupils to sing certain hymns which he had translated from the English. He was received with great cordiality, and the hall of the school-house was once put at his disposal for holding his Albanian service. The attendance, good from the first, went on increasing, and included Muslims of high position as well as Christians. Perhaps still more interesting was the scene in the school, when the pupils committed to memory and sang with delight Christian hymns, which, from the sentiments, or the music, or both combined, not infrequently attracted the parents to join their children in singing these sweet songs in their native tongue. More than one individual seemed to be impressed by the truth set before them, and Mr. Kyrias was not only charged to return soon again, but as urged to prepare and send weekly a short sermon in Albanian to be read to the people by the teacher. This was doubtless more than he could undertake, but it shows the deep interest awakened at Gortcha in Divine truth, and this we unhesitatingly ascribe to the labours of your Society in the dissemination of the Albanian Scriptures."

Page 527
Albanian Tosk (Adapted Roman Alphabet)

The Society's Albanian versions are in the Tosk and Gheg dialects. The Tosk is in the Greek character, and the Gheg in the Roman, and each has certain peculiar points and accents to indicate the numerous distinctive sounds of the respective dialects. An Albanian Committee has now been formed, consisting of Gheg and Tosk Christians and Muslims, and they have agreed to adopt the Roman alphabet, with some newly-invented characters added. In this alphabet they have published some elementary school books, and they have opened a school at Gortcha, and are opening others, where the new alphabet will be taught. The Albanian Committee has requested the Bible Society to bring out in the new character the Gospel of St. Matthew and the Psalms, and Dr. Thomson, the Society's Agent at Constantinople, has so heartily supported the application that the Committee have agreed to publish a tentative edition.

Mr. Kyrias will edit the work, and the Tosk, which is spoken by a more settled and civilised people than Gheg, will be taken as the basis.

85th Report, 1889

Pages 124–125
Turkey – The Work to be Done

It was the desire of your Agent to have every portion of the wide area entrusted to his care supplied with the Word of God by the hands of humble believing men. The task is not an easy one. To visit the countless islands of the Aegean, and not their little ports merely, but their inland villages; to penetrate into the uplands of Albania and Macedonia, the haunts of savage, bloodthirsty brigands who keep the land in terror; to testify for the truth of God amid utter indifference or mockery on the part of some, and fanatical hatred and violence on the part of others, and to maintain legal rights in opposition to local magistrates, who did not know, and were unwilling to recognise, the liberty granted to the Society by the very laws they were bound to execute, as was the case in Thessaly, Albania, and Crete; finally, to refute the pretentious infidelity and atheism so prevalent in Bulgaria—such was the work that had to be attempted in the name of the Lord. Your Agent is thankful to say that not a little has been done under all these conditions.

The Policy of the Government

It would be a matter for congratulation were the Government to recognise the Bible, in whole or part, as free to be sold in any language all over the Empire. This, unfortunately, is not the case. The Holy Scriptures are continually being seized and examined over and over again, and often detained, or sent from place to place, at great cost of time and money, while the colporteur himself is imprisoned or sent as a felon in charge of a policeman to headquarters. Such proceedings may often arise form ignorance or fanatical intolerance, but not infrequently from less excusable causes. Happily the Bible is making way for itself; but an aggravated case of this sort, the result of which is still unknown, calls loudly for some remedial measure.

Page 127
Notes on the Languages

Albanian exhibits the very considerable decrease of 108 copies as compared with the previous year. In Gheg the small decrease of eight is to be ascribed to the rivalry of a new system of alphabetic writing; in Tosk the large decrease was owing to the want of two permanent colporteurs for South Albania instead of one temporary one for eight months.

Pages 131–132
Macedonia and Albania

The circulation last reported in these provinces was about two thousand eight hundred copies: it has increased in the present return to three thousand seven hundred. The result would have been still better had the colporteur been freed from the vexatious opposition of which several instances are given. But the best evidences of progress are those given in some of the extracts below, and pointing to an awakening interest among the people.

Colportage Work

The Society's staff in this important section of the field was the same as before, except that colporteur Sotirios was sent from Constantinople to labour in South Albania, as that district was entirely without any colporteur, except in so far as Mr. Discus, the depositary, shut up the Depot for a time, and himself performed a tour, selling in less than three months 452 copies. Sotirios, who has long been an esteemed labourer in the capital, colported at first for over two months at Ioannina.

There is an important field for a zealous Greek missionary in that city; but there is, if possible, a still greater need for truly godly colporteurs, able to speak the Albanian language, to labour in South Albania. One Albanian, who was for a month or two in the Society's service in Greece, has been engaged on trial for six months, and put under Mr. Kyrias's superintendence; but another still is required.

Progress Made During the Year

Mr. Kyrias, who superintends from Monastir the Society's work in Macedonia and Central Albania, expressed great thankfulness that, under the vigorous and upright government of Rifaat Pasha, the land had enjoyed peace from brigandage, and our men had been able to go on their tours without fear.

Besides its increased circulation, last year was one of marked progress in respect of numerous districts having been visited, which formerly were inaccessible from fear of brigands. The important town of Prisrend was, till lately, such a place; and now another notorious haunt of brigands, Dibra, has been successfully visited by your old colporteur Michael, whose patient, prudent demeanour has so often elsewhere disarmed hostility. Michael gives only verbal reports in general, but his encouraging sales and his safe return were the best proofs of his success, and were the occasion of great thankfulness. Mr. Kyrias is anxiously considering what can be done for the still more inaccessible country and people of the 'Mirdites,' nominally Roman Catholics, but most of them unable to read, and intensely fanatical. It would seem that they must be approached through such of them as reside in Scutari, and some progress has been made in that direction. But obviously also, whoever would do anything among them must be an Albanian, able to speak to them the Word of Life in their own tongue, and assure them of our entire disconnection with anything political.

Page 440

A Record of Translation and Revision, 1888–1889

Albanian Tosk (Adapted Roman Alphabet) – The work of bringing out an edition of the Gospel of St. Matthew and the Psalms has been delayed by the Turkish police carrying off Mr. Kyrias' transcription of the Gospel of St. Matthew, with his other books. The preparation is now going forward, and at the request of the President of the Censor's office, an enlightened Albanian, the Committee have consented to publish with St. Matthew the Book of Genesis, instead of the Book of Psalms. Mr. Kyrias has gone to Bucharest to begin the work of printing.

86th Report, 1890

Pages 123–125

Signs of Progress – Macedonia, Albania, and Bulgaria

Considerable progress has been made during the past year in Macedonia and Albania, and also in Bulgaria, in reaching districts hitherto unvisited by the Word of God. The necessity of keeping this in view will be obvious when it is remembered that the colporteurs, in hiring mules, have generally to follow the main lines of the traffic, as the muleteers often refuse to go to places from which they fear they may have no return fare. As the colporteurs in Bulgaria have conveyances of their own, they are free to visit any village, and in Albania the difficulty has been met by engaging a muleteer for a circuit. There are still, however, two districts of Albania inaccessible to the colporteur—the country of the Mirdites, in which indeed little or nothing could be done, we fear, and the distant towns of Ipek and Jakova. This seems also the place to mention that though your Agent made a special visit to Cettigne, the capital of Montenegro, in order, if possible, to get permission to offer the Scriptures for sale in that principality, and was courteously received by all the members of the Council of State, he has received no reply to a formal application which he addressed to the President. An esteemed friend, who knows something of Montenegro, has suggested that I should try the power of importunity. At present, Montenegro is, perhaps, the only territory in Europe where the Society is denied admission for the Bible—a most unenviable distinction truly!

Notes on the Languages

In Albania the sale of 347 portions in the new Albanian alphabet in the concluding months of the year testifies to the deep interest taken by the people in the employment of their own language. Some of these were doubtless sold to Ghegs; but there can be no doubt that the fetters of Romanism still keep Ghegs far behind their Tosk brethren in the knowledge of God. ...

I would close these general remarks by observing that, as far as the work of your Society is concerned, the chief interest has been among the Greeks and Albanians. It would seem as if the Spirit of God were stirring up several among these people to break through the dead formalities of the past and offer to God a heartfelt and reasonable service. Offers of service as colporteurs were repeatedly made to your Agent by well-educated persons, for whom he had no room, but who were beginning to realise in their own hearts the importance of Divine truth. There is urgent need for zealous Greek evangelists, men full of faith and mighty in the Scriptures, to carry on the work which seems to have been begun in various places by the labours of your Society.

Pages 128–129

Macedonia and Albania

In this extensive territory, to use Dr. Thomson's words, 'the principal element of the population is the Albanian nation, and to this the efforts of the Society are chiefly directed.' The sales for the year were three thousand five hundred and twenty-seven copies; of these seven colporteurs sold three thousand one hundred and sixty-seven. There is a slight decrease compared with the

numbers of 1889, but the Scutari Depot—now reopened—
was necessarily closed for part of the year.

Colportage Work in Albania

The two colporteurs who laboured in South Albania
were Sotirios from Constantinople, and D. Tsoutses from
Greece; both natives of Epirus, and both called to bear the
offence of the Cross; for the former was sent as a felon
under guard to Ioannina from Philippiada, and the latter
from Metzovo, for no other reason than the enmity and
suspicion of the authorities. Happily, through the cordial
support of Mr. B. Kypriotis, Her Majesty's Consular
Agent, justice prevailed, and both were liberated after
some time of imprisonment, but at considerable expense,
besides annoyance and loss of time. Sotirios visited first
northwards as far as Tepelen, then returned by the coast
and proceeded to Prevesa and the intervening towns and
villages, and lastly visited again, as he did in 1888, the
important district of Zagora. His sales show the eminent
success of his labours, but they do not intimate the joy with
which this excellent brother discharges his duty, rejoicing
in proclaiming to all a free salvation through faith in the
Lord Jesus alone, and by his kindly manner disarming
hostility. On visiting one large village the steward called
a policeman to have him sent off, but after a few minutes'
conversation he became quite friendly, and at last bought
both a Bible and a New Testament. In many places he had
much discussion, but he was everywhere kindly received
– in many cases invited to visit the people in their homes,
and to return soon again.

In Central Albania colporteurs Tsiku, Michael, and
Soulis (the latter only for six months) have done good
work, and from the first and the last regular reports were

received. On the eastern side of Pindus, and particularly around Castoria, Colporteur Tsiku visited many places, where no colporteur had ever gone, meeting sometimes with not a little opposition, but in almost every case overcoming it by prudence, patience, and good sense. The rivalry between the Greeks and Bulgarians has had the effect of extending the means of education, doubtless with a view to the diffusion of the one or the other language. But in a region where both nationalities are found, and both languages spoken, education in either language is a priceless boon.

Northern Albania comprises much territory that is still inaccessible, especially the triangular-shaped Mirdite Country, encompassed by the Drin, and the valley watered by the White and the Black Drin, which unite not very far from Prisrend. These two sections are divided by mountain ranges, and are further marked by the prevalence of the Servian language in the eastern valley, while Albanian, Greek, and Italian are spoken on the western seaboard. The Society's station on the west is Scutari, which may be called the capital of Albania, and that on the east Uscup, a good way east of the valley of the two Drins.

Scutari

In Scutari, Colporteur Thoshe has done perhaps all that could be expected in that town so difficult to work. He made also two tours along the coast to Durazzo and Avlona, returning by Berat, Fieri, and Tiranna. Education is greatly needed, but we hardly know from what quarter to expect it. The Italian Government has established a school in Scutari with several male and female teachers; but of its character and influence it would be as yet premature to speak. Of all places in this field Berat—which was for several years the seat of the Society's Agency instead of Scutari—is the most hopeful, and we trust soon to devote special attention to that important city.

Page 438

A Record of Translation and Revision, 1889–1890

Albanian Tosk (adapted Roman alphabet) – The Book of Genesis and the Gospel of St. Matthew have been published in the new form of the alphabet.

87th Report, 1891

Page 141

Turkey

'During the year 1890,' writes Dr. Thomson, 'all the centres of circulation have been visited; careful and persevering efforts have been made to penetrate districts hitherto untouched, and with some success. An island of the Aegean has been visited for the first time with the Word of God, as well as another of which the scanty population and difficult access led to its being often passed by; more especially the western shores of Asia Minor have been traversed by our men as never before, for they have not only visited the towns at which the coasting steamers touch, but, going by land, have entered many villages and localities where a colporteur has never till now gone; and where in several instances they found a thirst for the Holy Scriptures. A similar account may be given of several districts in Central and Southern Albania, and even of Bulgaria and Greece.' The journals which follow give many separate instances of good results, but the most important matter is that the work has been done.

Pages 144–145

In Albanian the decrease of 55 copies is far more than accounted for by the loss of the services of two colporteurs for about six months each. There can be no doubt that the Albanian people are awaking to the consciousness of national existence, and are more disposed than ever to buy and study books in their own language, and with growing impressions of the importance of the message they contain. The increase in the Gheg circulation is doubtless due to the re-opening of the Scutari Depot; but the fact that only 268 copies of Genesis and Matthew in the new characters were sold during the year, while 347 were sold in the last quarter of the previous year, seems to indicate that the new Alphabet will be slow in winning its way, especially in the absence of Albanian Schools, and that the Society will do well to provide a good supply of Scriptures in the orthography it has hitherto used.

Pages 151–153
Albania and Part of Macedonia

In this extensive but thinly-populated region several things occurred to diminish the circulation. The growing interest of the Albanians in the spread of the Gospel in their own language seemed at last to require the removal of the Central Depot from Monastir, where they are but a colony, to Koritza, which is a thoroughly Albanian town. It was not without hesitation that we removed our head-quarters from the seat of provincial government and the protection of H.M.'s Consulate, but the result has justified the step.

Incidents of Colportage

Turning now to incidents of colportage, Colporteur Tsiku visited in the beginning of the year several remote villages in the district of Castoria, where no colporteur had previously been, and was well received, for the people were hungering for the Word of God—for something upon which they could earnestly rely. In one of the villages the people asked the teachers about God and His book, and were told, 'These men bring you the Word of God; they are the true orthodox, for they are doing what the so-called orthodox Church ought to have done long ago, and ought to do now. Instead of seeking to cheat you, they sell you for 4 pias a book costing 20.' In another village, the people of which were Bulgarians, but their clergy and Church service Greek, he stayed over the Lord's Day, and had acceptance with the people.

At the port of Durazzo, the ancient Dyrrachium, he found a boat from the district of Chimara in South Albania, and formed a brief but cordial friendship with two young Albanians of the crew. He spoke to them of divine things, and taught them to read Albanian in the Society's Greek orthography, while they showed that they warmly reciprocated his kindness. May this incident lead to the introduction of the Gospel into that wild region. Omitting for the present his visit to Scutari, I may mention that he encountered no small danger in fording the river on his return from the north, as the floods had swollen even inconsiderable brooks into furious torrents. In consequence of toil and exposure he had three attacks of fever and ague, which, however, he happily threw off.

In a town which he visited, the governor asked Tsiku many questions as to the light in which Christians regarded

Jesus Christ, and whether Protestants worshipped pictures or images. Tsiku assured him that they worshipped neither wood nor stone, but the One living, eternal, Almighty God, who knows the hearts of all men. 'Very good,' said the governor, 'but I hear that you are masons, and wish to destroy all religions.' 'Not so,' said Tsiku; 'but men have departed from God, and do the will of Satan, and our Society wishes to reform them by putting into their hands the Word of God Himself.' After some further explanations, the governor said, 'You are right; the whole world—Christians, Turks, and Jews—follow Satan, and I never understood till to-day how your Society labours. I bought a Bible some time ago, but, on showing it to our Hodja, he said it was not for us Mussulmans; so I laid it aside, and have not since looked at it. But now I shall begin and study it carefully.' He then added that he was sorry he did not know of the Evangelical services, otherwise he would have attended them. Such is very much the feeling of perhaps most Albanian Muhammadans.

In South Albania

It would be interesting to report at some length the labours of Colporteurs Sotirios and Tsoutses in South Albania, but I can only give a rapid outline. The latter visited chiefly in the extreme south—Paramythia, Parga, Prevesa, Louro, Konitza, &c. The first two are almost wholly Muhammadan, but experience abundantly proves that the Gospel is often as welcome to such—and it certainly is as necessary—as to nominal Christians. At Prevesa he was encouraged by Christian teachers and was well received.

Colporteur Sotirios visited the more northerly portion of Epirus, between Joannina and Argyrocastro. He writes that as a general rule he found the people very different from what they formerly were, being ready to hear him attentively and thankfully, and even asking him to stay longer with them. He was everywhere well received, and found a marked interest in the truth among the doctors, lawyers and teachers, the three most educated and influential classes of Greek society, except only at one of the villages, where an ignorant priest tried to expel him, and prevented many from buying the Scriptures. He stayed five days, however; sold 10 copies, and warned the priest that he was neither entering the kingdom of God himself, nor allowing those who wished to enter in. At Shahsta he sold 50 copies, and amongst others prevailed on a doctor to buy a Bible. He pored over it that evening, and returned it to Sotirios next day saying: 'We Greeks are the most ignorant of men, for we don't read the Bible, and so don't know it, but mock at it, while it is the wisest and best book in the world.' He asked many questions, and induced him to stay two days longer than we had intended. At Grevena he had an equally favourable reception from all classes, and much researching of the Scriptures.

Northern Albania

Turning now finally to the extreme north of Albania we have to notice in a few lines the re-opening of the Depot at Scutari, though the peculiar state of matters in that city might well deserve as extended notice as either Central or South Albania. Scutari is a city of at least 32,000 inhabitants, with nearly as many Muhammadans as Christians, and the latter consisting chiefly of Roman Catholics, but with a few hundreds of Orthodox, speaking Greek, Bulgarian or Servian. The Roman Catholic clergy are Jesuits, thoroughly avowed, and outspoken in their hostility, while the mass of the people are sunk in the deepest ignorance, and even the few educated persons among them are almost as much under a superstitious dread of their supposed spiritual power as the most illiterate. Hence the value of the Depot, not only for the sale of the Scriptures, but for affording an opportunity to all classes of the population to read the Scriptures, to satisfy curiosity and doubts of various kinds, and to receive religious intelligence. The Depot has in reality been in active operation only about six months, but in that time it was visited 1,600 times chiefly by Orthodox or Greek Christians, next by Mussulmans, and next in still considerable numbers, by Roman Catholics of various nationalities, Albanians, Slavs, Arabs and Armenians. Lastly it was visited several times by a Jewish army medical officer and his assistant. In a city where the Bible was utterly unknown, it is not to be wondered at that the people desire to know something about it before purchasing a book, which almost all their clergy represent as false and dangerous. Hence the value of the Depot in removing ignorance and prejudice. Mr. George Kyrias also, your depositary, seems to have exercised great prudence and tact in meeting the various classes of visitors. Numerous cases have occurred in which Mussulmans and Romanists have sat for hours reading for the first time with interest and wonder the Gospel narrative.

I should add that the Scutari dialect of Albania has peculiarities of its own which prevents easy intercourse at once with natives of other districts. Italian also is pretty current in Scutari, and Italian male and female schools have been opened there within the last two years, but the Word of God is not read in them, nor can we expect them to meet the wants of the general population.

Pages 159–160
Greece

It is well known that there is a large Albanian element in the population of Greece, an element, or section, which has never been neglected, but to which special attention was directed during the past year. The islands of Aegina, Poros, Hydra, Spetza, with the adjacent towns of Kranidion and Leonidion, the natives of which played so important a part in the Greek war of independence, are all Albanian, and were visited by Colporteur Papajordanes, who after a year's interval, was gladly welcomed back to the ranks of our colporteurs. He was generally well received, and especially by some to whom he had formerly sold the Scriptures. He visited also the prisons of Aegina, while in Poros, and in the other islands he saw proofs of former wealth and pious feeling in the numerous churches and charitable institutions, but found little appreciation of the gospel as the means of salvation. In Thebes and ancient Boeotia, Dr. Kalopothakes himself found the population, which is chiefly Albanian, equally indifferent to learning to read the Word of God in their own language. The people care more for farming and for military pursuits than for learning; and Dr. Kalopothakes very properly suggests that, in such circumstances the government should meet the people half-way and give them, even though but temporarily, instruction in their own language. Female education is unknown in that region. ...

Dr. Kalopothakes' Report

The colporteurs canvassed almost the entire country, including the Ionian islands and the Cyclades. They made also special visits to the places inhabited by Albanians in order to induce them to get the New Testament in their own language with the Greek letters. But, while they disposed a good many copies in modern Greek, they did not succeed very well in their efforts to sell the Albanian New Testament in Greek characters. Here and there some would buy a copy from curiosity rather than a desire to cultivate his own language. Unfortunately the Albanian people are not lovers of letters, preferring to devote themselves to farming. There are, however, a few among them who really desire to cultivate their own tongue, and if the government were wiling to them a little, a good deal might be done among this people. My desire is to do all I can to put the Word of God in their hands, be it through the Greek or the Albanian.

The Peloponnesus, as usual, as been the better field for the Bible colporteur this year, though the Ionian Islands, Hydra, and Spetza with Poros and others—all Albanian settlements—have shown a considerable readiness to obtain the Scriptures.

Page 467

A Record of Translation and Revision, 1890–1891

Albanian Tosk (Adapted from the Roman alphabet) – The work of publication, interrupted by the Turkish police carrying off MSS. and other books belonging to Mr. Kyrias, has been resumed, and the printing of the Book of Psalms is now almost completed.

88th Report, 1892

Pages 132–133
Turkey

'Over a large area,' writes Dr. Thomson, 'the steady and in some instances the increasing circulation of the Word of Life in the vernacular languages cannot but indicate a growing appreciation of Divine Truth, and a desire among the people to know for themselves what that religion really is, which thousands have hitherto ignorantly and carelessly professed. In short, among several nationalities, but especially among the Greeks and Albanians, the Spirit of God seems to be touching the conscience and awakening the intellect.' Such sentences could not have been written some years ago, and they are full of encouragement ...

One page in the report of the year is sufficiently dark; it is that which refers, here as elsewhere, to the universal prevalence of illness. The young wife of the Rev. G. D. Kyrias, the Society's superintendent of colportage in Albania and Macedonia, has been taken from him. Mr. Misaelides, of Smyrna, has lost his beloved eldest daughter, and Colporteur Kyriakos, of Volo, his son. Mr. George Kyrias, of Scutari, has been driven by failure of health from his post, and the list of the colporteurs shows a long record of sickness among the men. All this implies weakening of the available force and necessarily a reduction of circulation; but taking everything into account, it seems to Dr. Thomson that the deficiency is less than might be expected.

Page 136

Rouman is sold almost exclusively on the Bulgarian bank of the Danube, but the Gospel of Matthew in Macedonian-

Rouman is sold to the ancient Rouman colonies in Macedonia, Albania, and Thessaly, and would appear to be acceptable. It is peculiarly valuable as thus rendering the Gospel intelligible to the women, who seldom probably understand any other language. ... Servian sold in Eastern Albania and North Macedonia does not call for remarks; but your Agent is most thankful that with a reduced staff Turkish is only a single copy below the circulation of the previous year.

Pages 140–142

Albania and Part of Macedonia

Here, as in the case of Constantinople, illness and consequent reduction of the staff accounts largely for the lower circulation. This, it is hoped, will not be continued. The important city of Monastir, now relinquished by the American Bible Society, must be supplied by at least two colporteurs, and the needs of the Albanian speaking people are increasingly urgent. Details of colportage work supplementary to those given here may be found elsewhere.

In the survey of this region I begin with Uscup, the most easterly station. The people are poor, the towns far distant from each other, and robbery is not uncommon. The population, too, is very miscellaneous—Turks, Greeks, Bulgarians, Servians, and Albanians, with Spanish Jews and a few Europeans in some of the cities. The Osmanlis are the proprietors of the soil, and it was in this region that Turkish ascendency was achieved on the field of Kossovo. It seems to have been early occupied by Osmanlis of distinction, and some of its mosques, though small, are exceedingly interesting as specimens of early Mussulman architecture. Later, when the richer Osmanlis were attracted elsewhere, the difficulty was to find markets for the products of the soil; and this continued till railways were introduced. Three lines of railway now meet at Uscup, and it may be hoped that, in course of time, free communication will produce greater social comfort. I must add further that to the west and north-west, where the circuit embraces the eastern portions of Upper Albania, numerous mountains rise to the height of 6,000 and 7,000 feet, so that the climate is very severe, and the roads are passable only during about half the year. Being also a frontier province, bordering on Montenegro, Austria, and Servia, colportage used to be very much restricted, but has for some years been more free. The chief difficulty, however, remains to be mentioned, viz. the Roman Catholicism that prevails in North-Eastern Albania, with its centres at Scutari and Prisrend. The members of the Orthodox Greek Church, whether speaking Greek or any of the Slavic dialects, may be often ignorant and superstitious, but they almost always reverence the Holy Scriptures, and admit their authority as supreme. It is otherwise with Roman Catholics, who rely primarily on the teachings of their Church, and can seldom be induced to read, or hear read, the Word of God, far less to purchase it. If I have dwelt at some length on the characteristics of this circuit it is partly to do justice to the Society's colporteur, Jovancho, who has been labouring there now for seven years, in succession to previous faithful men. He complains of the poverty of the people preventing many from purchasing who would gladly do so, and especially of the inaccessibility of the Roman Catholics.

In these circumstances it is not surprising that he consoles himself, under the comparative fewness of his sales, with the opportunities he has for removing objections and misunderstandings, and proclaiming the Grace of God. He has everywhere, however, personal friends, with whom on each visit he holds religious meetings; and he feels assured that the truth is spreading. He mentions having been detained at home by robberies and murders in the region he had arranged to visit; and I should add that the extreme north-west portions of his field, including the towns of Jakova and Ipeko, an ancient ecclesiastical metropolis, have hitherto been inaccessible on account of brigandage, want of roads, and political difficulties.

Page 377

A Record of Translation and Revision, 1891–1892

Albanian Tosk (Adapted from the Roman alphabet) – On examination before going to press the version of the Psalms was found to be defective, and the Rev. Dr. Thomson and the Rev. Gerasim Kyrias, Superintendent of Colporteurs in Central Albania, are now revising the MS., and forty Psalms are ready for the press.

89th Report, 1893

Page 127

Linguistic Commentaries

Referring to the Linguistic Table we observe that Albanian, in its steady progress, has now exceeded considerably 1,000 copies, no small attainment among a people who had no written language till the Society gave it them, and who are still the least civilised of the races of European Turkey. The large increase of 489 copies is to be ascribed, doubtless, largely to a reduction in the prices; but that reduction would have produced no effect unless there had been a strong desire to possess the Word of God. Albania still lags behind, from the extreme ignorance of the people and their bondage to the Romanist Church, and partly from your Agent's inability hitherto to find a suitable person to occupy North Albania.

Pages 132–134

Albania

In this important section of the Agency two almost equally evident facts impress themselves upon the mind— one the prevalence of various forms of opposition, and the other a steady increase of interest in the Scriptures. The extracts which follow give sufficient information as to the general character of the field, and some glimpses of the ever varying experience of which the colporteur's life is made.

The table below exhibits the issues in these extensive regions.

	1892	1891
Sales from Joannina Depot	151	176
Sales from Monastir Depot per Rev. W. Baird	109 }	239
Sales from Koritza Depot per G. D. Kyrias	143 }	
Sales from Scutari Depot	14	21
Sales at Salonica per P. Crosby	26	—
By 5 regular, 2 occasional, and 1 aged colporteurs	3017	1852
Free Grants	10	158
Total Copies	3470	2446

Attention may also be directed to the very mixed population of these regions. Along the shore of the Adriatic, eastward, to the distance of front 50 to 100 miles, dwell the Ghegs (giants) in the north, the Tosks in the south, while Joannina and some other places seem to have been Greek colonies. North Macedonia is occupied by Serbs, central chiefly by Bulgarians, and the south chiefly by Greeks. On the range of Mount Pindus, from Thessaly up to the latitude of Durazzo, dwell the Vlachs, an ancient Roman colony, while in Joannina there is an ancient colony of Jews who speak Greek; and at Monastir a later colony speaking Spanish. South Macedonia has for upwards of thirty years been occupied by the Scottish National Bible Society, through Rev. Peter Crosbie of the Church of Scotland Mission at Salonica.

Joannina has been for about thirty years a station of prime importance in the Society's work; its population of more than 30,000, its gymnasium equal probably to any in Greece, and its political importance in the early part of the present century, all contributing to render the capital of Epirus a centre of deep religious interest. A Depot was opened for the sale of the Scriptures, and has been continued ever since 1865, with various colporteurs successively attached to it; though for the present Sotirios, one of the most successful, has, on account of domestic circumstances, been obliged to remove to Constantinople. The present depositary, Joannes Bosdoyannes, a young man of good education and Christian character, like Sotirios, is a native of Epirus. I shall only say of the work of Colporteur Sotirios that he everywhere met with a most kindly reception and found many thirsting for the Word of Life, and that in his native village of Delvinaki especially he was treated with unusual kindness, and could scarcely satisfy the desires of the people to have the Scriptures explained to them.

Koritza, on the old Egyptian way, derives its commercial importance as a transit station between the Adriatic coast on the west and Macedonia and the shores of the Aegean on the east.

The Albanian service and the sale of the Scriptures were mutually helpful to each other; and that while using every effort to avail ourselves of the Albanian language in order to reach the working classes, and, with but few exceptions, comparatively the whole of the females, it is being found more and more that the attraction of the national language has a powerful influence in gaining for the Gospel the ear of the Muhammadan population, composing probably a third of the nation. They are often, in fact, more ready to purchase the Holy Scriptures than their Christian brethren. But the Society's object is to circulate the Scriptures in whatever language the people best understand, and hence the Greek, the Bulgarian, the Servian, the Wallachian, the Turkish, and the Judaeo-Spanish Scriptures are all provided for the various nationalities of the extensive region under the immediate superintendence of Rev. G. D. Kyrias.

Our great antagonist in that region, as also in that between it and the Adriatic, is the Romish Church, of which Scutari is a stronghold. That city and North Albania were visited by I. Tsiku, who spent about six weeks in the northern capital, and was astonished, as almost all who visit that city are, at the ignorance and utter absence of independent thought or of a readiness to listen to reason and the Word of God, displayed by the Roman Catholic population. Only four persons had the courage to invite him to talk with them in their shops. These latter are all open booths, and the discussions he carried on were listened to by a multitude of people who were desirous, for one reason or another, to hear what the man said whom they had been so fearfully warned to avoid as believing in absolutely nothing at all.

Page 406
A Record of Translation and Revision, 1892–1893

Albanian Tosk (Adapted Roman Alphabet) – The Psalms, after long delay, have been printed, but are not yet in circulation. During the absence of Mr. Kyrias, several typographical errors crept into the text, and the first two sheets had to be reprinted.

90th Report, 1894

Pages 139–142

In the Turkish Agency the year 1892-3 has been one of "exceptional difficulty, but at the same time marked by very evident tokens of the divine blessing."…

One cause of decline in the circulation has been the too frequent interference of the local magistracy with the work of the men—an experience often most vexatious and unhappy, but attributable, Dr. Thompson is assured, rather to the over-zealous intolerance of individuals than to the Imperial Government …

The death of the Rev. Gerasim Kyrias is a loss of a different character, and of it Dr. Thompson speaks with natural sorrow.

Death of the Rev. G. Kyrias

It is difficult for me even now to estimate the calamity the loss the Society's work among the Albanians has sustained by the decease, in the very prime of life, of this devoted servant of our Lord. Mr. Kyrias had been labouring diligently for his people, we fear beyond his strength, till the closing exercises of the female school taught by his sister in Koritza. Just then commenced a remarkable succession of earthquake tremors, or shocks, which have continued with more or less severity and at generally increasing intervals till now. As Koritza was rebuilt, after the great fire of some twenty-five years ago[3], very largely in stone, such shocks were peculiarly dangerous; and, like most of the population, Mr. Kyrias slept under a booth in the court of his house. In consequence of this he caught a chill, which greatly debilitated him; but just then the interference of one of the Valis with our colporteurs made it necessary for him to move to Monastir to seek redress. I have little doubt that the constant vexation caused by such obstruction to the work greatly aggravated his illness. Shortly after, in July, I learned with alarm that his life was despaired of. The ablest medical advice was secured; hope revived under a wiser treatment, and great efforts were made to have him so far restored as to be able to remove to Athens for the winter. But it was not to be. He never was able to undertake the journey, the toil of which was then aggravated by quarantine regulations. His strength rapidly gave way, but amidst it all he enjoyed the 'perfect peace' which Jesus alone can give, and calmly fell asleep on January 2, 1894, aged thirty-five.

The Hardships of the Colporteurs' Life

I have specially to refer to the loss of time caused by sickness. Both influenza and cholera, in one form or other, have visited the Agency, in addition to the

---

3 There is documented evidence for significant Kortcha fires in 1822, 1858 and 1879 (according to Niko Kotherja, director of the National Museum of Education in Kortcha). Thomson may have misunderstood the year, or perhaps there was another fire around 1869 (D.H.).

malarial fevers to which our traveling colporteurs are peculiarly exposed. ... Colporteur Tsiku was seized with intermittent fever in the wild mountain region Ochrida, and was only with difficulty able to return to his home in Koritza at the end of three weeks. Georgios, at Rhodes, had to leave three islands in his field unvisited, from sickness either in his own person or in his family. And finally, during the five months of uttered exhaustion that preceded the dissolution of our lamented brother, Mr. Kyrias, some time was unavoidably lost from his inability to attend to the case of each colporteur under his care.

It is but fair, I think, in reviewing the labours of the past year, to mention the hindrances that were met, not to complain of them so much as to vindicate the faithfulness of the labourers, notwithstanding the apparently small results. Such a review may sometimes suggest the means of avoiding certain hindrances in the future, and if not, it may at least teach us to labour on in faith.

Scrutiny of the Linguistic Statistics

We observe that, while there is a total decrease on *Albanian* sales of 606 copies (475 instead of 1,082 copies), there is a slight increase in the Gheg issues. We note this with interest, as indicating that the Ghegs are beginning to be restive under the prohibition to read the Word of God and that when away from the vigilance of the priest, and perhaps, too, of their own brethren – for there were no Gheg sales in Scutari – they are desirous to judge for themselves of a book that is so jealously forbidden to them. It is encouraging to find that there was an appreciable demand for Albanian Scriptures in the Ionian Islands and in the Peloponnesus, proving that these tribes, that have hitherto been found quite indifferent to the Word of God, are beginning to sympathise with the work that is going on among their brethren in Albania. Still more encouraging is the fact that a member of the Albanian colony in Sophia, the capital of Bulgaria, stirred up by the good news from Koritza, assembled his countrymen for worship on the Lord's Day, and, as a mark of their interest in their country and the Gospel, sent a donation to the Albanian school that had been established there. The diminution of 606 in the year's sales is very considerable, but under the circumstances that have been mentioned, is not more than might have been anticipated. The steady sale of entire Testaments is encouraging, and it ought to be remembered that a large proportion of the people are quite illiterate, and that even for such as can read Greek, a certain degree of patience and acuteness is required in order to learn to read Albanian in any of the three alphabets in which it is printed.

Pages 147–148

Macedonia and Albania

Of all the cities of this Agency there is none, we must frankly confess, upon which less impression has apparently been made than on Scutari. The few Christians of the Orthodox Church, whether Greeks or Slavs, and even the Muhammadans, have bought and read the Scriptures with interest. But to the Roman Catholic Albanians, who are the bulk of the population, the sales have been very few indeed. But the explanation is obvious enough. The people have absolutely no literature at all except a small prayer-book and a catechism, while their religious instruction and all that they know of the Word of God is received entirely through the oral teaching of their clergy, who represent the Pope of Rome as the infallible Vicar of Christ on earth, and denounce as impious, and their Scriptures as falsified, all who do not acknowledge his authority. Patriotic feeling, too, supports the pretensions of the papacy, for Skanderbeg, the national hero, was a Roman Catholic. The people are sank in ignorance, and anything like independent judgment or inquire is unknown. Unable to find a suitable depositary, or to spare for that office the one colporteur who would be suitable, I was reluctantly compelled to recommend that the Depot at Scutari should be closed, which was accordingly done in August last. The only method left of seeking to introduce the Gospel is by sending our most suitable colporteur once or twice a year for a considerable visit, though past experience has taught us that the experiment is not unaccompanied with danger.

During two months at the beginning of the year, and again in August, he had a great deal of open, quiet discussion with the people, who feared, yet wished to hear, what he had to say. The result was that Tsiku did succeed in selling a few copies both in Tosk and Gheg, and, what was almost equally important, in convincing many that he was as firm a believer in Jesus Christ as themselves, and that his Gospel was the same with their own, notwithstanding all that their clergy solemnly declared to the contrary. Tsiku's subsequent visits to Berat, Durazzo, and other centres, were all interesting, but space will not permit me to add more than that he found in most of these towns, both Christians and Mussulmans earnestly seeking for some solid foundation of hope, and rejoiced to point out to them the Lord Jesus as an all-sufficient Saviour. Here and there he found enlightened Bible Christians.

Of Colporteur Sotiriades it is enough to say that he disseminated, for the locality, a fair amount of Scriptures, in regions that have long been the haunt of brigands, and directed the attention of both Christians and Muhammandans to the great question of human destiny beyond the grave, and to the Bible as the only unerring guide. The attitude of the teachers was generally favourable, but they were sometimes intimidated.

Within Monastir itself, and its nearest villages, good old Colporteur Michael has done a good work, and deserves warm recognition. It should not be forgotten that a year or two ago he was selected, on account of his age and his gentle, quiet spirit, as the most suitable of our colporteurs to visit Dibra, the capital of a region notorious for robberies, and that he performed successfully his mission, and sold some Scriptures.

Colporteur Marmaroff had his full share of annoyance, but writes gratefully of the exertions of H. M. Vice-Consul at Monastir, H. S. Shipley, Esq. His great and constant feeling is that the Word of God is working in the hearts of the people, so that they cannot remain indifferent. At one town he tells us the Bible readers have opened a Sunday reading-room, open to all who choose to come and read or hear the Bible. One village he mentions, which he was the first to visit with the Scriptures, and where the people were astonished to find so many copies of the Gospel, as they had never seen any but the large one in their church; while in another village, greatly infested with robbers, the people were thankful that he had had the courage to visit them, and received him with great kindness.

Perhaps none of our colporteurs have suffered more from the interference of local magistrates than Jovancho, and his solitary position as Uscup has aggravated his difficulties. But these seem at last to have been for the present removed. His field comprehends the region known as Old Servia, and extending to the frontiers of Bosnia and Servia. He is well known and has many friends, and he can defend the truth with tact and ability, but there is nothing in his report to call for notice.

At Joannina, the capital of Epirus, the voluntary services for public worship held by your depositary, Mr. Bosdoyannes, are attended by increasing audiences. Something also has been attempted for the outlying villages and districts unvisited till now, and not without success. But in no part, perhaps, of the Agency is the pressure arising from a diminished revenue felt more perceptibly than in the region of which Joannina is the centre. There are large villages out of the common routes which have scarcely ever been visited by any colporteur, while the territory is quite sufficient to occupy the time and strength of two vigorous colporteurs.

Table of Circulation (Macedonia and Albania)

	1893	1892
Sales by colporteurs (6); (1892, 8)	1,674	3,017
Sales from Monastir Depot	90	109
Sales from Koritza Depot	80	143
Sales from Joannina Depot	225	151
Sales from Scutari Depot	11	14
Sales at Salonica per P. Crosbie	—	26
Free Grants	10	158
Sales by Deacon Zalamichas	48	—
Total Sales	2,128	3,460
Free Grants	39	10
Totals (Decrease, 1,303)	**2,167**	**3,470**

Page 414

A Record of Translation and Revision, 1893–1894

Albanian (Tosk) (Adapted Roman Alphabet) – With a view to the completion and immediate publication of the Psalms, the Committee have set apart Mr. Athanasios Sinas to aid Dr. Thomson in the final revision and proof-reading.

91st Report, 1895

Page 142

The general aspect of the year just closed has not been specially notable. With hardly an exception the colporteurs have been undisturbed in their work, and had it not been for the prevalent want of money among the poorer people, the circulation of the year, instead of slightly falling behind, might have advanced. With the exception of this decrease, the review is favourable, and one of the memorable facts is that connected with the Albanian people and their Bible. For years the printing of Albanian Scriptures has been interdicted, and the restriction lay like a burden on Dr. Thomson's heart. That burden, like many another, has at length been removed, and 'now,' he writes, 'we look forward with joy to the work yet to be done for a brave and long-neglected people.'

Page 143

The Visit of Rev. J. Sharp and T. F. Victor Buxton, Esq.

I must now refer to the great pleasure with which we received the visit of the Deputation from the Committee, consisting of the Rev. J. Sharp, M.A., Secretary, T. F. Victor Buxton, Esq., a member of the Committee, and Rev. R. H. Weakley, the Society's Agent at Alexandria. It is not for me to say more than that our first place of meeting was

Smyrna, and that after careful inspection of the Society's work there, and pleasant intercourse with our American and Scotch friends, we sailed for Salonica to meet Mr. George Kyrias from Monastir, enjoying there the hospitality of our esteemed friend the Rev. P. Crosbie, of the Church of Scotland Jewish Mission, and sailed the same day for the Piraeus. In Greece the Deputation inspected the operations of the Depot and colportage under the direction of the Society's Sub- Agent, Rev. Dr. Kalopothakes, and as Mr. Bosdoyannes had come to Athens to meet the Deputation, Mr. Sharp resolved to accompany him on his return to Ioannina, and thus visit a town which has been a centre of the Society's earnest exertions for the last thirty years. On his return to Athens, the Deputation proceeded to Constantinople, and during their stay there were favoured with an interview by Sir Philip Currie, H.M. Ambassador, in order to lay before him the Society's request that the Imperial Government might be induced to permit the Society to go on publishing the Scriptures in the Albanian language, as they had been doing for the last sixty-seven years, with the express sanction of the censorship, and without interruption or complaint on the part of the local authorities. His Excellency had made himself acquainted with the facts of the case, and assured the Deputation that he would use his best endeavours in the circumstances to satisfy the benevolent wish of the Society.

Pages 144–145
The Albanian Bible

It had become obvious that it was desirable to elicit a decision from the Imperial Government on the important question of printing the Scriptures in the Albanian language, by addressing another petition to H.M. Embassy. This was done November 30th, and in due course the petition was laid in full force before the Turkish Government. The petition was referred by the Government to the Ministry of Education, who are understood to have granted us liberty to print freely not only the two editions of the Psalms but all the Holy Scriptures, and it is hoped also for others to print books of an educational and general character. This decision, which was communicated to your Agent January 31st, led us in deepest thankfulness to God to express our warmest acknowledgments to H.M. Ambassador, and through him to the Imperial Government for their generous response to our petition, as well as our deep conviction that the result of our circulation of the Holy Scriptures among the Albanian people could only be their advancement in intelligence, peace, and righteousness among themselves and towards their fellow-subjects of the Ottoman Empire. And thus after three years and a half of anxious waiting and repeated applications to the Government our burden is removed, and we look forward with joy to further labours for a brave but long-neglected people.

Page 146
Linguistic Analysis by Alexander Thomson

First, alphabetically, comes a nationality entitled to our deepest sympathy. It is still but the day of small things with the Albanians, but a really national movement must of necessity be slow; and it is not yet seventy years since the effort to diffuse the Word of God in the Albanian language can properly be said to have begun. Circumstances arising out of their past history as well as their geographical position among the Greeks, have retarded hitherto the cultivation of their own language; but now that the Imperial Government has given its sanction to the free publication of the Scriptures in Albanian, we trust, through Divine Grace, to see a wider diffusion of the Word of Life throughout their towns and mountain villages, and that the curse of brigandage especially may be soon unknown among them. Leaving out of view the issues reported in 1892, amounting to 1,082 copies, which owing to the late receipt of accounts included the sales of a large part of 1891, the sales we think of the last two years may be regarded as normal, or nearly so. The sales in Gheg, though fewer than in the previous year, show a continued interest in Divine Truth in that section of the nation, which we hope, by more systematic visitation of the northern parts of the country, to foster and diffuse. Specially worthy of notice is the sale of sixty-one Testaments, the largest number, we believe, sold as yet in any one year. But perhaps equally interesting is the sale of 206 copies in the new letters, though comprising only the Book of Genesis and the Gospel of St. Matthew, as evincing the growing desire, and a most reasonable one, for a national alphabet, accepted by the whole people, and adapted to represent the numerous sounds of their language. We value the Albanian circulation also because it is, with but few exceptions, the only means of presenting the Word of God to the women.

Albanian is one of the few languages in which last year's sales exceed those of the preceding year (551, and in 1893, 476).

Pages 152–154
Macedonia and Albania

As for various reasons it was judged expedient to connect South Albania, the ancient Epirus, with Greece under the more immediate care of the Rev. Dr. Kalopothakes, your Sub-Agent, the territory denoted by the title 'Macedonia and Albania' is very considerably less, while the circulation also is diminished by the abstraction of the sales from the Depot at Ioannina, and those of Colporteur Harisiades, which will be found in connection with the Report on Greece.

The stations occupied within this territory are Uscup on the east with Colporteur Jovancho, whose circuit extends northward to the borders of Servia and Bosnia, with a considerable Muhammadan and Servian population; Monastir on the south-west, with Colporteur Marmaroff and good old Michael for the city principally, and a population largely Bulgarian, but with Greeks, Muhammadans, and Israelites; and Koritza, further west, within the bounds of Albania, with Colporteurs Tsiku and Sotiriades, both Albanians; and with all Central and Northern Albania, as far as it is accessible—for a large portion to the north is not so—for their field. Jovancho had a serious illness at the beginning of the year, which recurred twice when he was on tours, compelling him to return as soon as he was able to travel; but latterly his health became more confirmed.

His sales are not large, but as large as can well be expected among a population so ignorant and fanatical, and among whom he himself may with justice be considered the first and chief evangelist. Perhaps his chief opponent is the Church of Rome, and he loses no opportunity of enforcing the right and duty of every man to read the Scriptures and judge for himself of their meaning, in opposition to the blind obedience to the teaching of the church which Rome uniformly requires. A Romanist, who had bought a Bible from him, told him that a priest had burned it. 'Did you ask

him to point out the errors with which he charged it?' 'No,'
he replied. 'Then,' said Jovancho, 'you were the servant of
men, and sacrificed to men the Word of God.' The man
did not venture to buy another, but invited him to lodge
at his house for further conversation if he should visit the
village where he lived. There the Christians heard for the
first time of the Bible Society, and highly approved of its
object, but did not venture to buy, fearing one another. I
am happy also to add that he met no impediment from the
magistracy.

Unhappily I cannot say as much in the case of
Colporteur Marmaroff, of Monastir. He was directed,
during the severe winter that prevails in that lofty plateau,
to visit the villages at no great distance all round Monastir.
The Vali, however, refused to permit him to do so, saying
that he could not permit him to visit any place that was not
governed by a Moodir, or at least by a Kaimakam. Much
time was lost in this way, but at last, by the kind offices of
H.M. Vice-Consul, Mr. Shipley, a certain amount of liberty
was granted. Michael does what he can within the city, and
directs special attention to the Jews. He is now an old man,
but his heart is young and eager to work for the Lord.

I rejoice to say that no obstruction whatever was met
with from the authorities at Koritza or in Albania by
Colporteurs Tsiku and Sotiriades.

One form of usefulness is mentioned more than once
by Tsiku, of which we have ourselves had some experience.
In a country like Albania, where khans or inns are not very
frequent, the driver often lodges his hirer in his own house.
This happened to Tsiku on a short tour he made to several
places on the Lake of Ochrida. He started on Saturday,
and a long ride brought him to the driver's village at dusk,
where he arranged to stay till Monday morning, as he

never travelled on the Lord's day. The driver knew well the guest he had with him, and at once invited a number of his neighbours, both Muhammadans and Christians, to come and hear the Word of God. On one such occasion Tsiku had an audience of fifteen robbers in that region, with whom, after a while, he ventured to remonstrate regarding their conduct. But on this occasion his hearers were quiet villagers, to whom he read Matthew v. and vi. with a few observations. On the Lord's day he read again largely Matthew vii. and xiii. and Luke xv., and enlarged on the love of God to sinful men, who, like the prodigal son, had forsaken their Father, and were vainly seeking happiness elsewhere. The simple villagers were delighted, and thanked him for reading to them these words of God, which neither priest nor teacher had ever told them.

But we must bring these notes to an end with a few words as to his visit to Scutari, which he reached after visiting every place of importance along the great coast line from Avlona northward. He was everywhere more successful than he had ventured to expect. At Scutari the people supposed that, as he had closed the Depot in the previous year, the Society had given up their labours there as hopeless. But he assured them that they had no such intention.

After a stay of a few weeks Tsiku had gained a good many friends, who were no longer afraid to converse with him, and had sold 65 copies, of which 39 were in Turkish, and only 5 in Albanian, 6 in Greek, 7 in Italian, 4 in French, 3 in Servian, and 1 in Greco-Turkish, an index this to the mingled population of the city. He afterwards visited various places, and returned to Koritza after a tour of four months and a half. To your Agent this tour has afforded ground for much thankfulness, as indicating that, after so many years of patient, though not quite continuous labour, the Lord was at last opening the hearts of the people of Scutari to listen to the Word of God, and to judge for themselves the meaning of that blessed Gospel which their church professes to teach but will not allow them to read.

Pages 162–163
Greece – Dr. Kalopothakes' Tours

I made four Bible tours during the year—two in Thessaly, one in company with Mr. Liaoutses, visiting several of the towns and villages on the plains of Thessaly, and examining more closely the condition of the people....

My last trip was to Epirus, and chiefly Ioannina. It was very pleasant to me, and I hope profitable to the Bible cause and the few brethren there. Through the labours of Mr. Bosdojannes a considerable number have been led to a knowledge of the truth; among them six prominent men in good circumstances. Mr. Bosdojannes is a faithful labourer, and there is great reason for thankfulness that such important results have followed the work of the Bible Society there. ...

The Deputation From London – Dr. Kalopothakes' Summary

Though I have already extended this report beyond its usual length, I cannot close without a grateful recognition of the pleasure and interest, and, I believe, permanent good, resulting from the visit of the Delegation from the Bible Society last spring. I am glad to feel that they follow every department of the work with intelligent and prayerful interest, and I trust that a large blessing may rest upon the beneficent Society in all its work of love for perishing souls here and throughout the world. I would particularly notice the good impression which the visit of Mr. Sharp made at Ioannina. I heard such frequent expressions from the brethren there.

Page 448
A Record of Translation and Revision, 1894–1895

Albanian (Tosk) (Adapted Roman character). – Mr. Athanasios Sinas has now joined the Rev. Dr. Thomson at Constantinople with a view to preparing two editions of the Book of Psalms for the press. Owing to several misadventures this work has been long on hand, and Dr. Thomson has devoted great care and pains to its completion, and it is now hoped that the work will be brought to a termination immediately.

Albanian (Tosk) (Greek character) – An edition of the above is being prepared in Greek for the older readers.

92nd Report, 1896

Page 128
Turkey – Linguistic Analysis of Issues

The Albanians are rejoicing in the use of their own language, and the circulation of the Scriptures continues to show a steady increase, amounting this year to ninety-one copies. Particularly interesting is the circulation in Gheg Albanian, amounting this year, as also last year, to only twenty-five, but indicating, we believe, a desire to escape from the mental tyranny exercised by the Romish clergy over the people in Scutari. In that town the fear of their neighbours and of the anathema of the Church has hitherto prevented any purchases by members of the

Romish Church. But in Stamboul there are several persons who seem to love the Word of God, and desire quietly to study it.

Page 131
Constantinople

Sotirios, perhaps our best colporteur, going one day to the restaurant he frequented, found there a Greek priest, who, on seeing him enter with his books, began to blaspheme and to revile him. Sotirios said nothing, but after finishing his meal, read, by way of defence, Eph. iv. At last the priest could bear it no longer, and exclaimed, "Why don't you beat the lunatic!' upon which two rude fellows rose up and struck him repeatedly on the head. The police office was close by, but Sotirios bade them not fear, as he committed his cause to God, and called on them to repent. Returning there three days after, the people begged his pardon. More pleasing was the following. Meeting one day with two Albanians, he told them what the Society had done for their nation, and showed them Genesis and Matthew in the national letters, and read to them. The men were both interested and grateful, and each bought copies, and said they now felt themselves to be Christians, for they had the Gospel in their own language, and they asked him to share their meal. He did so, and gave thanks for it in a prayer to which the restaurateur listened with deep attention. He was a Greek, but said he had never heard such a prayer from Christian, Jew, or Turk, and bought a New Testament to know the colporteur's religion.

Pages 133–135

Macedonia and Albania

In this important section of the field one colporteur was forced by bodily infirmity to resign his office, but has been succeeded by a man of energy and zeal who promises to render good service; while another has been promoted to be a preacher in the American Mission, and has been succeeded by a man of whom good hopes are entertained. In Macedonia the population is chiefly Bulgarian, but the rivalry of the Greeks, Roumans, and Servians has led them to establish schools for their respective nationalities, so that considerable attention is paid to education, the Albanians alone lagging behind, hitherto, at least, through fear of Government opposition. The past year has happily been free from those annoyances from the Government which were long so numerous, but just as we write (Feb. 3rd, 1896) difficulties have arisen with the new officer of the censorship which have compelled your Agent to apply to her Majesty's Embassy for protection. Amongst the Bulgarians there are numerous missionaries at work; but among the Albanians, with the exception of the help from the American Board in maintaining the Female School and public worship in Koritza, and the cordial aid of the Bible Lands Missions Aid Society, it is to the Bible Society that we have to look for the continued progress of the Gospel. With this object in view Colporteur Tsiku has, for the last two years, visited all the principal towns from Koritza to Scutari, twice a year, in spring and autumn, staying six weeks in Scutari each time, and with thankfulness we relate that a report just received intimates that some, even in Scutari, are at length perceiving it to be both their duty and their privilege to read the Word of God for themselves, notwithstanding the prohibition of their Church.

If one may judge from the reports of Colporteur Tsiku, who knows Albanian well, and is able to give to the people a Scriptural account of the great doctrines of the Gospel, perhaps there are few regions in Turkey in which there is more earnest inquiry after the way of salvation than just in Albania; and it is certain that in several towns there are not a few who eagerly desire that the Gospel were preached among them, and that they had truly Christian schools for their children. Nor is this spirit of inquiry confined to Christians. For Tsiku found a Muhammadan who made no account of the five formal hours of daily prayer, and longed for a more thorough cleansing than washing with water. And he found even a Jew, who was hated by his brethren as a Protestant for openly avowing the Messiahship of the Lord Jesus, though circumstances deterred him, as bethought, from professing Christianity. It is greatly to be desired that a preacher should itinerate in those towns, but meanwhile the visits of your colporteur are felt to be a great encouragement to those 'seekers' after God, to whom so many promises are made in the Holy Scriptures. We have said that the colporteur appears to have made some impression on Scutari. During the heavy rains that prevail there at this season he had visited a druggist's shop, when naturally the conversation turned on the right and duty of Christians to read the Word of God. During the prolonged discussion others entered, and among them an Italian lady, the teacher of a female school. It was pointed out how inconsistent the denial of the Scriptures to the people was with the example of the Lord and His Apostles, who preached openly to the common people, and how unreasonable it was that any human being should prevent his fellow-creature from reading that Word, which God had given to be 'a lamp unto our feet and a light unto our path.' At length, doubtless not a little impressed by the good sense and evident sincerity of your colporteur, the lady exclaimed, 'Well, after all, I am persuaded our friend is right. Here am I, a Roman Catholic, taught to reverence Mary, and this and the other saint, but really of the Gospel I know nothing. I am wholly dependent on the teaching of others, and am not allowed to judge of what most concerns me. They even forbid us to read the Gospel, but simply to keep by our profession as Roman Catholics.' The lady bought a French Testament, and the druggist a Croatian Testament and a copy of Specimens of Languages, for they praised the work of the Society and prayed for a blessing on it and their brother Tsiku, who had to suffer so much reproach and scorn. Soon after also two Croats came one evening to his room in the inn, and after much conversation on divine things bought a Croatian Testament. 'Who hath despised the day of small things?' May this be the beginning of blessing.

Page 142
Greece – Dr. Kalopothakes on the Work of the Year

As to the special work of the year. In the entire Greek Agency ten colporteurs have been employed, six in the old Greek kingdom, two in Thessaly, and two in Epirus....

Page 124 (Appendix)
A Record of Translation and Revision, 1895–1896

Albanian Tosk (Adapted Roman Alphabet) – The Book of Psalms, carefully revised according to the Hebrew, by Dr. Thomson, the Society's late Agent at Constantinople, and the late Rev. G. D. Kyrias, has been published in convenient form and with legible type, and it is hoped that the portion will prove a blessing to the Albanians, for whom Dr. Thomson has cared greatly.

Albanian Tosk (Greek Alphabet) – Dr. Thomson has presented to the Committee translations in manuscript of the Books of Ruth, Ezra, Nehemiah, Esther, and Job, made by the late Mr. Christophorides. The portions are in Greek character, and need to be rendered into the new national alphabet should they be published.

93rd Report, 1897

Page 122

This Agency of the Society has strong and deep roots. At an early date in the history of the Society, Malta was the centre for distribution in the Levant. A visit of Dr. Pinkerton to Constantinople and Greece led to the appointment in 1820 of the Rev. Henry Leeves as the Society's principal Agent in the Levant. Constantinople, Smyrna, Athens, and other places were centres from which he and his colleague, Mr. Benjamin Barker, directed translation and distribution. Greeks and Armenians, Turks and Jews, Bulgarians and Albanians have all been objects of unwearying care and love, many thousands of pounds having been spent on versions for them. Though much has been done, nowhere is there more to do.

Page 126

Albanian, with a circulation of 453 copies, does not occupy a very prominent place in our table of languages; but where, as in Albania, fanaticism and poverty are the hindrances, we can say that there is here, at least, the entrance of the Word that giveth light.

Pages 131–132
Macedonia and Albania
Circulation: 1636 copies, 1653 in 1895. Decrease of 17 in 1896

Practically, as the above figures show, the circulation remains at the same level as in 1895. There have again been changes in the staff of colporteurs. Jovancho has left the service and has been replaced by Marmaroff, who services as a preacher had been in the previous year applied for by the American Mission, but who has again been set at liberty on account of reductions in the mission. Christoff has joined the staff of colporteurs during the year, and an American Mission colporteur has been employed in the sale of our books at Monastir. Michael, whose increasing age and infirmities have incapacitated him for the toil of travelling in that difficult country, has also worked in Monastir. Tsiku is stationed at Koritza, and Marmaroff at Uskub. Mr. George Kyrias remains in charge of the Depot at Monastir.

In a country like Albania, where the state of political affairs is so uncertain and unsettled, it will be readily understood that our colporteurs carry on their work under considerable disadvantages. During the year, however, our men rarely have been interfered with by the officials, and when this has occurred it has been in small towns and villages under subordinate and often ignorant Government servants. Christoff was brought into Monastir in July under a guard of fifteen soldiers and put into prison. He must have been regarded as a formidable personage. When the matter was explained to the Vali Pasha, Christoff was set at liberty after a few hours' detention, all his papers being in order. The poverty of the people, as well as the state of political unrest, has also had its effect on our work. The result is described by a colporteur: 'Men's minds are filled with their present circumstances which entirely take away their taste for buying and reading the Bible.' No cause for discouragement, however, appears in the general review of the work. On the contrary, the colporteurs engaged in spiritual work, and quick to discern the growth of the hidden seed, mark, in various directions, where 'first the blade' begins to appear. Thus, among the ecclesiastics of the Orthodox Church are found many who value the Bible work and encourage their people to read and study the Word of God. These priests have shown hospitality to our colporteurs, have taken them into their houses and helped them on their way. The fanaticism of former years has been greatly softened, and a better spirit is described as being manifested generally 'among the men.' The women, no doubt, will follow in time. The question of national language is still a difficulty which to some extent affects our work. Under the head of Albanian we supply North Albania with the 'Gheg' in Roman characters, and South Albania with the 'Tosk' in Greek characters.

In North Albania, where we occupy Uskub, our work has not made any marked progress or impression among the scattered population of these wild and difficult regions. At Skodra, or Skutari, the famous northern stronghold of Albania, a colporteur has occasionally stayed a month at a time and succeeded in selling Scriptures to the value of two or three shillings; and these have been sold to the Moslems and Orthodox Greeks; hardly a Roman Catholic, of whom the population is principally composed, has bought a book. The people of North Albania use mainly the Italian language, but there is an impression that Albanian is making its way. In the towns in the extreme north, such as Pristina and Mitrovitza, where a good deal of work has been done, our colporteurs report encouragement and 'many friends of the Truth.'

In South Albania we occupy the capital, Monastir, and the town of Koritza or Kortcha. Here there has always been, and is now, more Christian work of various kinds than in the North, and the Albanian language is more widely spread and better understood. The people, too, seem to be less intractable than in the North and more open to receive impressions. Here also in towns such as Kastoria, Sachista, and Grebena, &c., much work has been done in former years, especially among the schools. There is no manner of doubt that the arduous labours of our colporteurs in this most difficult field, both in North and South Albania, have been blessed by God in these ancient lands, which have enjoyed so small a share of the blessings of progress and civilisation that have come to modern Europe. It is a work which has its blessings in store, too, and at the present shows some little need of organisation and development. Circumstances have not allowed me to pay a personal visit to this field, but, during the present year, it will be necessary to find opportunity for a tour of inspection among the Depots in Albania and Macedonia.

94th Report, 1898

Page 122
Turkey

The Agency which Mr. Hodgson directs from Constantinople embraces Greece as well as Turkey. Hence its past year has been full of vicissitudes, and the record of its Bible work presents a somewhat broken character. The war between Turkey and Greece interfered with our plans and operations in both these countries. In Greece, as will be seen, the opportunity was taken of reaching large masses of the population of the country by free distribution among the army. In Turkey the unsettled state of affairs and the political feeling roused by the war made it difficult for our colporteurs, mostly Greeks, to carry on their work. Parts of the field had to remain unvisited, and tours had to be curtailed. In Jannina our depositary was thrown into prison on an unfounded political charge, and we owe his release to the good offices of an influential friend in high quarters at Constantinople. Both in Epirus and Thessaly the work has practically been at a standstill. ... In Macedonia and Albania, if the work has not suffered to any great extent, it is entirely due to the order maintained by an able and upright Turkish official who filled the post of Governor of Monastir.

Page 127

Albanian, with its two divisions of Gheg and Tosk, has an increase [in sales] of 166 copies. Both in Albania and Macedonia there is a considerable sale of Scriptures in other languages.

Pages 130–132

Macedonia and Albania

(Circulation, 2,510 copies, against 1,636 in 1896. Increase of 514 in 1897)

Of the above total distribution in 1897 the colporteurs have sold 1,905 copies, and 245 have been sold at the Depot at Monastir. This increase in the sales for the year is encouraging, as the work has been carried on under what might have proved difficult circumstances. At the outbreak of the war between Turkey and Greece, writes Mr. Hodgson, I was myself in Monastir. Everything of course had to give way to the exigencies of the military situation. I met all our colporteurs and workers for a few days' conference, and then they separated for their various fields. For the remainder of the year our men have not been interfered with by the officials, nor prevented from travelling otherwise than by the difficulty of finding muleteers. I consider that great credit belongs to the authorities for the order maintained in these provinces at this critical time, and I have already stated that this has been due to a great extent to the excellent Vali of Monastir.

Expectations formed during my visit to Macedonia and Albania have been quite equalled by the work resulting from the opening of the new Depot at Monastir, the transfer of colporteur Luka from Koritza to Berat, and the arrangements made for the extension of the work in the Uskub vilayet. Mr. George Kyrias has faithfully fulfilled his duties as depositary and superintendent of the colporteurs. The staff has remained the same as in the previous year. Colporteur Michael, on account of age and infirmities, will now be placed on the retired list. Four Mission colporteurs, working in Monastir and in Old Servia in connection with the American Missions, have been employed in the sale of the Society's books.

Incidents of Colportage

Colporteur Luka Tira in the early part of the year worked among the towns and villages of North Albania. His sales were not large, and his own comment is 'though my sales were poor, yet I had a good time with the people.' At a small village he met an ecclesiastic 'who helped me much in the conversations we had about the Gospel with the people. He invited his friends to his house where we discussed the New Testament; and great pleasure was evinced when it was found that no difference existed between the New Testament used by the Church and the one I sold. The priest explained that the sole aim of the Society was to spread the light of truth throughout the whole world.'

Colporteur Tsiku also travelled in North Albania in the early part of the year. Of one place he says, 'the people are every religious and manifest great interest in the Gospel. Three years ago I sold a Testament to the keeper of a Kahn. He reads his Bible daily and has sold many copies for us.' Of another district he says, 'the souls of the people were just hungering for the truth.' Later in the year, in Macedonia, he met with some 'who think themselves wiser than they are,' and speaks of their persecution of a young man 'who always carried a pocket Bible about with him, and was not afraid to speak to others of the treasure he had found.' Like other colporteurs Tsiku receives hospitality from friendly priests, and the people are invited to meet him. But at one town he was beaten, at another he was left to lie out in the street with the dogs, and at a third town he was imprisoned. His sales amounted to 377 copies.

Colporteur Marmaroff, stationed at Uskub, speaks of the fanaticism of the people and the race enmities between Servians and Bulgarians as hindrances to his work. 'Often it happens that people come to me by night, through fear, to buy books and stay discussing religious questions until midnight.' He observes that 'the people are very religions, but I hope the time will come when they will be free to buy the Bible.' He notices that the hatred between the various nationalities is softened when they come together to read God's Word. He mentions a Servian priest to whom he sold a Bible. 'He told me that now he had found the book to satisfy his soul. When he comes to market he brings me the passages he cannot understand, noted on a piece of paper for explanation.'

Colporteur Christoff writes, 'It was market day, and in making my rounds a woman asked me what I was selling; I replied, God's Word. She shook out her purse and found sufficient money to purchase a Testament. A woman sitting by said, «Mind what you are about; it is an American (!) book.» She replied, «I am not buying men, I want a Testament, and these people are fulfilling the Lord's command to carry the Gospel.» At a certain village I was making my rounds and a woman stopped me and bought a New Testament, which she said she was going to give to the new church then building in the village. Another woman came up to prevent her, saying they were «Protestant» books (Protestant and American have come to be synonymous terms). The first replied, «If the priest will not have it I will keep it in my house, and get my brother to read for me God's words of Life.» Next day I visited the fanatical woman and had a long talk with her. She began to feel a little sorry, and brought me bread and cheese. Finally she bought a Gospel and brought two other women to buy Gospels, so that through her I sold several copies.'

95th Report, 1899

Pages 1–2

The Bible Society has been the great instrument in modern times by which God's Providence is accomplishing this wonderful work of translating and circulating the Scriptures. Already it has helped the Gospel to speak in some 350 languages and dialects. So that the Book, which a century ago was a sealed book to four men out of every five, to-day lies open, more or less completely, to seven men out of every ten in the world.

Pages 123–124
Turkey

"During the year," writes Mr. Hodgson, "I took what opportunities I could find to visit various parts of the Agency. A tour was made through Bulgaria and Macedonia, and later in the year Greece and Epirus were visited. The visits to Janina, in Epirus, completed my tour of our Depots, and in the course of 1898 I was glad to gain the personal acquaintance of those of our colporteurs whom I had not met before....

"I am reminded now, as I write, of one who for nearly forty years bore the burden of this Agency with courage and hope and faith. A few days ago Dr. Thomson passed away to his reward, full of years and full of honour, and his end may be counted happy in that his call did not come until work was over. How great and how fruitful that work has been, we who have entered into his labours can form some inadequate idea. So long as the Bible is distributed in Turkey, so long shall it be said of him that 'he being dead yet speaketh.'"

Page 128

In Albanian, with its two divisions of Gheg and Tosk, the circulation has increased by 151 copies, being 770 copies as against 619 in 1897. There is no doubt we should sell a larger number of the scriptures among this interesting people if we were prepared to offer more copies in the new or "national" character, a demand which we are now taking steps to meet.

Pages 131–132

Macedonia and Albania

(Circulation 2,485 copies, against 2,150 in 1897. Increase, 335.)

Of the above total distribution in this part of our Agency the colporteurs have sold 2,313 copies, being an increase of 408 over their sales for the previous year; and at the Depot at Monastir sales have amounted to 172 copies, being a decrease of 73. But when Mr. Hodgson visited Monastir in September he found that the Depot, which had been moved to new premises in the preceding year, was doing a very useful work, not only for the town, but for the whole of the surrounding district. It is kept open late at night for working men who are unable to come in the day, and the place seems to attract the people generally. Some thousands have visited the Depot in the course of the year, and though few, comparatively, buy, none can be said to go empty away. Under present arrangements we share the Depot with the American Mission at Monastir, and Mr. George Kyrias has continued to superintend our work with his usual diligence.

Colportage

In Albania, and Macedonia, we have five men, who are stationed at the widely-scattered centres of Monastir, Koritza, Berat and Uskup, and who travel extensively through their allotted districts. In the midst of the political rivalries, the racial and religious hatreds which have made Macedonia a menace and a danger to Europe, our men have gone about unmolested, quietly distributing the Gospel of good-will. This is owing to the character of their work becoming better known, and to the rule which it has been necessary to enforce strictly in this difficult part of our field, that they are neither to preach nor to stir up political or religious controversy. They are known simply as the men who carry the Book.

Colporteur Luka Tira has travelled principally in the northern or 'Ghegeri' part of Albania, visiting all the important towns and villages in the district. He is stationed at Berat, of which he says: 'The people are very friendly, and I do not remember to have met with any opposition or hatred, and I glorify God for opening the door of this place to our work. My system is never to speak about the doctrines of the Orthodox Church or any other religion, but I try to recommend to men the Work of God and to show them His Truth, which brings every blessing to mankind. Gradually their fanaticism disappears and they understand that the Bible Society's aim is to promote the enlightenment of all. His sales have amounted to 480 copies in some six languages, of which Albanian comes first and Turkish follows second.

Colporteur Jovan Tsiku, who is stationed at Koritza (Kortcha), has visited the beautiful central parts of Albania, inhabited by Christians, Moslems and Jews, among all of whom the Colporteur has laboured. He reports being 'greatly encouraged, that in many parts of the country the people begin to appreciate the value of the Word of God. They have been surprised and pleased at the moderate prices of the Scriptures, and at their being printed in languages which can be understood even by the ignorant. Many Albanians were exceedingly glad that the Testament was also translated in their own language. Tsiku has sold 618 copies in eleven languages. His largest sales are in Turkish, Greek comes next in order, and then follow Albanian and Bulgarian.

Colporteur Christoff is stationed at Monastir. From his very interesting report we take the following. He visited a village school where the teacher was very friendly and encouraged his scholars to buy copies of the Scriptures: he said, 'I have a great desire to help in this great and sacred work, but cannot do much on account of my poverty. But I can help in recommending the Bible to all my fellowmen, and I can pray for a blessing on all the workers and work.' 'A merchant called me to visit his son. On entering the room I saw a young man about twenty-three years of age lying in bed, who had been ill for four years. He asked for a copy of the New Testament, and said to his mother, " Mother, pray to the Lord that I may live a few days longer and read to you out of the precious Word of God." For three successive days I was able to visit the young man, and each time he bought some portion of the Bible.' Christoff's sales have amounted to 394 copies in nine languages. His largest sales are Greek, next comes Bulgarian, and then follows Turkish.

Christos Kyrias is the young man in charge of the Depot at Monastir. He has been employed since the beginning of the year, and has given satisfaction by his diligence and attention to his duties.

Mr. Hodgson adds; 'In Macedonia, as in other provincial Depots, I have dealt with individual colporteurs; for, not being directly under Agency control, it is necessary that each man's work should be brought into individual prominence. It is only at intervals that I can come into personal contact with these men, and the best we can do is to make them feel their personal responsibility in carrying on their work.'

Besides the five men mentioned above, we have sold Scriptures through four agents of the American Missions working in Albania and Macedonia. Their united sales have amounted to 618 copies in eleven languages, more than half of which are in Bulgarian.

We have also continued to supply the Agent of the National Bible Society of Scotland with Scriptures for his field, the headquarters of which are at Salonica, where, through a friendly arrangement with that Society, we have, consequently, no colporteur of our own. The American Bible Society also occupies a part of Macedonia, and their share of the work in this field is also the subject of friendly arrangement and co-operation. We hope and believe that to this distracted country all these united labours will bring the blessing which the Word alone can give.

Page 323 ...

A Record of Translation and Revision, 1898–1899

Albanian Tosk (National Character) – The Book of Genesis and the Gospel of St. Matthew having proved acceptable in the Roman character as adapted by the National Committee in Bucharest, the Committee have authorized the Rev. T. R. Hodgson, the Society's Agent at Constantinople, to have the Book of Psalms and the remaining three Gospels transliterated in the same manner. The only alterations that will be made in the text will be in the spelling and grammar.

Appendix

Foreign Depots: Turkey

Constantinople – Rev. T. R. Hodgson, Bible Depot, Pera
Constantinople – Bible House, Stamboul
Chios – Colp. Sevastides
Monastir, Macedonia – Mr. George Kyrias, Bible Depot
Koritsa, Albania – Colpr. Tsiku
Berat, Albania – Colpr. Luka

Uskup, Albania – Colpr. Marmaroff
Janina, Epirus –

96th Report, 1900

Pages 124–125
Turkey – Scriptures Printed and Published

In Albanian, editions of the Psalms and the Four Gospels in the new character have been prepared. The Psalms are practically ready for issue, and the Four Gospels are ready for the press. But the Turkish Government has raised difficulties about their publication, and for the present the work is stopped. After exhausting all other means, the negotiation of this difficult matter is now in the hands of the British Embassy at Constantinople.

Page 127
Languages

In distinctly Moslem languages, 4,189 copies were issued, 4,066 of which were Turkish, and the rest Arabic and Persian. The decrease of 454 copies on the sales of 1898 is accounted for by the biennial Bible tour in the Kastamouni vilayet not having fallen to the year 1899. The sales have been effected mainly in and about the city of Constantinople and in the Smyrna and Albanian provinces. ...

The languages of South-Eastern Europe are represented mainly by Bulgarian, with 4,724 copies—an advance of 234. Albanian, with a circulation of 1,080, is 310 copies ahead of the previous year. Slavic (312) and Servian (247) both show growth. Rumanian, represented by two dialects, remains about the same. The sum total of this group of languages, though not large, shows an advance.

Pages 129–131

Macedonia and Albania

Circulation, 2,609, against 2,485 in 1898. Increase, 124.

Of the above total, the Colporteurs have sold 2,383 copies—an increase of 70. At the Monastir Depot, the sales have been 226 copies, being an advance of 54. The returns would doubtless have shown a larger increase but for two causes: one is the absence of a Colporteur on leave for three months, and the other is the reduction in the staff of the Mission Colporteurs to one man only, whose sales have amounted to 46 copies, against 562 sold by the Mission in 1898. But the influence of the Monastir Depot is not confined to the number of books sold. Many of these sales were made to the surrounding villagers who frequent Monastir and find their way into the Depot.

The work of our Colporteurs has gone on quietly and persistently, with only one act of interference. A Colporteur was brought back to Monastir under arrest and put in prison, but on representation being made to the Vali he was at once released. This Vali is the same energetic and upright Turkish official whose excellent administration has been noticed in previous reports; he explained that the arbitrary proceeding was due to local disturbances quite apart from our work.

In Albania

The Albanian part of our work has great interest at present, when the Albanians are making such efforts in the cause of education and progress. Even very old men have begun to study their own language in order to be able to read; and we meet many pathetic testimonies to the appreciation of the people generally of the Bible Society's endeavours to give them the Scriptures in their vernacular. It is to be hoped that the objections raised by the Turkish Government to the publication of our Albanian versions now in the press will be speedily overcome. The question is not at all political, but it very closely concerns the right of religious liberty which Turkey is supposed to have guaranteed by treaties. Perhaps more than in other parts of the Agency the work in these Provinces has its special anxieties and difficulties; but we are thankful for another year of encouragement, whose result our Depositary, Mr. Kyrias, well sums up in the closing words of his last report: 'We can say that the Lord has greatly blessed us.'

Four Colporteurs have been travelling in these Provinces throughout the year. We have only space for a few characteristic touches to show the nature of their work.

Colporteur Luka Tira is stationed at Berat, in Western Albania, and in that difficult and little-known region he has visited several villages where no Colporteur had ever been before. He says: 'The people showed me great hospitality, took me into their houses, entertained me in every possible way, and with great joy wished to hear the Word of Life.' In another district, he says, 'The Lord blessed me abundantly. The priest and the teacher of the village helped me, and I sold 30 copies. Every day I heard the people speaking together of the treasure they had found in the Scriptures which they had purchased.' His sales were 353 copies, about half of which were Albanian, Greek coming next in order, followed by Rumanian.

Sealed with the blood of Christ

Colporteur Christoff is stationed at Monastir, and has travelled extensively in the central parts of Albania and in Macedonia. He recounts how, at one place, his books were objected to as not authenticated by the seal of the Patriarchate. A bystander supplied the unanswerable reply: 'Take the book, and if you read it carefully you will find that it is sealed with the blood of Christ.' At another place a Jewish Rabbi blessed him, saying: ' May the Lord bless you and your work, and prepare the hearts of the people to accept the word of God.' A priest, whose opinion was asked about the authenticity of the books, took a Testament in his hands and said: 'This is the Word of God: blessed is the man who makes it his daily companion. May the Lord reward the Bible Society and increase its influence, since it brings the richest blessing to the world.' Colporteur Christoff has sold 210 copies, chiefly in Greek, Bulgarian, and Turkish.

Montenegro

Circulation by Colporteur, 63 copies.
Deposited on sale at Cettinjé, 717 copies.

This is the first year that the little principality of Montenegro has been open to the Society's work. Through the kind offices last autumn of Mr. R. J. Kennedy, C.M.G., British Minister at Cettinjé, permission was granted by H.H. Prince Nicholas for our Colporteurs to enter this mountainous country. Its inhabitants number about 228,000, and are a primitive pastoral and agricultural people, belonging almost entirely to the Servian branch of the Slav race. Nearly all of them are adherents of the Greek Orthodox Church. Colporteur Stanko, who possesses a complete knowledge of the Servian language, was sent from Uskup, in Albania, and reached Cettinjé in October, armed with letters to the Metropolitan, &c. But on his arrival an unexpected difficulty presented itself, when he discovered that the sole right to sell books in Montenegro had been granted to the only bookseller in Cettinjé. The Metropolitan was exceedingly kind, and showed himself well disposed to our work. Through his influence Stanko was allowed to dispose of a certain number of Servian Scriptures, and sold 63 copies to willing purchasers....

Page 325
Editorial Report

Albanian Tosk (National character) – The Four Gospels and the Psalms are now transliterated and are ready for press. The work has been done by Mr. Sinas, and it is hoped that an edition will shortly be printed under his care.

Albanian (S. Italy) – Inquiry has been made as to the need of a special version for the old Albanian settlement in South Italy. St. Matthew was printed in the Calabrian dialect in 1862 through Prince Louis Lucien Bonaparte, but there is no Albanian about it. It remains to be seen whether there is a call for anything over and above the translations already accessible.

97th Report, 1901

Pages 130–131
Turkey – Scriptures Printed and Published

The Albanian versions of the Psalms and the Four Gospels in the national character remain where they were when the last report was published. Prolonged negotiations with the Turkish authorities failed to procure the necessary sanction to publish, and subsequent efforts of the British Embassy at Constantinople had no better result. The position and progress of our work in Albania, and the wishes of the Albanians themselves, may lead us to expect that this attitude of the authorities will not be persisted in, but in the meantime we have exhausted all the means at our disposal here.

Page 133

Languages

The languages of that part of South-Eastern Europe which is vaguely known as the Balkans come next in importance, and are represented by Bulgarian with 3,864 copies, Servian with 267, Slavic with some 200, and Rumanian with about the same figure. This group includes a few other dialects represented on the list, but special interest attaches at the present time to our Albanian versions. Reference has already been made to the obstacles raised to our work in this most interesting part of our field, but in spite of all difficulties 1,007 copies have gone into the hands of Christian and Moslem Albanians during the year.

Pages 135–137

Macedonia and Albania

Circulation. 2,672 copies, against 2,609 in 1899, and 2,485 in 1898.

Of the total circulation in these provinces, our four Colporteurs have sold 2,422 copies, showing an increase of 39: the Depot at Monastir has disposed of 232 copies, an increase of 6; and Montenegro has taken 81 copies. The slight increase for the year is in favourable contrast with the returns of our work in other parts of Turkey. There is no doubt whatever that Albania is ready to receive the Word of God, if we on our part were free to offer it.

The Obstacles in Albania

Allusion has already been made to the frustration of our efforts to meet the demand among the Albanians for freedom to read the Bible in their own tongue. The unrest among the people and the fears of the ruling race are certainly not excuses which will satisfy Englishmen, at least, that all the resources of an enlightened and Christian diplomacy are unable to procure this elementary measure of right and justice for an integral part of Europe in the twentieth century; and certainly no political compact or connivance can obscure the fact that Asiatic sloth, ineptitude, and futility have become an anachronism in Europe, even in its most remote and unhappy provinces. It is most significant that in this province, where trade does not exist and extreme poverty prevails, more Scriptures should have been sold than in any previous year. Education is as backward as material progress. In the whole of Albania there are only two Albanian schools, one for boys and one for girls, the latter supported by Christian Missions. Yet, at our Depot in Monastir there have been more than 5,000 visitors during the year, where, as our excellent Depositary, Mr. George Kyrias, says, ' Our talk is not of patriotism, but we speak that which will bring love and goodwill, not enmity, among the people.' The Colporteurs have traversed the length and breadth of the country with their message of peace, meeting with much kindness, and with very little interference from the Government officials. The province is blessed with an able and upright Governor, the present Valli of Monastir, and we have shared the benefits of his just and firm administration. And our men have learned to keep aloof from the fierce political and religious strife of contending factions which has given an unhappy prominence to Albania in our day.

Afoot with our Colporteurs

Some incidents of colportage, from the reports for the first half of the year, have already appeared in the Reporter for January, 1901. Space must be found for the following brief illustrations of the difficulties and encouragements of a work which is full of interest. From Colporteur Tsiku: 'An orthodox Greek bought a Bible from me a long while ago. This so wrought upon him that he opened a Sunday School for teaching the Bible. In my presence he delivered a discourse on the words 'Whosoever shall confess Me before men', &c. This is his favourite text, which he loves to dwell on and carries out in his life.' At a certain town, 'The Kadi, who is a good Albanian, defended me in the presence of the magistrate, and said, "These men are not troublers of the peace, but seek to bind the people in love: and in our place the people have need of such lessons." This Kadi proved my very good friend.' Colporteur Luka Tira has again visited Scutari, the famous fortress of Northern Albania. He says: 'This large town, with 30,000 inhabitants, seems as though it would never soften. It is full of Roman priests whose hearts only the Lord is able to unlock. Here I remained four weeks without much success: but when I first began my yearly visits I was unable to sell one-fourth of the number I dispose of now.' He met with an aged disciple. 'I sold him a Testament, and concluded he was at least 80 years old. I asked him if he could read. He replied that he could not, but would find some one to read to him: and added, "I mean to learn to read these sacred words, and then I care not how soon I may die."'

"Not of dead men, but of living"

Colporteur Christoff met a woman who wanted a book in which were written the names of the dead. I told her I had no such book, but I had the Word which told of the names written in the Book of Life. She asked me to read it to her, and said, 'I am 65 years of age and have never heard such sweet words.' She and another woman bought Testaments. He relates again:

> I met a traveller and he asked me what books I had. I told him, and he said, 'I know that Society; give me five of your Testaments.' Then he said, 'Now take them and give them to those who have no money to buy.' I rather demurred to this, as we do not like to give away our books; and with his consent I agreed to give them to the church at Monastir.

Colporteur Stanko went out one day with a friend for an evening stroll. They came upon seven Moslems sitting together reading the Bible. 'As I had sold some Turkish Scriptures previously at this place I concluded that these were the identical books. My friend said, 'These Moslems make us ashamed. We must try in some way to obey our Lord's command and speak the words of Life.''

In Montenegro

Population, 228,000

The sales in Montenegro, so far as reported, have been 81 copies since the commencement of the work. Mr. Kyrias, who visited the country in the early part of 1900, sends a long and interesting report, of which the following is a brief summary. We have again failed to obtain permission for a Colporteur to travel in the country. Mr. Peter Kaloudjerovitch has the sole right to sell books in Montenegro. With the consent of the authorities and the Metropolitan he undertakes to sell our Scriptures at his various depots, and we agree to allow him 50 per cent on sales. A special bookcase has been provided for the exhibition and sale of Scriptures at his shop in Cettinjé, and a constant supply will be deposited with him on our account. Meanwhile, Mr. Peter Kaloudjerovitch and his brother John, a Government professor at Cettinjé—both persons of influence and in favour with the authorities— will use every endeavour to obtain permission for a' Colporteur to travel in Montenegro: and we on our part will allow a royalty of 30 per cent, on his sales. It is to be hoped that the difficulties in opening up this interesting country to the free circulation of the Scriptures will soon be overcome.

98th Report, 1902

Page 131
Turkey – Scriptures Printed and Published

In Albanian, the editions of the Four Gospels and Book of Psalms in the national character remain where they were at the close of the previous year. After the failure of the British Embassy at Constantinople to obtain permission for us to publish and issue these editions, the time seems approaching when other and more efficacious means should be tried to influence the Turkish authorities in favour of our being allowed to supply Albanian Christians with the Scriptures in their own language.

Page 133
Circulation by Languages

In the Balkans we have a group of languages of which the most important is Bulgarian, with 5,828 copies, against 3,864 in the previous year. Albanian has 1,063 copies, Servian 265 copies, Slavonic 218, all showing an increase. In spite of the very disturbed condition of this part of South-Eastern Europe, in many districts of which our Colporteurs travel with considerable danger, more copies of the Scriptures have been sold.

Pages 137–139
Albania and Macedonia

Circulation, 2,858 copies against 2,672 in 1900, and 2,609 in 1899

The total circulation in these provinces both by our Colporteurs and through the Depot at Monastir shows a slight advance. On the other hand, the sales credited to Montenegro have only amounted to three copies. No Colporteur has yet received permission to travel in this little Principality, and the bookseller who has the sole right of selling books in Montenegro did not care, for certain reasons, to show himself too active in our interests. But we need not despair of the prospects of our work in this rocky corner of the Balkan field.

The Outlook in Albania

We can only very briefly recount some of the more suggestive and interesting details of colportage in Albania. For obvious reasons it is undesirable here to refer in any other than the most general way to certain aspects of Bible work, which have a most profound and personal interest to our men in these provinces. Here, for instance, is a document which ends, 'I will not keep a copy of this report, nor will I sign it. I can only send it through our friend, under cover of his own dispatches. It is unfortunate that there is no British official here to whom it is possible to appeal.'

Brigands of Various Kinds

For money extorted for political purposes, 'a regular receipt was offered, but who would keep such a dangerous paper?' One of our Colporteurs escaped capture by brigands through a friend's timely warning, but of other travellers less fortunate 'a score are still in captivity, and unable to pay any ransom.' Nevertheless it is but justice to record that we hear no note of complaint against the lawful authorities of the country; on the contrary, 'the Government has been the cause of no hindrance whatever.' And mention is again made of the just and excellent administration of the Turkish Governor of Monastir, 'who has done so much for the good of the people, and the improvement of the place.'

It is encouraging to find that the Depot in Monastir, which, with the direction of the Colporteurs, is in the hands of Mr. George Kyrias, has increased its sales. More books are sold in the Albanian language than in any other. We read of Albanian soldiers economising on their scanty pay in order to buy copies of the Gospels. While the Depot, of course, forms a standing witness and a centre for our work, which all men may know and see, it is to the labours of the Colporteurs that we must turn for the results of most interest and importance. A few characteristic incidents of their Bible-journeys can be recorded here, while a volume might be written of their extensive travels in these hardly explored countries, during the course of a single year.

Colporteur Tsiku, whose headquarters are at Koritza (or Kortcha) has travelled extensively in the central parts of Albania. From one town he writes, 'I had a pleasant time with my friend the Kadi, who is an Albanian. He used to oppose me, but after buying and reading a New Testament, he grew interested and became quite friendly.' One day Tsiku sold a Testament to a peasant woman, and followed her to her village. The people were all out in the fields, where he joined them, and read to them out of the Gospels. They had no money in their pockets, so he sold nothing, but adds, 'Next time I expect to make good sales there.' In crossing Lake Ochrida the boat was in danger from a storm, and our Colporteur had an opportunity to comfort the passengers with the words of Scripture. . . . He speaks of the risks of these journeys, and owns that God has saved him from many perils. His sales have amounted to 517 copies.

Colporteur Luka has his station at Berat, which is not far from the Adriatic coast, almost opposite to Brindisi. His sales are the largest of any of our Albanian Colporteurs, being 816 copies, principally in Albanian, Turkish, and Modern Greek.

'How lovely are the Messengers'

He speaks of a boy who in three months saved up sufficient money to buy a New Testament, and was accused by his father of having stolen it. But the boy began to read to his parents, and as a result, says Luka, 'the father's hatred of me turned to love, and now he says, "You are the man who has brought peace into my house," and in every possible way they endeavour to show their gratitude.' At Scutari, the famous stronghold of North Albania, he finds the influence of the Roman priests hostile to his work.

A young man who bought a Testament was threatened, and finally deprived of the book by the priests. A village priest of the Orthodox Church who bought an Albanian Testament, said to his parishioners, 'Sell every other book you have and buy this, which every Christian ought to possess.' Among a company of people at another place he found it necessary to put an end to an unprofitable discussion: 'I am neither a preacher nor a theologian; I am a graduate of no university. I am only a Colporteur, whose business it is to sell these books, without which no Christian can have wisdom.' They bought twenty-two copies, and some of them said, 'God prosper your Society in its high aims.'

Colporteur Stanko is stationed at Prishtina, in the extreme north of Albania. He is a simple, earnest Christian, who finds a difficulty in putting the record of his labours into suitable language. In the town of Uskub he sold many Scriptures amongst the Turks. And in his simple, cheerful way he records of other places he has visited—'I met with numerous friends and good success.' His sales are 620 copies, chiefly in Bulgarian, Servian, and Turkish.

'God will take care of the Sales'

Colporteur Christoff travels from Monastir, which is the centre of his interesting district. He was greatly encouraged by a lady of Krushevo. 'Do you sell Bibles?' she asked him. 'Not so many as I should wish,' replied Christoff. 'Do not be discouraged,' the lady rejoined, 'it is God's Word, and He will take care of the sales.' At Florina 'the people seem to have a hunger for the books. I sold forty-three in ten days—an unusual event.'

Medicine for the Soul

Christoff sold two Gospels to a poor sick boy, who was reproached by his friends for wasting the money; 'better buy some physic and get well,' said they. 'I have plenty of physic for my body,' said the lad, 'but I need some medicine for my soul.' At an Albanian village Christoff sat in the market with his wares, and presently another bookseller came up with other kinds of books, which drew away all the people. 'Don't worry,' said a youth standing by, 'we will sell your books.' Then, exhorting the people to give heed to the Word of God and not to fables, he induced them to buy twenty copies. A village priest also befriended Christoff. 'Why should we brand these books as Protestant?' said the good man. 'It is the Bible, and a treasure, and you are still ignorant of it.' The result was the sale of twelve copies. Elsewhere another ecclesiastic spoke out thus: 'We live in darkness, and instead of being grateful to this Society, we despise the Scriptures it offers. If you have the money, buy the books, and by so doing you will inherit the blessing of those who know God's Word.'

In Macedonia

Altogether during 1901 we have sent out 4,592 copies into Macedonia and Albania—those unfortunate provinces which form the neglected and forgotten members in the family of Christian Europe. Yet we are still forbidden to publish and issue the Scriptures in the character and language which the people of Albania themselves desire and demand.

Colporteurs in Conference

Our Colporteurs in Albania assembled at Monastir at the close of the year for conference and prayer under the leadership of Mr. George Kyrias, the Depositary. After the week of meetings they write:

> All the gatherings were helpful and inspiring, and we return to our duties with renewed courage. We regret to hear that the Society is compelled to make retrenchment in its expenditure. To Mr. Kyrias's question whether we should be willing, under the circumstances, to pay our own travelling expenses to and from this gathering at Monastir, we gladly answered in the affirmative. We also engage to observe the strictest economy in our travelling generally. The meetings have proved so beneficial in every way that we feel it would be well that we should come together again on a future occasion.

Page 373
Editorial Report

Albanian, Tosk (National character) – The Rev. R. Thomson, missionary at Samokov and son of the Society's late Agent for Turkey, pleads that part of the Cocker legacy should be used to give the Albanians those portions of the O.T. which would provide them with a complete Bible. But further efforts to induce the Porte to permit the issue of the new editions of the Gospels and Psalms have been abortive.

99th Report, 1903

Pages 128–129
Turkey – Scriptures Printed and Published

Albanian – An edition of the Psalms, 3,000 copies, as stated in previous reports, has long been ready for issue, but permission to publish has hitherto been refused by the censorship. The Four Gospels are also ready for printing, and are withheld by the same difficulty. All our efforts have hitherto failed to overcome the objections of the Turkish authorities to the issue and distribution of the Scriptures in the Albanian language, other than in the Tosk and Gheg versions which the Bible Society long ago gave to the Albanians.

Circulation by Languages

In the Balkans the disturbed political atmosphere has to a certain degree affected our work, although not to the extent we might have feared. ... Albanian has fallen from 1,063 copies to 594. Servian remains about the same, so do Slavonic and Ruman.

Page 130
Colportage

Of the six Colporteurs, one is an Albanian, four are Greeks, and one is a Scandinavian. Their work is one of continuous patient labour among a poor, debased, and for the most part fanatical population.

Pages 132–134
Albania and Macedonia

Circulation, 2,801 copies, against 2,858 in 1901. Decrease, 57 copies.

The total circulation in these provinces shows a slight falling off, but less than might be expected considering the disturbed conditions which have prevailed. Of the total of 2,801 copies our Colporteurs have sold 2,446 copies, and the Mission Colporteur at Monastir has disposed of 20 copies. At our Depot at Monastir 308 copies have been sold, and the sales in Montenegro through the medium of the State bookseller have amounted to 27 copies. The decrease on the total of last year's sales is represented by 57 copies. It is a matter for great thankfulness that our work has been so slightly affected.

'Order my footsteps in Thy Word'

Our Colporteurs have laboured and travelled in constant peril and under great difficulties. The mountainous regions are infested by brigands, and the towns and villages are terrorised by Revolutionary 'Committees.' The lawful Government is suspicious and alarmed, and the revolutionary organisation is itself an *imperium in imperio* which issues its own laws, enforced under penalty of death. Women are forbidden to wear ornaments, everything being turned into money for arms. Drunkenness is punished by a fine for the first offence; the second is death. This is to avoid the risk of a man talking too freely when under the influence of drink. Our Colporteurs out of their scanty pay have been forced to contribute largely to this organisation. Between the upper and nether millstone the lot of the people has been one of misery, and under such conditions our men have carried on their work.

How Turkish Justice is Administered

Mr. Kyrias, our Depositary in Monastir, was placed under arrest and ordered to proceed to Salonika to be tried by the Turkish Courts. Colporteur Sinas was arrested at Berat, his license was taken from him, and all his books seized; he was deported to his native village, the entire population being required to stand guarantee for him; his house was ransacked and all his private papers taken away. Now, after an interval of some five months, it is understood that the prosecution in both these cases has been dropped owing to the very efficient intervention of the British Ambassador, although no official intimation of this has yet been forthcoming. But as the only charge against the men was that of selling Albanian books, and as each copy of these books bears the official permission of the Government censorship, it is perhaps too much to expect that the authorities will be in any haste to own to such arbitrary and oppressive proceedings. The question of our full right and freedom to sell Albanian Scriptures has yet to be decided. In the meantime the Colporteur in Albania needs courage and faith and wisdom, and our constant prayers that the Word which he carries to others will bring light to his own path in these critical and eventful times.

Colportage

Five colporteurs are on our list for the year, but two of these, Tsiku and Sinas, have only laboured three months each. Tsiku, after some twenty years' service, has retired, and later in the year Sinas was appointed to the vacancy. He is probably one of the best Albanian scholars of the day, and to him was entrusted the first draft of the transliteration of the Four Gospels and the Psalms into the new Albanian character. He is deeply interested in our Albanian work, the sphere to which he has been specially appointed, and the cause for which he has so greatly suffered. Before his arrest his sales amounted to under 200 copies, mainly in Albanian, and this constituted the crime for which he was prosecuted by the authorities.

Colporteur Luka Tira was transferred from Berat to the pleasant Albanian town of Kortcha in the latter half of the year. He has always been happy in his work, and writes of much encouragement despite hardships and opposition. He has made the largest sales of all our Albanian men, 839 copies, principally in Albanian, Turkish, Bulgarian, and Greek.

A Liberal-minded Official

Colporteur Stanko has for his field the northern part of Albania, bordering on Servia and the Austrian frontier, and known by the generic term of Old Servia. ....

Colporteur Christoff, whose headquarters are at Monastir, has travelled extensively in the surrounding parts of Albania and Macedonia. With his quiet, pleasant, and earnest manner he wins his way with the simple villagers, and especially amongst the young. His sales amounted to 607 copies, mainly in Bulgarian, Modern Greek and Turkish.

The Depot at Monastir has been moved into more commodious premises. It is the centre of much interesting and useful work in the town and district. The sales for the year, while not large, have been distinctly encouraging.

Mr. Kyrias, our Depositary, through whom the Colporteurs' reports are forwarded, says that they never complain of their trials, but on the contrary feel that they are helped by them, while they realise more and more that the harvest is great and the labourers few. ...

The National Bible Society of Scotland.

The veteran Agent of this Society at Salonica, the Rev. P. Crosbie, has been supplied by us during the year with 956 copies of the Scriptures. These have been circulated by his Colporteurs, and they swell the distribution in Macedonia and Albania for the year to 3,757, each copy a silent messenger of peace and goodwill where men have heard only the sounds of hatred and passion and strife.

100th Report, 1904

Page 131
Turkey – Circulation by Languages

Bulgarian gives us a circulation for the year of 6,910 copies, an advance on the previous year of 1,483. Other languages throughout the Balkans show a decline, especially Albanian, with the small total of 541 copies. ... Returns of the free distribution in connection with relief operations have not yet come in.

Scriptures for the Albanians

After three years we still await the permission of the Turkish Government to publish and issue the Albanian Psalms, 16mo, 3,000 copies. An edition of the Four Gospels in the same language is also ready for the press, and is withheld for the same reason. During the year this matter was again brought to the notice of H.B.M. Ambassador at Constantinople, who, while sympathising with the issue of the Christian Scriptures for the use of the Christian subjects of the Turkish-Empire, considered that the time was not propitious for urging upon the Ottoman authorities the grant of this small measure of religious liberty to Albania. The Albanians themselves, both Christian and Moslem, have given the strongest proofs of their desire for the Scriptures in their own language and character. The Tosk and Gheg versions, which the Bible Society long ago issued for the Albanian race, do not sufficiently meet their needs.

Pages 134–138
Albania and Macedonia
Circulation, 2,399 copies, against 2,801 in 1902, and 2,858 in 1901.

The circulation in these provinces during this troubled year has been as good as we had reason to hope or expect. Our four colporteurs have disposed of 2,121 copies. At the Monastir Depot 238 copies have been sold, and in Montenegro, where no colporteur has been allowed to enter, 31 copies have been sold through the medium of the state bookseller at Cettinjé.

To Relieve the Distressed
Mr. Kyrias, our Depositary at Monastir, and our entire staff of colporteurs have been engaged in assisting to administer the Relief Funds provided by associations in England and America for the starving peasants in those regions which were ravaged by the insurrection. To this work of mercy our men devoted the whole of their time during the later months of the year. The Committee of the Bible Society granted vernacular Scriptures for free distribution in connection with this relief work, and up to the end of the year 225 copies were given away to the sufferers side by side with the temporal relief administered. These copies are not included in the returns for 1903, but will appear in next year's report, when (it is hoped) the relief operations will be completed.

All our men, in spite of their labours and perils, have been mercifully preserved from harm and danger. We are specially indebted to Herr A. Kral, the Austrian Consul at Monastir, for his valuable services in times of great difficulty. The Committee have passed a resolution of thanks to this gentleman, and have presented to him a German Bible, with a suitable inscription.

Our Staff

In Albania and Macedonia the past year has proved a time of great anxiety, considerable hardship, and no little peril. During its latter months Mr. Kyrias has been entirely occupied with the burden of relief operations at Monastir, in carrying out which he rendered most valuable and humane service.

Colporteur Sinas had been under arrest by the Ottoman authorities in Albania in the early months of 1903; since being set free, he has been engaged in the relief operations. Colporteur Luka worked in Albania for the greater part of the year, his headquarters being at the town of Koritza. He also has been employed on the relief operations during the latter part of the year. Colporteur Stanko, whose field is old Servia, worked in that district during the revolutionary troubles, until towards the end of the year he was called into the Monastir district to assist in the administration of relief. Colporteur Christoff, whose district is the Monastir Vilayet, has pursued his labours under great difficulties in that disturbed province. He was also drawn into the relief work at the end of the year. Colporteur Christo Kyrias, who has charge of the Monastir Depot, was pressed into the relief work at an early period of its operations.

Under the terrible circumstances of the year we have great cause for thankfulness to God's providence which has brought our men safely through the perils that have surrounded them. Indeed without their efficient and willing assistance it is difficult to see how the relief could have been satisfactorily administered to the sufferers. We are glad to record that H. E. Hilmi Pasha, the Inspector

General of the Vilayets, has dealt justly and honourably with our Colporteurs; so far as the disturbed condition of the country has allowed, he has not interfered with their movements or the work of the Bible Society, while his administration has been marked by extraordinary energy.

The Report of Mr. George Kyrias

Mr. Kyrias writes:

At one time thousands and thousands of Turkish soldiers were moving on the roads, in the cities and villages, and among the mountains; villages were plundered and burned on every hand, while news of the murdering of men, women, and children reached us every day. Nevertheless, our Colporteurs were seldom molested.

Before the outbreak the Colporteurs were regularly at work—with some restriction; and considering the circumstances and the poverty of the people, their sales for the first six months were better than had been anticipated. During the latter half of the year all the men were engaged in relief work, which was the means of saving thousands from perishing with hunger. The aid which the Society's men were asked to administer to these poor unfortunate sufferers came from England and America. Relief work is still going on, and has been most successful. And the British Relief Committee highly appreciate the valuable assistance that is thus being rendered by the Society's servants.

Free Grants to those in distress

The Bibles given by our Society to the poor villagers who had lost their all were as important as the giving of daily food to prevent their starvation. Many of these downtrodden people have found great solace in the faithful promises of God, and especial comfort has been given to some unfortunate prisoners to whom—with the assistance of Herr Kral—we presented Bibles and Testaments. The prisons are full of villagers and citizens, and the Scriptures are gladly read by the more intelligent of these people.

Work at the Bible Depot has been uninterrupted, and numbers of poor people have applied for copies of the Scriptures. When the supply for free distribution was exhausted, hundreds came whom we had to send away disappointed. At first the relief work was conducted at the Bible Depot, until it grew to such huge proportions that it became necessary to rent a dwelling with eight large rooms and two large halls, and this at present hardly suffices.

Among our Colporteurs

In the three following paragraphs Mr. Kyrias gives us glimpses of our men at their normal work.

During the year the colporteurs have had many encouraging experiences, which help them the better to bear the discomforts and hindrances. Colporteur Christoff writes: 'In the market of Florina a villager asked me for a book entitled "The God-born Son: A Dream of the Virgin Mary," when an educated citizen who chanced to be near asked the man if he could read. The peasant replied that he could. "I am sorry," said the other, " that you know how to read and yet you seek such false stories. Take this Holy Testament and read it, and you will see how the words of Jesus will stir your soul. In it you will find comfort for all occasions, and if you will follow its directions you will be blessed." The citizen then read a few verses, for which the peasant was very grateful and immediately bought a New Testament and ten copies of the Gospels. Some days later I again met the villager, who was very cheerful, and said, "I am sorry I did not know before that there are such good and cheap books. Every day I read this book, and I find great delight in it." He then pulled out his purse and bought six more copies of the Gospels, and as he departed he said, "I have friends who I am sure will be pleased if I give them these beautiful little books."'

The Book of the Cross

Christoff relates an incident which occurred in Krushevo: 'One day, as I was going about with my books, I came to where a group of people were sitting. As soon as they saw me one man remarked, "What blessed books this man sells!" They inspected my books, when one of them said, "These books are Protestant, and not according to the Orthodox Church." The first speaker exclaimed, "It is a shame for us, who are called Christians and have reached the twentieth century, to be so ignorant of the Gospel as to talk such empty words. Tell me where is the mistake in these books?" "But these books have no cross," said the other. And the first man answered, "Truly there is no cross printed on the outside, but read the book with attention and faith, and you will find the cross inside, and you will understand what that cross means." The result of this conversation was the sale of several portions of Scripture, and ever since, whenever I pass their shop, these men invite me to speak to them on religion.'

Albanian Scriptures

From conversations held by Colporteur Sinas with Christian (Orthodox) Albanians and with Moslems, it is evident that, if the Turkish Government withdraws the restrictions placed on the sale of Albanian books, large sales may be expected. Many inquire with deep interest if the whole Bible is soon to be printed in Albanian, because they say and believe that it is the Bible alone that can raise up their nation from its fallen condition.

Not Politics, but Humanity

Some of Sinas' anecdotes are very interesting. He sold a portion to an Albanian officer who had a strong desire for the spread of the Gospel among his people. 'I have found,' he said, 'very great delight in this book, and truly its teachings are the very best means for the moral education of mankind.' While the colporteur was talking with the officer, another officer joined them and said, 'These are the only people who do not meddle with politics and who endeavour to do good to humanity.'

Races and Languages

All the races in this polyglot part of South-Eastern Europe are included in the Society's operations. The Bulgarians, who probably form the mass of the population in the heart of the Macedonian region—a sturdy, sober, and industrious peasantry—have always been open to the work of our colporteurs, and a very considerable proportion of our circulation in those regions is in their language. The Greeks, who are found principally in the large towns, and along the coast of the Aegean, form a community of considerable importance from their wealth and business capacity; and in a country where creed so often stands for race, their claim to represent the elder, or Patriarchist branch of the Orthodox Church has given them a certain intolerance which places them out of sympathy with the Bulgarian Exarchists. Our circulation in Greek (principally in modern Greek) is somewhat smaller than in Bulgarian. The peculiar term, 'Graecoman,' would seem to signify a native not a Greek, who has attached himself to the Patriarchist Church, and who is probably ignorant of Greek. The Patriarchist Church also claims the allegiance of the Rumans, or Kutzo-Vlachs, whose settlements are scattered about the centre of Macedonia. They are nomads, shepherds, carriers, and muleteers, and in a few towns such as Krushevo (destroyed in the fighting) have acquired a certain status of wealth and position. For these we provide Scriptures in the Ruman dialect which they use, and which, for want of a better term, we describe as Macedo-Ruman. The sales, however, are at no time large. The Serbs, chiefly found in the Kossovo Vilayet, in Old Servia and in Uskub, do not form a considerable or important element of the population; and although pure Slavs like the Bulgarians, they have not hitherto shown much sympathy with that nationality. Political rivalry in Macedonia is too keen. Our circulation in Servian, some 350 copies in the year, is almost entirely in Macedonia.

In Albania and Macedonia

The Moslem races, Albanians and Turks, form an important element in the population. Christian Albanians (principally found in the Skutari Vilayet, but scattered more or less throughout the whole of Albania), are probably neither more nor less friendly to our work in Albania than the Albanian Moslems. The smallest impression of all is made on the Roman Catholic Albanians of Skutari, in what is called the Ghegeri country. For these we provide the Gheg versions of the Scriptures. The Tosk versions are more widely spread and are used by the Albanians who read the Greek character. It is a matter for regret that the Ottoman Government has hitherto steadily withheld the necessary permission to publish the versions which, in response to an almost universal demand, we prepared for the press in the 'new' character which the Albanians have adapted to their peculiar and little-known language. Amongst none of the races of the Balkan Peninsula does the Bible Society meet with greater appreciation than among the Albanians, and the regard in which England is held by this interesting race is certainly to some extent due to the labours of our Society. The Turkish population in Macedonia and in Albania is still considerable, and, holding a privileged position, forms an important element of consideration in our relations to the people of the country. A large proportion of our sales of Scriptures are in the Osmanli-Turki language. It is extremely difficult to arrive at any reliable data or statistics as to the races inhabiting this part of South-Eastern Europe. Probably a moderate computation of the Muhammadans in the country would be something like half a million. No reasonable estimate would put the number higher than one million.

Page 407

Editorial Report

Albanian, Tosk (National character) – A fresh appeal to the British Ambassador respecting the Four Gospels and Psalms which are in type, but have been refused publication by the Porte for three years, has not produced any change in the position. Both Christian and Moslem Albanians have given strong proof of their desire to possess the Scriptures in this national form, but nothing that fosters their national aspirations is approved by the suzerain power.

101st Report, 1905

Page 125
Turkey – Publication

The Psalms and the Four Gospels, in Albanian, 3,000 copies each, in the national character—these editions, after being in the press for four years, still await the permission to publish of the Turkish Government, which no efforts of H.B.M.'s Embassy at Constantinople nor of the Bible Society itself have hitherto been able to obtain. For Albanians—Christians and Moslems alike—we are still constrained to provide only the imperfect versions which we already possess in the Tosk and Gheg dialects. Extremes meet: Turkish Albania and Christian Greece are the two countries in Europe where the Bible in the vernacular tongue is a forbidden book.

Page 126
Turkey – Circulation by Languages

Bulgarian stands at practically the same level—6,749 copies. Of the other Balkan languages Albanian has a circulation of 754 copies—an increase of 213.

Pages 128–129
Albania and Macedonia

Circulation, 2,918 copies, against 2,399 in 1903, and 2,801 in 1902.

During another troubled year of suffering these unhappy provinces have manifested an increased demand for the Scriptures. The sales by our four colporteurs have been 2,282 copies—an advance of 161 on the previous year—while the Mission colporteur at Monastir has sold 68 books. The sales at the depot at Monastir have been

228 copies. The little Principality of Montenegro, which lies outside the disturbed area, has taken 20 copies only. The free distribution of Scriptures in connection with the Macedonian relief work—which was mainly administered by our colporteurs—has been a total of 388 copies, the cost of which was partly provided from private sources.

All accounts go to show that English sympathy has touched the hearts of the suffering population, both Moslems and Christians, and has aroused a special feeling of friendly interest in the Bible Society which brought assistance and comfort in their hour of need. And in spite of poverty and hunger and actual suffering, many a poor peasant has found it possible to save a penny to buy a portion of the Word that speaks of hope and comfort and a better life.

A Call from Albania

Mr. George Kyrias, our depositary at Monastir, is himself an Albanian. Letters in Albanian, mostly anonymous, have been addressed to him full of gratitude and thanks for the work of the Bible Society. The burden of all the letters is to implore the Society to complete the Albanian translations, and to give to these people in their own tongue the precious boon of God's Word. Would that the Turkish Government might be led to remove the prohibition which alone prevents us doing this! Colporteurs Sinas and Luka, who have worked and travelled exclusively in Albania and whom no dangers daunt, send the same appeal in every report. Albanian men and women, they say, are hungry for the Word of God, which in a foreign tongue gives them neither comfort or pleasure. When the time comes for the Scriptures in the Albanian language to be circulated freely, the results—so both men agree—will give cause for thankfulness and joy.

From Saul to Paul

Thus colporteur Christoff describes the case of 'a fierce and vicious youth,' who from a persecutor became a follower and helper of the Gospel. One day in the house of a friend he found an old and well-worn Bible, and borrowed it out of curiosity. After reading it he brought it back to his friend and said, 'This is the real Orthodox Bible and no "Protestant " book.' 'My friend,' said the man, 'that is what you call the "Protestant" Bible which you have so long persecuted.' Whereupon, says the colporteur, this youth from an enemy became his warm supporter, all through reading that tattered Bible . . . 'by his assistance I was able in a few days to sell 59 copies of God's Word in that place—a rare event in our work.'

Turning the Other Cheek

Colporteur Stanko, who was arrested by the authorities at Uskup, had, before that event, visited a neighbouring town. On reaching the place, some one went off to accuse him to the Chief of Police as a suspected person. That official sent for Stanko and began the interview by smiting him on the face. In the end, however, the patience and good faith of the colporteur won upon him, and his wrath was turned against the denouncer. 'After that,' says Stanko, 'he treated me with kindness and humanity.'

This incident is related as an instance of what may happen at any time to a colporteur; accusations, false charges, ill-usage, often arrest and imprisonment, and then diplomatic intervention, inquiries, delays, loss of time to the man and of his services to the Society; and then in the end the man's innocence is established, and he is let off with a warning 'not to do it again'!

102nd Report, 1906

Pages 3–5

Until the spring of this present year we had not discovered the full meaning of the Bible Society's title.... The name "British" now covers nearly a hundred times the area of the United Kingdom, and our fellow-subjects include a quarter of the whole human race. Kind Edward VII rules over four hundred millions of mankind, only a small minority of whom are white. ...

Such overwhelming figures bring home to us a solemn sense of God's calling and election, which have thus entrusted to Britain the headship and guidance of so huge a fraction of the world. Surely it must humble us profoundly to feel this burden laid upon our people. Surely we who are Christians are doubly bound to send the Gospel to our own fellow-citizens.

Yet again, if 'British' means much, 'Foreign' means far more. The Bible Society's title proclaims that its enterprise can recognise no frontier. Its mission is ecumenical and universal – like the Book which it exists to carry into all countries and kingdoms. And that mission will be fulfilled when in every land God's redeeming Love speaks to every man in his own tongue in which he was born....

The list of languages in which the Bible Society has promoted the translation, printing, or distribution of at least some part of God's Book now includes four hundred different tongues.

Pages 119–121
Turkey

The review of the work of this Agency during the past year calls for thankfulness, and, we may add, also for hope, since it has survived in the face of difficulties which threatened its continuance. The Turkish Government imposed new restrictions on the movements of the Society's colporteurs which would have effectually stopped their work. The British Ambassador in Constantinople was able, however, to induce the Sublime Porte to modify a policy of repression which the Bible Society by no means deserved after its half-century or more of continuous labours in Turkey. It is acknowledged that the Society's men and methods have been entirely free from political, controversial, or subversive meddling, and have been confined to distributing the Scriptures. In no case has any personal charge been brought against a colporteur, nor have any suffered personal ill-treatment. Yet our colporteurs have been in some cases detained in idleness for lengthened periods, while the provincial governors who had hindered them were being dealt with from Constantinople. Under such untoward circumstances the results of the year's work as described in the following pages are better than we had dared to hope for.

From the *Times* Correspondent

Under the heading of "The Bible Society in Turkey," the *Times* for October 24, 1905, published the following special article, dated Constantinople, October 16, *From our own Correspondent*: "For many months past the British and Foreign Bible Society has had to complain of the hindrances which are placed in the way of its work by local officials in various parts of Turkey. Its colporteurs have been prevented from going about their work in Monastir, Mosul, Bagdad, and many other places. The worst cases have occurred at Castamuni and Scutari, in Albania, where the colporteurs have been kept waiting six months and more for the renewal of their licenses, without which they cannot travel. The British Embassy has made frequent representations on this subject; but as soon as one difficulty has been settled another has arisen, until it would seem as if the Turkish Government had made up its mind to cripple the activity of the Society. In reply to the latest representations of the Embassy, the Porte has acknowledged that the colportage of the Scriptures ought to be freely permitted, but claims the right to refuse to allow it in towns and districts where the circumstances are exceptional, and insists that every colporteur shall find a resident in the locality to go bail for his good behaviour. The Bible Society objects to these restrictions, especially to the last; for it exercises great care in the selection of its agents, and does not think any further guarantee than its own to be necessary. The kindred American Society is subjected to the same annoyances, and protests similar to those of the British Embassy have been made by the United States Legation."

Printing and Publishing

The Psalms and the Four Gospels in Albanian, 3,000 copies each, in the new Albanian character, have now been stopped in the press for the past five years by the censorship of the Turkish Government. Neither our own efforts, nor those of H.B.M.'s Embassy at Constantinople, have been able to overcome the suspicions or fears of the Turkish authorities in regard to any attempt to give the Albanians the Scriptures, or indeed any kind of literature,

in their own language. We can only wait and hope for a
door to open in God's good time.

Pages 125–127

Albania and Macedonia

Circulation, 2,700 copies, against 2,918 in 1904, and 2,390 in 1903

Unrest and insecurity, internecine strife, fierce passions
and jealousies, outbreaks and outrages, lawlessness and
repression, have again made these provinces a troubled
field for Bible work. The unsafe and unsettled state of
the country and the hostility of the Government have
made colportage a difficult and almost impossible task,
dangerous in some districts, forbidden in others. Our
staff of colporteurs has been reduced to its lowest limits,
consisting last year of three men only, and of these three
men only one has been allowed to travel at all freely. Yet,
in spite of these difficulties, we may take encouragement
from the fact that our circulation of 2,316 copies by
colportage shows that the Word of God finds many hearts
and homes to which it brings its message of hope and
comfort. From the depot at Monastir 393 copies have been
sold during 1905 – a larger number than in any previous
year.

A Welter of Racial Strife

Bulgarian Exarchists and Greek Patriarchists at deadly
strife; Servians who are friendly to neither; Wallachians
who side with Bulgarian and Servian against the Greeks;
Albanians divided among themselves, the backbone and
the tools of Turkish ascendancy; Turks who play one
faction against another and betray and oppress each in
turn; such a welter of political and racial confusion is not to

be soothed into order and peace by "reforms," which only irritate the wounds they were never intended to heal. With such political pharmacy we have nothing to do; our work is to cast out devils which these mutterings of incantations will not reach. Only "the finger of God" and His Word can effect this, as the following paragraphs serve to show. They are taken from the journals of our colporteurs, and they cast some bright revealing rays through the dark shadows that have hung so long over the mountains and valleys of this beautiful and blood-stained land.

In the Open Day

In Albania Colporteur Sinas was detained for four months at the town of Scutari; not only was permission to travel refused to him, but he was also forbidden to sell Scriptures in the town. Nevertheless, he was not idle. From his frequent visits to Scutari he is well-known and respected; his work, as he says, 'has been done in the noonday and under the eyes of the authorities.' Amongst Moslems, even more than among the Roman Catholics of Scutari, he finds encouragement and acceptance. 'Here is the book I bought from you last year,' said a Moslem, producing a well-thumbed copy of Proverbs. 'It is my guide and companion.' To his copy of the Proverbs this man now added the New Testament, and the Psalter. A priest, who had bought an Albanian Testament, said to Sinas, 'Alas for the people to whom I have been appointed to show the way of the Lord! Now that I have the Word in my own tongue, I understand what a heavy charge has been laid upon me.' And this priest has now begun earnestly to read and preach to the people 'the way of the Lord.'

Nunc Dimittis [cf. Luke 2:29–32]

An old man brought his little store of money to purchase an Albanian Testament. "Now I am ready to die," were his words, "because in these books I have found salvation for my soul." With such a *Nunc Dimittis* many an old Albanian has blessed the colporteur. One aged priest is said to have possessed himself of every Albanian edition issued by the Society. He bought copies for those of his village flock who could not afford to buy for themselves. He wrote and published a Brief History of the Old and New Testaments for Albanian readers. His zeal and his patriotism cost him his life. He was murdered by a band of insurgents. Whose was the secret hand that sent them forth to punish the teaching of Albanian as the worst of crimes?

In the Heart of Albania

Mr. George Kyrias, our depositary at Monastir, made a tour, under exceptionally favourable circumstances, into the heart of Albania. He may be said to have reached the heart of his country in the more intimate sense than the physical. In the important town of Elbasan he says there is not a single house, either Christian or Moslem, which does not possess one copy at least of our Albanian Scriptures. The Beys of Elbasan – the Albanian chiefs – whom he met by invitation, requested him to urge the Society to print more Albanian Scriptures. These people have a high idea of the Bible Society, and think it all-powerful; they were left, they said, being Moslems, in the darkness of ignorance, which they did not attribute to the Bible Society.

Sunday at a Moslem Village

A Sunday was spent with the hospitable chief of an Albanian village. Mr. Kyrias proposed to read the Bible to these Albanian Moslems, when his host produced a Book of Psalms and invited him to read out of that. Later in the day people from the neighbouring villages were called to come and listen. The host provided supper, and Mr. Kyrias was detained far into the night, speaking to this assembly of Albanian peasants. On the following day the villagers escorted Mr. Kyrias two hours' distance on his road, and made him promise that books should be sent to them. Of this tour Mr. Kyrias reports that everywhere he found the fruits of the labours of our two Albanian colporteurs, Sinas and Luka, and an immense regard and reverence in the hearts of the people for the Bible Society.

Page 354

Editorial Report, A Record of Translation and Revision

Albanian Tosk (National Character) – The 3,000 Psalms and 3,000 Four Gospels have now for five years been debarred issue from the press by the censorship of the Turkish Government, which fears to let the Albanians have literature in their own language.

The Albanian Dictionary, prepared by the late Mr. Christoforides when in this Society's employ, has been published by the Greek Foreign Office at Athens. The gift of some copies has been obtained for the Society. Two of them have reached the Library in London.

Appendix

Foreign Depots: Turkey

Constantinople: Rev. T. R. Hodgson, Bible Depot, Pera
Constantinople: Bible House, Stamboul

Janina, Epirus: Mr. Stergios Nousios
Kortcha, Albania: Colpr. Luka
Monastir, Macedonia: Mr. George Kyrias, Bible Depot
North Albania: Colp. Sinas
Prishtina, Albania: Colp. Stanko

103rd Report, 1907

Page 126
Turkey

The political and other troubles that beset our path in 1905 have, happily, grown less formidable, and we have been enabled to carry on our work more peaceably. Ottoman Government officials have been less inclined to interfere, and we have utilised all the advantages which such improved relations have given us. We praise God for this, and for His protecting care of us all in this field, and for the work given us to do.

Pages 127–128
Printing and Publishing

After six years the Albanian Four Gospels and Psalms still await the removal of the prohibition by the Turkish Government, which forbids the Albanian race to possess a literature in its own tongue. ...

Circulation

Albanian shows a falling off, with only 382 copies; for this, the disturbed state of the country and the long delays of the Turkish authorities in issuing the necessary permits to our colporteurs may be given as reasons, but the result is none the less to be deplored.

Pages 132–134

Albania and Macedonia

Circulation, 1,961 copies, against 2,709 in 1905 and 2,918 in 1904.

In these unhappy provinces our work has again been carried on under many difficulties and trials. Of the four colporteurs remaining in the field at the beginning of the year, one was removed to take charge of the work in Bulgaria. Another, Christoff, died in June, 1906, after much hardship and suffering. Another, Luka, was for some considerable time under medical treatment at the Greek hospital in Monastir. Colporteur Stanko alone has worked steadily throughout the year, his field being principally the district of old Servia. One suitable candidate was found to add to our scanty and inadequate staff; and to him the Turkish authorities refused for a period of four months to issue the permit without which he would not be allowed to work. We must now go through the same protracted negotiations in the case of a second candidate. Under such circumstances the sales by colportage, the work mainly of two men, amounted to no more than 1,527 copies, a not unsatisfactory total, when we also consider the distracted state of the country and the evil passions that have filled the dreadful years with murder and revenge, hatred and despair. To oppressed and oppressor alike, to the avenger of blood on his ruthless errand, to the innocent victims of man's injustice, to the outlaw with his life in his hand, and to the toiler in the fields who seeks only to eat his bread in peace, these copies of the Divine Word have brought their message and their witness of the kingdom of peace and righteousness which is God's kingdom and may yet be man's.

The Depot at Monastir

The sales from our depot at Monastir, under the efficient care of our depositary, Mr. George Kyrias, have been 434 copies. This depot has also fully taken its share in ministering to the spiritual needs of the suffering and the destitute.

In the Prisons

Moved by the miserable condition of the 1,200 prisoners in the Monastir prisons, and anxious to bring some consolation into their wretched lives, Mr. Kyrias applied to the authorities, and after consider-able delays and references here and there, and not without a little outside official pressure, he obtained access to the prisons, where in a short time copies of the Scriptures in Greek, Bulgarian, Turkish, and Hebrew—181 copies in all—were placed at the disposal of the prisoners. For the sake of those who cannot read, the Greek and Bulgarian priests who are themselves also imprisoned 'read the Bible all day long.' One young man confined for life said to Mr. Kyrias: 'Since I have read of the sufferings of Christ, and how the penitent thief at the last hour of his life found salvation, I believe there is compassion for me too, although I have been an evil-doer.'

At the Hospital

During the time that Colporteur Luka lay ill in the Greek hospital at Monastir, Mr. Kyrias, who visited him, was led to take interest in the other patients. The members of the Protestant community at Monastir collected some money, and 52 copies of the Scriptures were distributed, with the permission of the hospital superintendent, among the patients. A youth, smitten with incurable disease just after he was removed from the hospital to die, said to Mr. Kyrias, 'I cannot repay you; but the Lord will, I know. My life has come to an end, and I am not sorry. I am going to where I shall be no longer strapped to my bed, and where there will be no more pain.'

The Trials and Compensations of a Colporteur

In June, 1906, Colporteur Luka was arrested by the Turkish police at Starova. He was brought before the Governor, who was for stopping his sales and expelling him; but the Council would not agree to this, and not only advised that the colporteur should be set at liberty but also bought some copies of the Scriptures. Through the good offices of the British Consul at Monastir the Vali sent an order for Luka's immediate release, and the result of this incident was, he says, that he sold many more books in the town than he otherwise would have done.

Reading the Gospel in Prison

From Starova Luka proceeded to Struga, where he was again imprisoned and not even allowed to send off a telegram. 'That night in the prison,' he says, 'I shall never forget.' He had in his pocket St. Matthew's Gospel, which he read to the other prisoners, who were all Albanians. He had to read all night long, and his hearers became so enthusiastic that they made him promise to send them Gospels into the prison after his own release. The next day Luka was escorted with an armed guard to Ochrida, whence he was able to telegraph to Monastir, with the result that an order was obtained for his freedom. The Council at Ochrida scoffed at the ignorant zeal of the Struga official, and here also many of the members bought copies of the Scriptures. Luka returned at once to Struga, where he stayed for five days and did good work; his first business was to send fifteen copies of the Gospels to his Albanian friends and fellow-countrymen in the prison.

In the town of Uskup, Colporteur Stanko was detained for forty days until the Turkish authorities could decide as to which places he should be allowed to visit. This list was finally made out, according to agreement, with the British Consul's approval and consent. In Uskup itself Stanko worked freely and with good success, among both Moslems and Christians. At the various places he was allowed to visit in this somewhat fanatical district he met with great encouragement. At one small town he sold to Turks and Christians sixty copies, at another fifty copies, and at Mitrovitza, where both the Roman Catholic and the Moslem population are said to be fanatical, he sold seventy copies.

'Let him Sell his Garments and Buy one.'

We hear of a man who, after becoming the happy possessor of the New Testament, did not cease exhorting his friends, saying, 'Whosoever has money, let him buy a Bible, if he wants the riches which are worth more than all the world; and whosoever has not money, let him sell his garments and buy one.'

A Blood Feud

In last year's Report mention was made of the murder, by an insurgent band, of an aged Albanian priest, who was deeply beloved by the Albanians, a zealous friend and supporter of the Bible Society, and the author of several books in the Albanian language, among which the best known are a brief Bible History and the Acts of the Apostles, with notes. This good priest, Papa Christo, was killed by a Greek band for the crime of being an Albanian patriot. His murder led to the death of the good Bishop Photios of Kortcha, who in his turn was killed by an Albanian band to avenge the blood of their beloved priest Papa Christo. This second deed of blood has led to a third. Spiro Kostouri, a well-known banker of Kortcha, was marked down by the Greeks and slain in Salonica, where he had gone on business. This last brutal murder has roused the frenzy of all the Albanians, a fierce and vindictive race; and who can say when and where these unchained furies of murder and revenge will stop in their devastating career? We give this tale of horror as an illustration of the scenes among which our Bible work is done; the colporteur with his message of peace and good-will and the love of God moves as an herald of light amid the gloom and terror which have covered this unhappy land. 'How beautiful upon the mountains are the feet of them that publish good tidings!'

104th Report, 1908

Page 151
Turkey – Printing and Publishing

The Albanian Psalms, in the 'National' character, still await, after seven years' delay, the permission of the Turkish censorship. This edition of 3,000 copies is ready for issue. For the same length of time an edition of the Four Gospels, in the same character, has been ready for the press. The Turkish Government continues to forbid the Albanian race to possess a literature in its own tongue.

Page 152
Circulation

Albanian gives us a circulation of 635 copies; while for the greater part of the year supplies have been stopped by the embargo which the Turkish Government has placed on the importation of our books into Albania.

Pages 159–162
Albania and Macedonia

Circulation, 3,852 copies, against 1,961 in 1906, and 2,709 in 1905.

Another year's work in these afflicted provinces has been brought to a close, and we can record with thankfulness that it has not been without its measure of encouragement. The circulation has been larger than in any previous year, nearly 2,000 more copies of God's Word having been sold than in 1905; it would have been larger still but for the stoppage of our large consignments of Albanian Scriptures in the Salonika customhouse by the Turkish authorities.

Our four colporteurs have sold 3,402 copies. One of the four, Colporteur Stoykoff, with eight months' service only, made 1,052 sales; while another, Colporteur Natchi, has eleven months' service only. At our depot in Monastir 450 copies of the Scriptures have been sold. The total of 3,852 copies is a testimony that the Bible Society has not laboured in vain, notwithstanding the fact that the colporteurs are greatly restricted in their freedom of movement, and that they labour among a people whose minds are distracted by all the evil passions that ruthless cruelty, despair, and revenge can rouse in the human heart. No words can exaggerate the dreadful reality of the scenes among which our silent and steadfast work is done—like that of Him who shall not strive nor cry, who shall not fail nor be discouraged, till He have set judgment in the earth, even in such a sad spot of the earth as this.

Rival Nationalities

There is no doubt that the Turkish administration has succeeded, by intrigue and the lavish use of funds, in weakening the powerful Bulgarian 'Comitat,' with the result of breaking up this formidable organisation into parties distrustful of each other. The Greek 'Committee,' on the other hand, with a plentiful supply of money from Greece and foreign sources, and by means of ruthless and relentless methods of terrorism, has gained a political influence and importance quite out of proportion with its hold on the sympathies of the people. The efforts of this organisation to strengthen its position by an alliance with the Albanians, who are all more or less disaffected, have not been attended with success. The latter nationality, not to be behindhand, have 'Comitajis' of their own, who at present find the freedom they will strive and die for only among the fastnesses of the wild and rugged mountains of their native land. The short-sighted repressive policy of the Turkish Government, the futility of all attempts at reform, the insecurity and slight value of human life, the restlessness and recklessness and despair of men who will die to earn the right to live, form the elements of a tragedy whose gloom seems hardly relieved by the little we can do to bring the light and the comfort of God's Word into such darkened souls. Even what we are able to effect is too often ruined by the same political perversity which has raised the passion for freedom in these lands to the heights of martyrdom.

A Forbidden Land

In the district of Elbasan there is a community of twenty-three villages. No traveller in Albania is allowed to see these villages, no colporteur may visit them. The dwellers in this secluded valley are Christians, but bear, all of them, two names—a Moslem name, which they use when they frequent the market at Elbasan; and a Christian name, by which they are known in their own homes. They neither pay taxes, nor are they liable to military service. What these villages are to the outer world, such is Albania to us—a forbidden land. While our colporteurs have travelled in the country, often at great risks and with many difficulties, the Turkish Government has prevented our Albanian Scriptures from reaching them, closing the door at the port of Salonika. For nine months our much-needed supplies have been lying at the custom-house of that port, and although, through the good offices of the British Embassy at Constantinople, an order was procured for their release, the delivery of them is still delayed on pretexts which give ground for supposing that the order was not intended to be obeyed.[4] The Government dreads the cohesive influence in Albania of a national language and literature: but it might as well attempt to shut out the sunlight and the air. We, of course, cannot countenance contraband methods to circulate the Bible; but at the present time Albanian newspapers, all of them hostile to the Turkish Government, edited in London, in Boston, in Trieste, in Alexandria, in Sofia and Bucharest, are largely circulated and read throughout Albania.

---

4 The books have been released since this was written, after being detained for a year.

On Tour in Albania

Mr. George Kyrias, our depositary in charge of the work in Albania and Macedonia, made a tour in Albania, of which he sends an interesting report. At Skodra (Scutari) where he resided fifteen years ago as a colporteur, he finds a remarkable change in progress. The fanaticism and intolerance of the powerful Roman Catholic element has given place to a friendly interest in our work; which Mr. Kyrias attributes to a feeling of gratitude to the Bible Society for its efforts to give the Scriptures to the Albanians in their own language. Formerly in Scutari Albanian Scriptures were sold with difficulty: now the Roman Catholic ecclesiastics, who are all Albanians, encourage their people to buy the Scriptures, and the sales are large and encouraging. Petitions have reached us from the leaders of the community for the completion of the entire Bible in the Albanian language. Mr. Kyrias also speaks gratefully of the friendly services rendered to the work of the Society by the Dragoman of the British Consulate in Scutari, and of his kindness to the colporteur. Travelling through Albania, Mr. Kyrias found, as on former occasions, what he describes as 'an astonishing feeling of affection' towards the Bible Society on the part of Beys and peasants, rich and poor, Moslems and Christians alike. He says they gave him 'a good time,' and everywhere, in town and village, in shops, and in private houses of all degrees, he found treasured, and much read, copies of our Albanian editions.

A Visit to Montenegro

When at Scutari, Mr. Kyrias took the opportunity of crossing over into Montenegro, where, under the cold shade of official displeasure, our work has languished for seven years, and where no colporteur is allowed to travel. During these last seven years only 132 copies of the Scriptures have been sold in Montenegro, through the medium of the rigorously supervised State-bookseller at Cettinje, and no plans or proposals for extending our work in this little principality have been found possible of acceptance by the patriarchal despotism, which keeps this rugged little State in strict subjection and seclusion. Mr. Kyrias hopes for great results from the expected grant of a constitution.

Incidents of Colportage

In Albania and Macedonia colportage offers excitement and risk enough to satisfy the most adventurous. It is full of dramatic situations and scenes and contrasts—prisons and brigands, friends and foes, food and friendly shelter to-day, weariness and danger on the morrow, now some bloodstained, smoking ruin, now the pure freedom of the mountain heights. Through it all the colporteur passes on his way, faint, yet pursuing, content if he can leave the message of God's love behind him, and rejoicing whenever a heart is open to receive it. Travelling from Ochrida to Resen—a wild mountain road—Colporteur Natchi found himself benighted, and was offered hospitality by the Albanian guards stationed on the road. One of the guards, who could read, spent the night reading aloud out of the New Testament to the others. All who had money bought copies, and those who could not read vowed to begin to learn without delay. Many ears have been attuned to that voice which from those lonely mountain heights went up to the midnight sky.

'Bonds and Afflictions Abide Me'

Colporteur Stoykoff, who has done excellent work in Macedonia, found a Bulgarian purchaser one day for the Book of Proverbs. Stoykoff was urgent with the man to buy a New Testament also for his soul's good. The man said, 'Very likely I shall find myself in prison one day, then what good will this book do me?' 'The very reason you ought to have one,' said the colporteur. 'It is God's Book, and will give you the consolation you will then be in need of.' The man's premonition came true, and when in prison he was said to be rejoicing in the possession of the Testament, which gave him patience in tribulation and hope for the future.

'Idle Talk'

Colporteur Stoykoff, in the market-place at Prelepe, was invited to enter a shop, where he found a number of men discussing politics. The shopkeeper said, 'Now let us leave this idle talk, and let us listen to what our friend here has got to tell us.' The colporteur produced a Testament, and read aloud to them the Sermon on the Mount. All listened with deepest attention, and every man in that company bought a New Testament, some of them two copies apiece.

A Moslem Witness

Colporteur Stanko has his field in Old Servia, and in the northern parts of Albania, bordering on the Bosnian territory. It is a disturbed district, and includes eleven Albanian towns which the Turkish authorities have forbidden him to visit, where he has met in former times with great encouragement. Sixteen towns remain on his list, of which the population is largely Moslem. In one of these a Moslem called him aside, and earnestly besought him for copies of the Old and New Testaments. 'I do not wish,' he said, 'to be seen, because the Turks are suspicious, and will not understand what treasures are to be found in these sacred books.'

Trying Experiences

Colporteur Luka, who has laboured with encouragement and success, has been through what are described as trying experiences. In the year 1906 he was for a long time in hospital at Monastir, where he underwent an operation. In 1907 heavy floods carried away his house and furniture at Kortcha, and a good deal of his time had to be spent in building himself a house to live in; but he has tried honestly and faithfully to do his duty through all the difficulties that have beset him.

In the Depot and the Prisons at Monastir

Mr. George Kyrias, our depositary, has made excellent use of the opportunities afforded by this depot for reaching the great mixed population that is at all times to be found in the town of Monastir. The large Jewish community has manifested unusual interest in the study of the Bible, having formed several associations for that object which meet on the Jewish Sabbath. Numbers of them frequent the depot, where they buy Hebrew Scriptures for free distribution among the poorer members of their race. Mr. Kyrias is struck with the contrast presented by their 'Christian' neighbours, who only meet together to plot murder and revenge. The little Protestant community, however, was not less charitable or zealous than the Jews, and raised a sum of money for the distribution of the Scriptures among the unfortunate prisoners who fill the

Monastir prisons to overflowing. In these prisons there are 1,400 unhappy captives, whose state is described as wretched in the extreme. Mr. Kyrias was able, however, to distribute about 150 copies of God's Word among them in the Greek, Bulgarian, Servian, and Rumanian languages. The authorities refuse to allow Turkish and Albanian Scriptures to enter the prisons. In different ways the poor prisoners express their thankfulness for the books thus given them. Mr. Kyrias, with an intimate and life-long knowledge of the region, the races, and the languages, laments the futile and inadequate efforts that have yet been made for any real amelioration of the unhappy state of these countries; he cherishes the lingering hope that a people so willing to sacrifice life and all that life holds dear for patriotic aims, may yet be found ready to sacrifice much for the sake of eternity.

105th Report, 1909

Page 155

Turkey – Printing and Publishing

The following editions are in the press; some of them, especially the Bulgarian, have been greatly delayed, and are now urgently called for: Albanian Four Gospels, 32mo, 5,000 copies; Albanian Psalms, 16mo, 3,000 copies. ...

Albanian revision and printing will have to be taken in hand, and for this delicate and difficult task proposals and plans and persons have been under careful consideration ever since the commencement of the new régime in Turkey, which has given us an open door in Albania, where formerly our work was carried on under circumstances of great difficulty owing to the suspicious and hostile attitude of the old despotic government. The two Albanian editions now in the press (see above) have remained for the last eight years under the ban of the old censorship.

Page 157
Circulation by Languages

Albanian gives us a return of 1,278 copies—more than double that of any previous year. One result of the new era of freedom is the liberty we have never possessed before to circulate the Scriptures widely in the Albanian tongue. We have now in this case, as in Bulgarian, to face the problem of a suddenly increased demand which we have had exceedingly limited facilities for meeting.

Pages 162–164
Albania and Macedonia

Circulation, 4,810 copies, against 3,852 in 1907, and 1,961 in 1906.

We have an increase of practically 1,000 copies in our sales throughout these provinces during the year; the increase is the result of the work of the second half of 1908, and is due to the new era in Turkey. The total sales have amounted to 4,810 copies, of which number our four colporteurs have sold 3,524—an increase of 122; while the depot has sold 1,286 copies, an increase of 836. Scriptures in Albanian account for the greater part of the increase; of these, 1,278 copies were sold—more than double the sales in any previous year. As might have been expected, the results of the revolution in Turkey have been more marked in this part of the Agency than in any other.

The Depot at Monastir

Mr. George Kyrias, our depositary at Monastir, has found his labours and responsibilities very largely enhanced by the wonderful changes of the year, changes which had their beginning and origin under his immediate observation—at his doors, so to speak. His Albanian fellow-countrymen made urgent calls upon his time and strength, to which he has endeavoured to respond at considerable sacrifice to himself. The Albanian National Congress for the settlement of the alphabet question, held at Monastir in November, 1908, invoked his services as acting- president, as secretary, and as general organiser, and our new Albanian editions of the Scriptures, now asked for, will be very largely determined by the conclusions of this important Congress.

During the months preceding the revolution Bible work of great interest was carried on in connection with the prisons. The authorities forbade Turkish and Albanian versions to be introduced; but Greeks, Bulgarians, Vlachs, and Servians were supplied with the Scriptures in their own languages. Some of the Moslem prisoners in this way grew deeply interested in the Bible, and although Mr. Kyrias would not consent to let Bibles in forbidden versions be smuggled through, these Turks and Albanians found their own means of buying the books at our depot—with the result that 'the men were both enlightened and reformed.'

With our Colporteurs

In the early part of the year the colporteurs were much discouraged by the hostility and persecution of the authorities and by the unscrupulous attempts of police agents and spies to entrap them. After many years' faithful service, Colporteur Luka wished to resign, but the prospects of freedom under the new regime restored his courage. Colporteur Natchi, after two years' service, gave up his position, to which he has not returned. Colporteur

Stanko, whose work is principally among the Servian population of 'Old Servia,' has been greatly hampered by restrictions on his movements, but now enjoys a larger freedom which encourages him to hope for better days. In Central Macedonia Colporteur Stoykof has made excellent sales, and has been more free from molestation than the others. It is difficult for us to realise all the circumstances of danger and suspicion and uncertainty under which our men have hitherto pursued their difficult labours in these provinces, and we must give them credit for courage and earnestness of intention. Our hearty sympathy will go with Mr. Kyrias's words when he says: 'The Lord has protected our men from all dangers, and has given them to find happiness and blessing in their trials.'

Hopes and Prospects

Mr. Kyrias writes: 'The marvellous changes which have happened in our country mean much for the people of the Balkans, and not less for the Bible Society, since the doors have been opened wide for the Scriptures, which bring light and salvation. When I think of our troubles and difficulties and hindrances, of the fear which possessed every Albanian who dared to buy a copy of the Scriptures in his own tongue, all that has happened seems to me like a dream. I can hardly believe that, when our books arrive now, we can put them forthwith into the hands of the colporteurs; whereas formerly months of valuable time were wasted in endeavours to get them sealed and stamped by the local censors. Our prayer is that the new era of freedom will continue and extend, especially in Albania, whose unhappy sufferings have been beyond the power of words to express. Sales in Albania have never been so high as they have been since the Constitution was proclaimed. Many schools have been opened in Albania, and the Albanian language is to be taught in the Turkish schools there. This reminds me of the need for hastening the translation of the entire Bible into Albanian, which the Albanians are looking for with the greatest eagerness. The Albanian nation will never cease to be grateful for the kindness, interest, and sympathy of the Bible Society. Our colporteurs reach the remotest corners of the country, help the poor shepherd, comfort the sick and the prisoner, and every human soul. On my last tour in Albania I was amazed to find what the people knew of the Bible Society, and how much its work is appreciated. The harvest which the Society is bountifully sowing will be reaped in God's good time. Though the people are generally uneducated, yet the Bible can be found in homes where you would least expect it.'

From an Orthodox Priest in Albania

Mr. Kyrias has received the following letter from an Orthodox priest in an Albanian village, who was too poor to purchase a Bible:—

The kindly readiness with which you complied with my request and gave me copies of the Holy Scriptures for myself and my household has laid upon me the obligation of writing to express to you my feelings of profound thankfulness, and to assure you that I will not cease during the whole of my life to pray to the High God and to our Lord Jesus Christ for your happiness and for the success and progress of the venerable Bible Society of which you are a worthy representative.

The National Bible Society of Scotland

The total circulation for Albania and Macedonia given above, 4,810 copies, represents our own direct sales by colporteurs and at the depot. Besides these, we have supplied to the Rev. W. M. Tait, the Agent of the National Bible Society of Scotland at Salonika, 2,398 copies of the Scriptures for circulation by their own colporteurs in the Vilayet of Salonika, which, by arrangement, is left to the care of the Scottish Society. Including the Scriptures supplied to the N.B.S.S. we have, therefore, sent into Albania and Macedonia during the year no fewer than 7,208 copies of the Scriptures, probably the largest yearly distribution on record.

106th Report, 1910

Page 135

Turkey – Printing and Publishing

The following editions remain in the press at Constantinople; Bulgarian New Testament, 32 mo, 11,000 copies; Bulgarian Psalms 32mo, 10,000 copies; Graeco-Turkish Reference Bible, 8vo (plates), 5,000 copies; Albanian Psalms, 16mo, 3,000 copies.

At Monastir the Albanian press, recently established under the auspices of the Albanian Association, has in hand for us an edition of the Albanian Four Gospels, 16 mo, 5,000 copies. This is undergoing a thorough revision, which we hope will be extended to the remainder of the Albanian New Testament should the issue of the Gospels encourage us to persevere with this important work. The revision and completion of the entire Bible in Albanian come within our plans for the future, and our tentative efforts in that direction will follow the settlement of the vexed question of a standard national alphabet for the Albanian language and literature.

Page 137
Circulation by Languages

Albanian, with 1,732 copies, gives us the largest total yet attained in this language, and is an earnest of what this virile race, awakening to new hopes of freedom and progress, may yield in promise and fulfilment to the long-continued labours of the Bible Society in Albania.

Pages 141–142
Albania and Macedonia
Circulation 4,745 copies, against 4,810 in 1908, and 3,852 in 1907.

The year's circulation in these provinces practically maintains the level reached in 1908. Three colporteurs have worked throughout the year; two others, new men on the staff, did only three months' work each; and the united sales of these men about to 3,505 copies. The depot at Monastir has sales of 1,240 copies. Of the total sales, Scriptures in Albanian account for 1,732 copies, the largest circulation in this language of any previous year.

The Depot at Monastir

Mr. George Kyrias, our depositary in charge of this depot, has been actively engaged in the Albanian part of our work during a rather memorable year. National feeling in Albania runs high, and the work of the Bible Society, which for many years in its editions of the Scriptures in the Albanian language has published the only literature available in Albania, has attracted an amount of interest and sympathy which even Mr. Kyrias, himself an Albanian, finds surprising. Many Albanians come to the depot; they want to see the whole of the Bible printed in their own tongue, and the sales at the depot have been mostly to Moslem Albanians.

The question of their national alphabet is one of vital interest to all Albanians. Our edition of the New Testament now being printed at the Albanian press at Monastir is in the Latin character, adopted and recommended by the two successive national conferences at Monastir and Elbasan. Attempts, partly political and partly religious in their origin, to force the Arabic character upon Albania are doomed to failure, and if persisted in will be fraught with disaster. Patriotic Albanians, Moslems and Christians, disillusioned as they have been by the tardy dawning of the brighter day they hoped to see, have, nevertheless, made efforts and sacrifices without parallel in the history of their race in the cause of the national progress, unity, and enlightenment. Within the short space of less than two years since the proclamation of a Constitution Albania has been covered by the beginnings at least of a national system of education; a normal school has been founded at Elbasan at a cost of £700, raised on the spot, and has now fifty pupils. Besides the printing press at Monastir, others have been established at various centres. Eight newspapers in the Albanian language are now issued in the country. The leaders in this movement anticipate that as a result of their efforts 50 per cent of the Albanian population will in a few years be able to read. All this will have a very considerable bearing on our Bible work in Albania, and even now we have abundant cause for thankfulness to Almighty God for the way it has developed from its first small tentative beginnings in darker and more difficult days.

The report of a tour through Albania which our Agent, the Rev. T.R. Hodgson, accompanied by Mrs. Hodgson, made in June and July, 1909, was printed in the October and November numbers of the *Bible in the World*.

The Colporteurs

Our staff of three men with which we commenced 1909 was increased at the end of the year by two more, raising the number to five. No difficulties have been experienced by any of the men, a contrast to the time not far distant when bonds and imprisonment awaited the colporteur in Albania. Two men have worked in Macedonia, one of whom, Colporteur Stoykoff, had sales for the year of 1,052 copies. Colporteur Stanko, who works mainly in the Kossovo Vilayet, reports a softening of the fanatical spirit of the population. His sales were 849 copies, mostly in Servian, Turkish, and Albanian. Colporteur Luka in Central Albania disposed of 1,197 copies of the Scriptures among a population largely illiterate, but friendly and eager to learn the words of the Bible. The two new colporteurs have worked three months each: both have had previous experience, and both have to prove their fitness in their respective fields, one of which, Colporteur Elia's in North Albania, is a hard and difficult soil.

Famine in Albania

During the exceptionally severe winter of 1908-9 great distress was experienced in the district of Berat, and the famine-stricken population among whom our colporteurs were well known, turned to the Bible Society as the only friends they could appeal to in their hour of suffering and need. The Government distribution of corn was inadequate and tardy; the district is remote and inaccessible; before we could even deal with such an appeal much suffering and hardship fell to the lot of these poor Albanians. From friends of the Bible Society in England and elsewhere about £10 reached us. Colporteur Luka's report of the distribution of this money says: 'I found the famine not so bad as it had been, as the people had begun to work in the fields, and many of them had obtained small supplies of corn or wheat. There was still great scarcity of bread and great distress. The Rev. Mr. Theona and Mr. George Carbonara assisted me to find the families in extreme need, and among these we distributed the money in small sums.' He sends a list of seventeen families who received sums of from 5s. to 10s.

Page 468

Editorial Report

The B.F.B.S. has hitherto published its Albanian version in three distinct characters. The Gheg version, for the Ghegeri districts of North Albania, is in Latin character; the Tosk, or Southern Albanian version, is in Greek character; and there is, besides, the so-called National character, which is an adaptation of the other two. The Gheg has proved more acceptable from its use of Latin characters. At the Albanian National Congress, held at Monastir in November, 1909, the Bible Society's representative was appointed Vice-President. The question of the alphabet was discussed, and the Latin alphabet was adopted as a basis, adapting each letter to the phonetic needs of the language. It is proposed that another Congress should be held in two years, with the object of deciding further questions concerning Albanian orthography and literature. The provision of the new Albanian version is a large question. But the way has been perceptibly smoothed by the adoption of a uniform alphabet.

Revision of the four Gospels has proceeded, and an edition of 5,000 is being printed at Monastir. If this is found to be acceptable, the remainder of the N.T., and afterwards the O.T., will be taken in hand.

107th Report, 1911

Pages 132–133
Turkey

We have to record a whole year's Bible work under constitutional government in Turkey. On July 24, 1908, an Imperial Irade was suddenly issued restoring the constitution of 1878. On April 27, 1909, Sultan Abdul Hamid, having failed in a nefarious attempt to upset the constitution he had been compelled to grant, was deposed, and Muhammad V succeeded to the throne. In those two troubled years of revolution our work in Turkey went quietly forward amidst all the fears and hopes which attended the birth of the new era. .... Martial law in Albania and elsewhere; the boycott of Greek commerce; the outbreak of cholera in the later months of the year, and the strict enforcement of quarantine regulations: these events in particular have adversely affected our work as they have affected almost every interest in Turkey. But the Government of the country has probably recognised that by peaceable and loyal methods we have endeavoured to cooperate in the progress and advancement and development of the people. Where colporteurs have been arrested by local officials, as in Albania, they have immediately been set at liberty upon application to the proper authorities. The closing, under martial law, of the Albanian press in Monastir put a stop for a time to the printing of our Albanian editions of the Scriptures; but, with the help of our Albanian friends, this prohibition was eventually removed, and the press has now resumed the printing of the much-needed editions. We come to a review of our work in 1910 with feelings of humble thankfulness for another year of God's protecting care and mercy.

Printing and Publishing

We have received the following editions from the press. ... *In Albanian*: St. Matthew and St. Mark, each, 2,000 copies.

The following editions remain in the press: ... Albanian four Gospels, 16mo, 5,000 copies. With the exception of the Albanian, all these editions are issued from the press at Constantinople. Reference has already been made, in the introductory paragraphs, to the Albanian press at Monastir which is now occupied in printing our Albanian editions. Unless there should be further interference with the press by the authorities—which we have no reason to expect— we hope that the revision and the printing of the Albanian Scriptures in the new Latin character will go steadily on until we are able to give the Albanian people the complete Bible in their own language.

Page 135

Circulation by Languages

Albanian has the largest circulation yet reached in that language, namely, 2,014 copies. Albania has become wonderfully receptive of the Scriptures in recent years, and a demand has arisen which we are endeavouring to meet. Among a population so remote, so scattered, and so illiterate, our colporteurs have a hard and trying task, but they never meet with any but the warmest welcome, and are always cheered by a reception of their message which in many cases can only be adequately described as enthusiastic. And this among Christians and Moslems alike.

Pages 137–140

Albania and Macedonia

Circulation, 6,410 copies, against 4,745 in 1909, and 4,810 in 1908.

The circulation for the year is the largest yet reached in these provinces, being 1,665 copies in excess of the sales for 1909, about the same increase on the sales for 1908, and almost double the sales of any year preceding that date. The six colporteurs now employed in these provinces, of whom one has worked nine months and another three months only, have sales amounting to 6,030 copies. Of the total sales 23,014 copies have been in the Albanian language, the largest circulation in, Albanian of any previous year. Circulation in the Bulgarian, Turkish, and Greek languages, with some few sales in Servian, formed the bulk of the remainder.

The Depot at Monastir

At the depot in Monastir 380 copies were sold—a great falling oil as compared with the previous year. This is largely accounted for by the continued ill-health of our depositary, Mr. George Kyrias, who says, 'Owing to my sickness I have been unable to see so many visitors as in former years. Yet many friends have called, and all express their deepest interest in our work. The common desire of all, expressed in many ways and repeated again and again, is to have the entire Bible completed in the Albanian language, their mother-tongue.'

The Albanian Press

Reference has already been made to our printing operations at this press. Two years ago, soon after the proclamation of the Constitution, the Albanian Association in Monastir, known as the 'Bashkim,' summoned the first National Congress to consider the language question. This Congress met in Monastir, and its outcome, among other things, was the establishment in Monastir of this excellent press, at a cost of some £2,000 subscribed by patriotic Albanians. From the first the press has been placed at the entire disposal of the Bible Society, and the earliest work undertaken was a revised edition of the four Gospels in Albanian. In 1910, when Albania fell upon evil days, and all her hopes and efforts and sacrifices for enlightenment and progress were rudely dashed to the ground, the press was closed by the Government and our half-completed Albanian printing was suspended. After many months the Government was induced to relax this stringent measure, and the press has now resumed its operations. It is through this Albanian press that we hope to be able to respond to the earnest desire of all Albania and to give her people, thirsting for knowledge and light, the complete Bible in their own tongue.

The Colporteurs

The staff of colporteurs now consists of six men instead of the four men of previous years. During 1910 the average number was five. All the colporteurs have done excellent work, especially Colporteur Elias, who now occupies the difficult field of Scutari in North Albania, and whose sales amounted to 1,327 copies. One other colporteur is at work in North-Eastern Albania, one in South Albania, and another in Central Albania. Two men are at work in that part of Macedonia which is attached to our Monastir depot. The field is fairly adequately occupied, and the staff remains under the experienced supervision of Mr. George Kyrias, our depositary at Monastir.

The Albanian is not the man to sit down in patient endurance under oppression and wrong. He is a European, proud of his high traditions of race and freedom. 'Never,' says Mr. Kyrias, 'has their zeal for knowledge and the blessings of civilisation been so strong and passionate as to-day. And to the praise of the Albanians let it be said that our colporteurs have everywhere been received with the warmest welcome, now, as always before. They will never forget the benefits they have received from the Bible Society, the only source to which they owe now, as in the old bad days of Abdul Hamid, the one Book in their native tongue which can enlighten their minds and enrich their souls.'

With Colporteur Stanko.

This colporteur's field is far up in North-Eastern Albania, and he works among a scattered, remote, and somewhat fanatical population, very poor, and mostly illiterate. He tells of a Moslem youth who bought a Bible from him two years ago in Ipek, the boy's home. Every time the colporteur came to Ipek the boy sought him out for instruction in the Bible. Recently he travelled to Prishtina, where Stanko resides, to beg for further instruction, and spent two days in the colporteur's house engaged in reading and prayer. At another small town a Moslem young man, having bought a Bible, roused such a spirit of inquiry among the people that, on his next visit, the colporteur sold 25 copies of the Scriptures in three days. Stanko reports a more friendly feeling among the Roman Catholic population of his district, and gives instances of certain priests coming, or sending to him secretly, for the purchase of Bibles. Stanko's sales for the year amounted to 991 copies.

With Colporteur Elias

This colporteur, who is stationed at the northern Albanian fortress of Scutari, has the hardest field of all our men in Albania. He travels extensively, and reports that from Moslem and Christian alike he has received the greatest hospitality. At Berat he was entertained by a little company of Moslem ecclesiastics, with whom he passed some days in friendly discussion, and who, on his departure, bought for themselves a number of Bibles. At Elbasan he was brought before the authorities and severely questioned, and for a time feared he might suffer the fate of many other victims of martial law. Fortunately, his excellent command of Turkish stood him in good stead, and after some little detention they let him go. His sales are the largest in Albania, amounting to 1,327 copies.

With Colporteur Spiro

Colporteur Spiro, stationed at Janina, reports many interesting experiences of his work among the Moslems of Southern Albania. He tells of a Turkish military officer who entered a shop and began to rail at the Moslem shopkeeper, who had just bought a Bible. A little crowd gathered as usual, but the colporteur's demeanour so disarmed his hostile critics that the officer himself bought three copies of the Scriptures and others were sold to the bystanders. At Permet a Moslem teacher bought an Albanian copy of St. Matthew, and having gathered a little audience began to read aloud the 23rd chapter. Then he said, 'The Christians are thus taught to read their book in their own language; not as we Moslems, who have to read our Koran in the Arabic language, of which we know nothing.' On his persuasion many of the people bought copies of the Scriptures.

With Colporteur Stoykoff

This colporteur, who is stationed at Monastir, works mainly among the Bulgarian-speaking population. He says that the minds of the people are so full of their misfortunes and sorrows that they give little thought to higher and spiritual things. He speaks of great encouragement from many Bulgarian priests, and of their assistance to him in selling the Scriptures to the people. ...

In Macedonia

The work of Colporteur Kartalis, in Macedonia, has been full of interest especially among the young in village schools. Some of these children, he says, who have read and studied their Bibles, had, by the testimony of their teachers, not only improved in knowledge, but in character as well. He tells of a certain innkeeper who was unwilling to receive a man who sold Bibles into his hotel, but was persuaded to buy a Bible. Two months later he bought from the colporteur twelve Bibles, one for each room in his hotel, and said, 'Now I have the richest hotel in the world, for I have given it the richest furniture. Many a man will find here a cure for all his sorrows and sins as I have found for mine.' Women, too, in these little villages are frequent purchasers, and delight in hearing the Gospel story so near and so like their own homes and lives. The women and girls, gather round the colporteur and listen to the story of the Samaritan woman, deplete his store of Scriptures, and send him rejoicing on his way. They are kindly folk in these Macedonian villages.

Page 445
Editorial Report

The printing of four Gospels at the Monastir press was delayed for some time, owing to the closing of the press during the recent political troubles. The press has now been re-opened, and the work is proceeding.

108th Report, 1912

Page 3

Amid the troubles in the Near East we are at length—after being for ten years forbidden by the Turkish authorities—now allowed to issue the Four Gospels in *Albanian*, printed in what is known as the "national" character. It has been arranged to prepare and publish in this form the complete Albanian Bible.

Page 142
Revision

Two important revisions are in hand about which we are able to report some degree of progress; a beginning in one case and an under- taking in the other. The Albanian revision has made a beginning with the New Testament now being issued from the Albanian press in Monastir. Some of the books of the Old Testament are also ready for the press, and we hope to see the issue of the complete Albanian Bible within a period of three years.

Printing and Publishing

Albanian: St. Luke and St. John, 16mo, completing the Four Gospels, 5,000 copies; Psalms, 3,000 copies.

Albanian: New Testament, 16mo, 5,000 copies.

Page 144
Circulation by Languages

Albanian has a circulation of 1,560 copies, which is some 500 copies less than the circulation of the previous year. The disturbed state of the country is entirely accountable for the smaller circulation. With our new editions of the Albanian Scriptures ready for issue, and with the necessary freedom and safety for our colporteurs to move about the country, we have reason to anticipate that Albania will absorb more and more copies of God's Word, for the gift of which, in her darkest and saddest hours, she has shown herself so deeply grateful.

Pages 145–146

Mr. Sinas, in charge of the depot at Rustchuk, was appointed during the year to the charge of the revision and printing of the Albanian Bible, and after some preliminary work on this important undertaking under the direction of the Society's agent in Constantinople, proceeded to Monastir, where the new edition will be carried through the press. His place was taken in Rustchuk by Mr. John Kartalis from our staff in Macedonia, who has proved himself well qualified for this responsible post.

Pages 148–150
Albania and Macedonia
Circulation, 5,813 copies, against 6,410 in 1910, and 4,745 in 1909.

A Troubled Year

Mr. George Kyrias, our depositary at Monastir, has continued in charge of the work in these provinces, and returned from prolonged sick-leave somewhat restored in health. In his report regarding the past year he writes, "The political situation was decidedly not a help to our work." After three years of "constitutional government" many hopes have been shattered; insecurity, poverty, destitution, and civil war have ripened to their unhappy harvest—just as the ungathered crops and untilled fields of Albania have deepened the common poverty of a people who at the best of times find the struggle for existence hard and bitter. The scourge of cholera spread its paralysing shadow over the face of the land, and stirred to unwanted panic a population grown callous to murderous deeds of bloodshed and crime. Under these conditions our work has been carried on throughout the year with results that have not belied our hopes, nor left us without encouragement. A total circulation of 5,813 copies of the Scriptures, 1,560 of which were in the Albanian language, represents some 600 copies less than the circulation of 1910, when the circumstances were more favourable. At the depot in Monastir 461 copies have been sold and the balance of 5,352 copies have been sold by the united labours of our six colporteurs, four of whom have worked and travelled mainly within the limits of Albania.

The Albanian Bible

The New Testament is approaching completion in the Albanian press at Monastir. The Psalms have been issued, the book of Proverbs is ready for the press, and the revision of the Pentateuch is steadily proceeding. Mr. Sinas has been set apart for the charge of this important work and of its issue from the press, and it is hoped that a period of three years' steady work will see it brought to a completion. Mr. Kyrias writes that the Albanians gratefully acknowledge the long and patient labours of the Bible Society, which for fifty years has endeavoured to bring to them the knowledge of God's Word in their own tongue; and that they believe that it is mainly owing to these labours that they have attained to whatever moral and intellectual enlightenment they now possess.

With the Colporteurs

Our staff of colporteurs has consisted of six men, four of whom have worked in Albania and two in Macedonia. In the daily records of their lonely and adventurous journeys there is much of exceeding interest, much valuable information about the people and the country, and, above all, much testimony to the saving power of the Word of God over the hearts and lives of rude and simple folk who know little of "modern progress" and very little more of life than the bare struggle for existence.

A Young Macedonian

Colporteur Kartalis gives us the following simple narrative. A Macedonian youth had a great desire to possess a Bible, but extreme poverty baffled his hopes. His earnings amounted to seven pence a day, and out of this the lad had to support his aged mother and little sister. The happy thought occurred to him of saving out of his food, and so reducing his daily expenditure of seven pence to six pence, which in twenty days would provide the 10 piastres wherewith to purchase a Bible. At the end of that time he sought out the colporteur, and became the happy possessor of the long-sought treasure. Kartalis, who afterwards visited the little home, bears testimony to the happy influence of that Bible. ...

A Moslem Reader

Colporteur Stanko, described by Mr. Kyrias as "the good-hearted old worker with his pleasant ways," moves among a somewhat fanatical population in Albania. Many years ago he sold a Bible to a young Moslem, the fruit of which is to be found in a touching letter which has just reached the agent. Stanko also writes that not only for himself alone does this man love the truth, but he never ceases to recommend it to his friends and neighbours and to testify of the joy and comfort he has found in serving and following the Lord.

Moslem and Christian Testimony

Colporteur Spiro, working in South Albania, says that the influence of the Scriptures is spreading not only among the common people but also among those who claim to be educated and civilised. He met two lawyers, one a Moslem, the other a Christian, both of whom had purchased and read the Bible, who asked him how he was getting on with his work. He replied that it was God's work and He would take care of it. Both men then agreed that nothing would bring peace and happiness to the world except the knowledge of God's Word. The Christian lawyer went on to say, "As for me, nothing has brought me to the knowledge of myself more than the teaching of this Book. Since I have read it I have begun to understand my aim in life and my end." He spoke of the work of the Bible Society, whose story he said he knew, and producing a copy of the Society's "Specimens of Languages" from his pocket, said to his little audience, "This is an example of the most beneficent work which the world can show."

A Sad Catalogue

Colporteur Elias, whose field is North Albania, enumerates his experiences in a terrible catalogue of miseries that have affected his work during the year. Cruelties, insurrection, starvation, poverty, cholera, quarantine, the outbreak of the war with Italy, conscription, the blockading of Albanian ports, the closing of Albanian schools—through all of these he has pursued his labours and his journeys with the conviction in his heart, as he says, that all these dreadful troubles have not availed to hinder the spread of God's Word among his countrymen, and in proof he points to his sales of 1,039 copies of the Scriptures during the year.

In Albanian Villages

On one of his journeys, Colporteur Elias joined two peasants returning home to their village at nightfall, and they offered him hospitality for the night. The next day the chief of the village gathered all his little clan together to hear the colporteur read to them out of the Albanian Bible. The chief then gave orders that all who were present should buy, each of them, a copy of the Scriptures. Some of them had no money, and for these the chief himself bought copies, so that on that one day 35 copies of the Albanian Scriptures found entrance into that remote village. A peasant, passing through a village in another part of Albania, heard one of the villagers reading aloud from the Albanian Testament. He asked where this wonderful book was to be procured, and he was told if he went to the neighbouring town he would find a man who would sell him one. This was rather sad news for the peasant, who had no money to spend. However, nothing daunted, he collected a load of wood with which he went off to the town, and having sold his load, sought out Elias, and returned rejoicing in the possession of his Albanian Gospel. This man was unable to read, nor, until that time, did he know of the existence of such a book in the Albanian language. Thus the seed is sown among the mountains and the valleys of Albania. The time will surely come when both sower and reaper will rejoice together.

The National Bible Society of Scotland

We have sold to this Society 1,191 copies of the Scriptures for circulation in Macedonia. during the year. These are in addition to those sold through our own direct agency, thus bringing our issues in these provinces to a total of 7,004 copies for the past year.

Page 453
Editorial Report: Albanian

At last we are able to report the publication of the Gospels and Psalms in Albanian, printed in the national character, and bound at the Monastir Press. The revision of the remainder of the N.T. is proceeding. In the O.T., Proverbs has been completed and Genesis almost finished. Messr. A. Sinas and G. Kyrias, two of the members of our own staff, assisted by Mr. Simon Sutariki of Elbasan, and Albanian teacher of the Orthodox Church, form the Revision Committee.

109th Report, 1913

Page 7

Colportage

In Albania a man was first robbed by Turkish soldiers and then made prisoner by the Greek troops and carried off to Athens. Yet in every country we find colporteurs loyal to their calling and blessed with wonderful success.

Pages 154–155

Turkey

Peace had hardly been ratified when Bulgaria, Servia, Greece and Montenegro simultaneously declared war upon Turkey, and European Turkey was at once aflame. All our fields of work were closed by the military operations, and all our labours to bring the message of 'peace on earth and good will toward men' seemed, for the time, to be frustrated and overthrown. But God is greater than our hopes and fears, and the sorrows of men are His opportunity and His care. We have to record, with thankfulness and wonder, a circulation of God's Word throughout the agency which is probably larger than in any previous year. ...

Our edition of the Albanian New Testament, 16mo (5,000 copies) had practically passed through the press at Monastir in November, 1912, when its issue was stopped by the war. Peace will bring this good gift among others.

The preparation, revision, and translation of the Albanian Old Testament under the care of Mr. Sinas, went on steadily at Monastir until the outbreak of the war. Some of the books are ready for the press, and only await more peaceful times for their issue.

Pages 157–158

From Macedonia and Albania, since the investment and capture of Monastir by the Servians, we have no official returns. All our available stock of Turkish, Greek, Albanian, and Servian Scriptures in the Monastir depot has been freely distributed, and we have been unable to get further supplies through. ...

Albanian has a circulation of 959 copies, which is 601 copies fewer than in 1911. This decrease must be attributed solely to the disturbed state of Albania. For the last two years our colporteurs have found their work increasingly difficult and dangerous in Albania. In the other Balkan languages we have a circulation of 1,218 copies, principally in Slavonic and Servian.

Pages 161–162

Albania and Macedonia

Circulation (for nine months of the year only) 4,018 copies. In 1911, 5,813 copies, and in 1910, 6,410 copies.

The full returns for the year's circulation in Albania and Macedonia have failed to reach us, and the futures given are the results of nine months' work only. From the time of the investment and capture of Monastir by the Servians, communications with that town, where our central depot is situated, have been entirely cut off.

We have also to deplore the death of Mr. George Kyrias, who since 1894 had been our depositary at Monastir, and who was called away suddenly on December 30th. During all these years Mr. Kyrias has served the Society and the cause of the Gospel among his fellow-countrymen faithfully and well, and we shall miss the benefit of his knowledge and experience. Mr. Sinas, our depositary at Rustchuk, who was already in Monastir engaged in the work of translation and revision of the new Albanian Bible, has for the present succeeded Mr. Kyrias in the charge of the Monastir depot. But the last quarter's returns and reports have been unavoidably delayed by our sad loss.

The Colporteurs

For the first three months of the year six colporteurs worked in this field, two in Macedonia, and four in Albania. For the remaining nine months five men only have been employed. Their sales, for the nine months of the year for which their returns have reached us, have been well up to the average, in spite of the troubles, difficulties, and perils in the midst of which their labours have been carried on. In Albania, Colporteur Stanko and his family have been shut up in Prishtina, where their home is, enduring great privations; the same fate befell Colporteur Visso at Kortcha and Colporteur Spiro at Yanina. Colporteur Stoykoff, has been confined to Monastir before and since hostilities commenced. Colporteur Elia, who is stationed at Scutari, has been able, as usual, to make his adventurous journeys through some of the most troubled regions of North Albania, and has worked in Scutari, Antivari, Durazzo, Elbasan, Avlona, and through all the intermediate regions, with sales of 1,076 copies of the Scriptures. One of his adventures may be given in his own words:

Fallen Among Thieves

At Avlona, one day towards evening, I was returning from the harbour to the town. A company of Turkish soldiers, seated under some olive-trees by the wayside, called me, and thinking they would buy my books, I went to them. As I began to open my books two of them attacked me and held me down, and others searched my person, and found my purse, containing 1,085 piastres (about 10 pounds)'. They took the money, and after threatening me with death if I should report this to the authorities, they let me go. With this money it was my intention to go and see my wife and children, and now what am I to do? It is impossible for me to visit my family.'

Elia, who had not seen his wife and family for three years, had saved this money with many privations. However, the way home was opened for him in a manner none of us could have foreseen or expected.

After reaching Durazzo at the end of October and going on board a steamer, Elia, and several other passengers who wore the fez, were taken from their steamer by the captain of a Greek vessel and carried off to Piraeus. After an examination at Piraeus, Elia was liberated and the others detained in custody. 'By that time,' Elia complains, 'I was a little sick', which is hardly a matter for surprise after his experiences. On his recovery, he pursued his labours at Piraeus until an opportunity offered for him to proceed to his home, where doubtless his excellent wife was greatly rejoiced and relieved to welcome him in safety once more. 'My wife is anxious, and I am afraid for my family,' he wrote from Piraeus; 'please do what you can to comfort and protect them until my arrival.'

All our other colporteurs in this field have had similar experiences, and have endured great privations and hardships. They and we can join in giving thanks to God who has mercifully preserved them from greater dangers and kept them safe while working in the midst of trouble. And they can truly say, 'Thy rod and Thy staff they comfort me.'

Among Sick and Wounded Soldiers

The flight of the Turkish troops from Monastir, and the sudden and unexpected entry of the Servians, greatly taxed the resources of our depot in that town, the diminished supplies of which we have been unable to replenish. Among the sick and wounded Servian soldiers who were brought into Monastir on its capture some 400 copies of the Servian Scriptures were gratuitously distributed, thus exhausting the entire Servian stock at the depot. The hasty flight of the Turkish troops left no opportunity for the distribution of Turkish Scriptures.

During last year we have sold to the National Bible Society of Scotland, for its work in Macedonia, with headquarters at Salonika, 1,321 copies of the Scriptures. This brings our total issues in Macedonia and Albania, as far as they are accounted for, to 5,339 copies.

Page 452

Albanian – Owing to the outbreak of war it has been found impossible to publish the N.T., though it is practically complete. Mr. A. Sinas, one of the members of the Revision Committee, has died [*This is an error in the original: George Kyrias died, not Sinas, D. H., 2017*]

110th Report, 1914

Pages 122–123

Turkey – Printing, Publishing and Revision

The following editions have been issued by the press during 1913:

In Albanian: New Testament, 16mo, 2,000 copies; Genesis, 16mo, 5,000 copies; Proverbs, 16mo, 5,000 copies.

The translation and revision of the Albanian Bible, in spite of war and the troubles arising from the Servian occupation, have proceeded steadily at Monastir, under the care of Mr. A. Sinas. The Albanian press at Monastir issues the books as they are separately completed. An article on "The Albanian Bible," by the Rev. T. R. Hodgson, appeared in *The Bible in the World* for 1913, p, 358.

Page 125
Circulation by Languages

Albanian, with 604 copies, has fallen to one-half the circulation of the two previous years. This is accounted for first, by the prohibition of the sale of Albanian Scriptures in the territories occupied by Greece and Servia—which, in the case of Servia, still continues—and secondly, by the almost complete stoppage of colportage in Albania during the war.

Pages 128–130
Albania and Macedonia

Circulation 3,121 copies, against 4,018 (nine months) in 1912, and 5,813 in 1911. War distribution by free grants, 2,573 copies.

For this part of the agency it will be convenient for the purpose of the present report to retain the names given in the heading of the section. Geographical and political boundaries have been altered by the war, and much of what has been known vaguely as Albania and Macedonia is now Greek and Servian territory. Our work in this field has been greatly hampered by the war, and the freedom which we enjoyed under Turkish rule has been greatly restricted or altogether denied to us in the case of the large indigenous populations which have passed under the Greek and Servian Governments.

The Depot at Monastir

Mr. Athanase Sinas, our depositary at Monastir, has faithfully held a difficult and trying post during this troubled time of transition. The Servian occupation of this important and pleasant town was accompanied by harsh, arbitrary methods, which were applied with especial rigour to our men and our work. The ruthless treatment of the large Bulgarian and Albanian population and the proscription of their two languages practically put a stop to the work of the depot and of the colporteurs. It was made a crime to sell the Scriptures in the Bulgarian and Albanian versions, a crime for which some of our men suffered in prison. The Albanian Press was forbidden to print books in other than the Servian language, and for a time the printing of our Albanian editions ceased. The depot was never actually closed, but as only Scriptures in the Servian language were allowed to be sold, we can only record 214 copies as the result of the depot sales for the year. Summing up the many difficulties and trials of his work, Mr. Sinas wrote last December in a very desponding tone, "We were better off under the old Turkish rule. Monastir is a decaying town: great numbers of Moslems, Jews, Bulgarians, and Greeks have left, or are leaving. The value of all property has decreased by one-half, and you may now understand that the former importance of Monastir has gone for ever."

The Colporteurs

Six colporteurs are on our list as having laboured more or less in this field during the year. Of these six, none has been able to do continuous work. Two of the men, whose field is now Servian territory, have not been allowed to travel; Stanko in Prishtina, and Stoykoff in Monastir, have been detained in these places, idly and fruitlessly, since the Servian occupation. Of the two colporteurs in Albania, one, Visso, has spent many months in prison, in exile, and in fruitlessly demanding a passport to enable him to travel. Elias, who was allowed to come to Constantinople to visit his family, was unable for many months to return to his field. The two colporteurs in South Albania were harried and escorted back to their homes by the Greek police, and the Scriptures they had sold were demanded back by the police, and eventually returned to them. Under these circumstances the united sales of the colporteurs—2,907 copies—are probably as much as could be reasonably expected in such a trying and difficult year.

War Distribution

To the Turkish, Greek, and Servian soldiers 2,573 copies of the Scriptures have been freely distributed from the Monastir depot during the war. These books, once given, have passed out of our cognisance: they are as the seed which the Sower went forth to sow, and the harvest is only known to God.

Prospects

Monastir has hitherto been the centre of our work for Albania and Macedonia, from the Adriatic to the frontiers of Bulgaria. Our depot is there, from which our colporteurs draw their supplies: the Albanian Press is in Monastir, where our new editions of the Albanian Scriptures are being printed and bound under the supervision of Mr. Sinas our depositary. Albanian, Turkish, and Bulgarian versions have hitherto formed the bulk of our issues from the depot. Since the Servian occupation we have been forbidden to circulate the Scriptures in these languages, and our colporteurs in the new Servian territories have been refused permission to travel about the country. Whether these harsh measures will continue to be enforced and maintained it is impossible to say, but our efforts to obtain a relaxation of them have hitherto been without effect. It would be fatal to our work and our aims to have to confine our operations to the circulation of Servian editions alone. For the present we can only wait upon events, and hope and pray for better days. Mr. Sinas, writing at the close of the year, sums up the position and prospects for us in words we can well make our own. "The difficulties are terrible, but God is Almighty, and He will open to us a wide field for our work. If God be with us, who can be against us? The Divine Word will not be held down by men. Let us continue to labour, and God will bless our work and workers."

A Colporteur in Albania

From the only colporteur, Athanase Visso, who has remained in Albania during the troubled year under review, we have a long and graphic report. A brief extract may be given to illustrate the dangers and difficulties that beset him. Kortcha (Koritza), where his home is, was occupied by the Greek troops, and the police authorities at once forbade him to sell Albanian Scriptures, and pressure was brought upon him to withdraw from the service of the Society. "At last," he writes, "they found their opportunity." This occurred when some friends asked him to send Albanian Scriptures to Avlona. A police spy seized the books, and Visso and his friends were arrested. "They put us in chains, bound us with cords, marched us through the streets, and sent us under escort to Salonika, where they thrust us into a miserable prison, and kept us there seventeen days. We were not allowed to see our advocate, and we were not examined. They then put us on board a steamer, three Albanians and fourteen Bulgarians, under the charge of two policemen, with orders to land us in Crete." On arrival at Crete, they heard such terrible reports of the treatment of exiled prisoners that they refused to land. The captain of their steamer, an Austrian Lloyd boat, stood by them, and refused to allow the police authorities to take them off. He seemed to have been convinced that their lives were in danger, and he offered to land them at Avlona, in Albania, if they paid their passages. "So we landed in Avlona, where we received a great welcome. A banquet was given to us in the Town Hall, at which many speeches were made by our Albanian hosts in praise of the Bible Society's work in Albania."

During Visso's enforced absence from Kortcha, 30 Greek soldiers were quartered in his little house. News reached him that his mother died suddenly during that time, and a letter from another source says, "All the men suppose and believe that his mother was killed by the Greek soldiers in the house, and all his household goods plundered." Since the departure of the Greek troops Visso has returned to Kortcha and his desolated home, after a detention of three months in Monastir by the Servian authorities.

Such are the trials of a colporteur's life, which, for all we do, can neither be alleviated nor prevented. And Visso's case is only one among thousands of other victims of this fratricidal strife, which, in some at least of the forces engaged in it, has disgraced the sacred name of Christianity.

Page 445
Editorial Report (Albanian)

Editions of the N.T. and of Proverbs have been issued. Genesis is now ready, and a beginning has been made with the printing of Exodus. The member of the Revision Committee who died in 1913 was Mr. [George] Kyrias— not Mr. A. Sinas, who is still engaged upon this important work.

111th Report, 1915

Page 7
Bible-women

Besides its colporteurs, the Society maintains nearly 500 native Christian Bible-women, mainly employed in connection with missions in Eastern lands.

Page 11

Since its foundation in 1804 the Bible Society has issued over 263,000,000 copies of the Scriptures. Of these, more than 90,000 have been in English.

Page 122
Printing, Publishing and Revision

In Monastir, at the Albanian Press: *Albanian* editions—
– Exodus, 16mo, 4,000 copies;
– Deuteronomy, 16mo, 5,000 copies;
– Job, 16mo, 5,000 copies;
– Ecclesiastes, 16mo, 5,000 copies;
– Four Gospels, 16mo, 2,000 copies.

The Albanian revision and translation have been going steadily on at Monastir under the capable supervision of Mr. Sinas, our depositary in that town. Previous translations have been carefully revised, and of the books of the Bible of which no translations existed, translations have now been made. Besides the books already printed, some of the prophetical books are ready for the press. Printing operations, however, have been stopped by the lack of paper and other materials, for which we must wait until peace is restored and communications re-opened.

Page 123
Circulation by Languages

Albanian has a total of 1,742 copies, mainly in the new revisions and translations of separate books of the Bible now being printed.

Pages 127–128
Albania and Macedonia
Circulation 2,678 copies, against 3,121 in 1913, and 4,018 in 1912.

For the part of the agency which has always hitherto come under the above designation it would be difficult for the present time to find a sufficiently distinctive name corresponding to political boundaries. Part of the field is now Serbian territory, and another part is Greek territory, or is either claimed or occupied by that kingdom; and the remainder is a kind of No-man's Land, of which it would be difficult to say what the government is, or even whether any government exists. Our field of Bible work covers the same regions as before the Balkan war; but the population is shifting and unsettled, chafing under changes of government and administration, and under the burden of military exactions, impoverished and discontented. In many extensive regions, such as a large part of Albania, the inhabitants are without any reasonable security for life and property, and have no prospect, at present, of any better lot. In this part of the agency Moslems have always been our best purchasers of the Scriptures.

Depot and the Colporteurs

The depot at Monastir, in Serbian territory, remains under the charge of Mr. Sinas, who has filled a difficult post with his usual prudence and ability. Communications with Constantinople ceased during the later months of 1914, and only by indirect means has it been possible to keep in touch with Mr. Sinas and the colporteurs, and to make provision for their needs. Mr. Sinas laments that the sales of Scriptures are "almost nil"; at the depot the sales for the year only reached 194 copies. The five colporteurs working under this depot, one of whom has only eight months' work in the year, have sold 2,484 copies of the Scriptures, mainly in Albanian, in which language, as mentioned above, there has been a circulation of 1,742 copies.

Colporteur Zarifzappas, after some months' devious and difficult wanderings through the disturbed regions of Albania, finally reached Skodra (Skutari) towards the end of the year, where for some time he was laid up with a bad fever brought on by his privations. He was heard from via Italy, by which route it has been possible to communicate with him through the kindness of Mr. Summa, the British Vice-Consul at Skutari. His sales for the year amounted to 1,137 copies.

Colporteur Visso was compelled to fly from his home at Kortcha early in August, being driven out with most of the Albanian population, by what he described as "the Greek terror." He and his wife travelled on foot to Durazzo, and both immediately fell ill; but were kindly ministered to by some of our friends in that town. On recovery, Visso being afraid, apparently, to stay in Durazzo, where continual fighting was going on, left that town and went to Bucharest. There he has remained ever since, having thus only eight months' service to his record for the year. His sales amounted to 316 copies.

Colporteur Mladenovitch, who has remained throughout the year in his district, the headquarters of which is Mitrovitza, in Serbian territory, had sales of 469 copies.

Colporteur Stoykoff, who is stationed at Monastir, continued at work throughout the year, with sales of 312 copies.

In South Albania Colporteur Vasilion, who remained at Janina in Greek territory, had a circulation of 250 copies.

The colporteurs dwell on the difficulties and hardships of their work which, no doubt, have been many and severe. Some of them have shown courage and endurance worthy of all praise, and out of the five men only one has left his sphere of duty from feelings of fear and discouragement. Their devotion to duty is nourished from the secret springs of faith in God and in His protecting arm: they know that their work is His work, and they have learned that in the service of the Bible Society the faithful endeavour to do their duty will not fail of support and acknowledgment.

112th Report, 1916

Page 104

Albania and Macedonia

Circulation (nine months), 1,394 copies, against 2,678 in 1914, and 3,121 in 1913.

From Albania we have received returns for nine months only. In that period the circulation of the Scriptures has amounted to 1,394 copies, against 2,678 in 1914. Three colporteurs have been more or less at work during the year, and secured the sale of 1,270 copies. Of these three men, Colporteur Elias has been detained in the town of Skodra (Scutari) for some six months, unable to travel and waiting for an opportunity to leave for a less restricted field of labour. His sales for the nine months for which we have returns have been 549 copies, mainly in Albanian. At Monastir, where Mr. Sinas has remained in the faithful discharge of his duties, the depot sales were 124 copies. In this field, as elsewhere, difficulties of communication have greatly hampered our work, and our little staff of Bible-sellers, who have bravely stuck to their posts and carried on their labours, deserve a word of praise for their fidelity and courage.

Up to the present date we have distributed about 200 copies of the Scriptures, through the courtesy of the authorities, among prisoners of war at Monastir and in the interior.

113th Report, 1917

Introductory note about the war:

The difficulties by which we have been confronted have only increased our determination to surmount them. ... Suddenly the familiar pattern of our world has grown obsolete ... Though the axis of the earth may seem to have shifted, the Bible points to the same changeless pole-star of righteousness and peace and joy. And this star shines not for us only, but for all the scattered and sorrowful children of God.

The paragraphs which follow set forth a brief summary of how the Bible Society has fulfilled its mission during the most tragic year we have ever known.

Page 84

From our Monastir depot we have sold by colportage 883 copies, at the depots 612 copies—a total (including 342 copies as grants) of 1,837 copies.

At Monastir the Society has for many years past maintained a depot from which our colporteurs in Macedonia and Albania have drawn supplies of books which they sold. Letters reached London at the end of May, 1917, from our depositary, Mr. Athanase Sinas, who gives a vivid picture of the ordeal through which he is passing:

> Since five months our town is increasingly bombarded by the enemies, and always we are in danger of being killed. We live in the cellars, and there also without many hopes of safety. The losses are enormous and terrible; but as for us, glory to God, till this moment we are alive and in health and the depot is safe.

> With the Serbians, thanks to God, we have bread enough, and the poor are fed by the Government, gratis; but all other victuals and things necessary for life either are missing or very dear—at least ten times dearer than in normal times. Indeed, our actual life is intolerable—but God is merciful, and we hope for better days as soon as possible.

> Since six months I have no letter from the Rev. T. R. Hodgson, and it is impossible for me to write to him. And from our colporteurs—one who was in Elbassan, Albania, and another who is in Prishtina—since six

months I have no news, and I do not know how and where they are, and what they are doing.

For the present, selling the Scriptures is impossible; the market is destroyed, the streets are deserted, and communication with the environs interrupted for the bombardment.

I am here with Colporteur Stoykoff and our families. His house has been destroyed by the shells, and now he is living in the American Mission school. We are in most terrible danger. May our God send a right peace as soon as possible."

114th Report, 1918

Pages 52–53
Turkey including Albania and Bulgaria

When Turkey entered into the war early in 1915, direct communication with Constantinople was interrupted. Our veteran secretary in that city, the Rev. T. R. Hodgson, courageously resolved to remain at his post....

We cannot wonder that Mr. Hodgson should warn us that his stocks of books in languages, editions of which are usually imported from abroad, are getting dangerously small. He is able to obtain a sufficient supply of editions of the Scriptures which are printed in Constantinople; but his stock of these is kept low.

Monastir

The Bible Society has for many years maintained a depot at Monastir, from which our colporteurs in Macedonia and Albania have drawn supplies of the books which they sold. Letters have reached London intermittently from our depositary, Mr. Athanase Sinas.

Writing from Monastir in May 1917, Mr. Sinas describes the terrible bombardment which had then gone on, uninterruptedly, for nearly seven months, until the town was half-destroyed and abandoned by the greater part of its inhabitants. His wife and daughter had suffered so much in health that he was compelled to remove them to Vodena. Though numberless shells had fallen round the Bible Society's depot, killing many persons, the depot itself was still safe.

Writing from Vodena on Dec. 28th, 1917, Mr. Sinas reported that in Monastir conditions remained unaltered. The people were all living in their cellars, but the Society's depot was still untouched.

115th Report, 1919

Pages 71–73
Turkey including Albania and Bulgaria

For the four years, 1915–1918, the circulation is here given for the agency at Constantinople. But it must be understood we have complete returns for the entire agency in 1915 only. In the three following years no returns are given of the circulation in Greece, Macedonia, Albania, the Greek Islands, and Asia Minor, from which parts of the agency we have been totally cut off by the war. ...

From Albania word comes that although much of the town of Monastir has been destroyed during months of bombardment, our depot there has escaped serious injury.

116th Report, 1920

Page 61
Monastir and Albania
Colportage sales in 1919 from Monastir, 5,440 copies.

As yet, we have not received from Mr. Sinas his long-promised report of the work in this region. The Scriptures were sold last year under great difficulties. The Serbian Government forbids the sale of editions in any but the Serbian language; and as only the officials in Monastir are Serbian, it may be imagined how difficult our position is. The bulk of the population speak Bulgarian, although most of them are now reckoned as Serbian subjects; but we cannot give them the book they want in the only language they understand.

Mr. Sinas hopes to take a three months' journey this spring into Albania to explore the conditions and prospects there. He is an Albanian himself, and longs for his countrymen's conversion to Christ.

An article by the Rev. T. R. Hodgson on "Albania and the Bible Society" appeared in *The Bible in the World* for November, 1919.

117th Report, 1921

Page 69
Albania

The region known as Albania was made up of the Turkish Provinces of Scutari and Yanina, and of the parts of the vilayets of Kossovo and Monastir, which bordered upon those Provinces. The Albanians are divided into two principal groups—the Ghegs, who live in the north, and the Tosks, who live in the south.

Depositary: Mr. Athanase Sinas; Depot at Korytza.

From the depot at Monastir (now removed to Korytza) our sales last year amounted to 152 copies, besides 3,675 copies (returns incomplete) sold by colportage.

One most painful result of the great war has been the way in which in certain countries our Society lost sight of some of its colporteurs. In Albania a Greek Christian colporteur named Elias Zarifzappas had been employed by our Society since 1910. During the war, however, he dropped entirely out of sight. Happily, towards the end of 1920, he was rediscovered. We learn that, after the Austrians entered Albania in the early months of 1916, they came upon Zarifzappas with his books, and threw him into prison as a dangerous character, "for he was in the employ of a British Society." After a time he was taken out of prison and compelled to do forced labour for many months, by way of further penalty for "having been in the service of a British Society." Depositary Sinas writes: "His adventures have been terrible, indescribable, and I am astonished that he is actually alive." Zarifzappas fell ill, as his nerves had suffered greatly, and for several months he found shelter at the Greek Convent of St. John, near Elbasan.

Sinas wrote again on Dec. 30th, 1920: "At Kortcha [or Korytza] I met Elias Zarifzappas. He was weak enough for want of food, without money, and almost naked. Through his calamities and endurance Elias has gained a great influence among the Albanian people, both as a national and Christian martyr. Their sympathy and love towards him were shown by their lending him money that he might not die from hunger and cold." Elias is our best and most expert colporteur in Albania. Early in 1921 he recommenced his work.

"The Serbian people regard the Albanians as an awful thorn in their side. Indeed, Albania has been described as Serbia's Ireland." There are, of course, a good many Albanian tribesmen inside the Serbian borders. In the region of Kossovo, for instance, around which Serbian song and legend centre, Colporteur Stanko Mladenovitch, who has his headquarters at Pristina, is in frequent contact with Albanians, though, seeing that he is a Serb, he finds it difficult to gain any entry among them.

Monastir, too—also in Serbian territory—lies close to our Albanian fields of work. It, was, indeed, from Monastir that our depositary, Athanase Sinas, himself an Albanian, has for long made his expeditions into the wilds of his native land. He and Zarifzappas are our witnesses among the Albanian people.

The disturbed state of South-eastern Europe is reflected in the experiences of Sinas last summer, when he left Monastir and set out to take supplies of Scriptures into Albania. What followed was described in *The Bible in the World* for March, 1921.

Page 279

The American Bible Society has published a diglot edition of St. Mark in Albanian and English, the Albanian text being reproduced from the B.F.B.S. edition.

118th Report, 1922

Pages 87–88
Albania

The Albanians are divided into two principal groups—the Ghegs, who live in the north, and the Tosks, who live in the south. Estimated population about 1,000,000, two-thirds being

Moslems and the remainder either Greek Orthodox or Roman Catholic Christians. The adherents of the Orthodox: Church are found mostly in the south, and the Roman Catholics in the north.

Secretary: Mr. J. W. Wiles (Belgrade)

Assistant Secretary: Mr. A. L. Haig, (Pera, Constantinople)

Depositary: Mr. Athanase Sinas, Bible Depot, Korytza (Kortcha).

Circulation, 2,616 copies, as compared with 3,827 copies in 1920.

Albania is a wild and mountainous region, without railways and mostly without roads, peopled by a hardy, turbulent, yet hospitable and in some ways attractive race. Our Society first published the New Testament in Albanian in 1824, and has since translated and sent out most of the Old Testament books. Today the B.F.B.S. is preparing to print the whole Bible, which has at length been completely translated and revised. In April, 1921, the Albanian Minister of Education sent an appreciative letter to the Society, asking for a new edition of the separate Albanian Gospels for use in schools, and offering the help of a literary committee attached to the Ministry of Education in preparing the MS. in 'national' character. The Albanian Government has recently granted our Society permission to import all its editions duty-free into Albania.

Last year our depot was transferred from Monastir (which has been Serbian territory since the Armistice, and no longer serves as a centre for Albanian work) to Korytza, or Kortcha, a town of over 20,000 inhabitants in Southern Albania. Owing to official hindrances and inertia this transference took nearly six months to effect, and it was not until the autumn that our depositary, after a narrow escape from drowning in the Lake of Ochrida, stepped on to Albanian soil with his books.

As one consequence of the war the famous town of Monastir, which used to be a kind of Mecca as well as an emporium for Macedonia, has suffered a fundamental change. It has lost its "hinterland," has been half-destroyed by repeated bombardments, and has become a provincial town of Yugo-Slavia where the local Serbian officials are very jealous of the distribution of any editions of Scriptures not in the Serbian tongue. Since its depot was removed from Monastir the Society maintains in that district a colporteur—Naum Stoykovitch—who may best be described as a "Macedonian" Christian. Amid people who have been literally torn to pieces by racial and political strife, Stoykovitch—shrewd old saint that he is—holds his head serenely high in his difficult sphere of operations, seeking to minister to all alike the healing message of the Gospel of Christ.

Our depositary, Athanase Sinas, reports that many Albanians who had emigrated to America and are now back in their own country, have begun to realise the value of the Bible in forming not only individual but national character. Indeed, he says, a great new ferment has begun to appear everywhere in Albania, and the Gospel would progress if there were just now a good Christian newspaper and some Christian literature in the vernacular. He laments the five centuries of oppression which his race suffered under the Turk. He regrets not less the frequent opposition of both the Greek Orthodox and Roman Catholic Churches. Of Albanians not more than 3 to 5 per cent. gain any education and knowledge of foreign languages; and for these their smattering of Western education proves often only a snare. "But, glory to God! The Bible Society has set down in our language the Gospel. The Albanian people need the written message; indeed, the written message is above all necessary in a wild country like ours, where you cannot gather big congregations for preaching. The printed page can penetrate everywhere, into every house, while preaching can be only in a town and to men who already have some interest in the Gospel."

Colporteur Stoykovitch sold 871 volumes in Albania between December 1, 1920, and August 31, 1921, when he was transferred to Serbia.

Colporteur Elias Zarifzappas, an Albanian, who has been sixteen years in the Society's service, works around Kortcha. Owing to the disorganised state of the country he went short of books for some time, but he distributed 1,026 copies during the year. During the war Zarifzappas suffered a good deal from enemy treatment—because he worked for a British Society—and what he thus endured has increased his influence among his own people.

Page 308

Albanian: The draft translation of the Bible in Albanian, Tosk Dialect, prepared by Mr. A. Sinas, is now being examined with a view to publication.

119th Report, 1923

Pages 100–101
Albania

The region known as Albania includes what were the Turkish Provinces of Scutari and Yanina, with the parts of the vilayets of Kossovo and Monastir which bordered upon those Provinces.

The Albanians are divided into two principal groups—the Ghegs, who live in the north, and the Tosks, who live in the south.

Estimated population about 831,000, two-thirds being Moslems and the remainder either Greek Orthodox or Roman Catholic Christians. The adherents of the Orthodox Church are found mostly in the south, and the Roman Catholics in the north.

Circulation, 3,040 copies, as compared with 2,616 copies in 1921, and 3,827 in 1920.

Depositary: Mr. Athanase Sinas, Bible Depot, Korytza (Kortcha).

At the initiation of the B.F.B.S. the Gospel of St. Matthew in Albanian was, for the first time, printed in 1824 by the Ionian Bible Society. In subsequent years the B.F.B.S. issued its own editions and distributed them.

The prospects of the Society's work continue to brighten in this country. An unheralded, but nevertheless very important, revolution has been effected in the Albanian Orthodox Church. In September last this Church was declared independent, and the ancient liturgy and services were translated into the language of the people. An Albanian can now worship God in his church in his own language. At the same time Albanian priests have taken the place of the Greek priests, and, in some cases at any rate, the Gospel is being faithfully preached and the reading of the Word of God encouraged. The Government has proved itself tolerant by decreeing that there is no state religion. This is interesting in view of the fact that two-thirds of the population are Moslems. The people, also, are generally more sympathetic to our work, and this is in part due to the influence of Albanians who emigrated to the United

States and have returned to their own country. These men bring back new ideas as to the Gospel and civilisation.

Colportage

We are glad to report an increased circulation of the Scriptures. Our only colporteur in this country, Elias Zarifzappas, worked the town and district of Kortcha for the first six months, and for the remainder of the year made Berat—a town in Central Albania—his headquarters. Very little effective opposition is met with, although Moslems are in the large majority. If we had the means, we could usefully employ more colporteurs.

Mr. Sinas relates the following incidents:

> One day I entered a coffee-house, where I found a Moslem whom I had known for many years. After the usual greetings, he began to talk about our Lord Jesus Christ and His Gospel. He had been a violent and bad man in his youth, but now in his old age he is different. He spoke respectfully about the teachings and parables of the Gospels and gave Jesus Christ the name 'Our Lord,' although when speaking of Mahommed he merely spoke of him as 'Mahommed.' The other Moslems present listened to him attentively. I then learned from him that he had bought a Turkish New Testament when he was at Constantinople.

> Some time ago I met a man in the street with a book under his arm. I asked him what it was. He showed it to me, and I found it was a New Testament, evidently well read, for it was much marked. The man said, 'I have had this book for many years, and it is my guide for the present life and also for the future and everlasting one.'

"Such examples," says Mr. Sinas, "show that the Holy Spirit is continually working through the Word of God and bringing men to repentance."

120th Report, 1924

Page 89
South-Eastern Europe

This Agency includes Yugoslavia, Rumania, Bulgaria, Turkey, Albania, Greece, and the Islands of the Aegean.

In South-Eastern Europe the year 1923 has, at the best, been one of the untranquil peace. There has been wide-spread disturbance with bloodshed in Bulgaria, and Greece has passed through yet another year of crisis. ... The territory covered by the Agency falls roughly into two halves, a northern and a southern. ... The southern half may be described as practically Graeco-Turk, with the trackless wilds of Albania in the background.

Page 93
Yugoslavia continues to be a place of polyglot demand. During the year 1923 the Scriptures have been circulated from the Belgrade Depot in the following tongues; Serbian (Cyrillic character), Serbo-Croatian (roman character), Slovene, Ancient Slav, Russian, Bohemian, Polish, Bulgarian, Rumanian, German, Hungarian, Ancient and Modern Greek, Latin, Hebrew, Albanian, English, French, Italian ..."

Pages 105–106

Albania

Circulation last year, 2,997 copies, as compared with 3,040 copies in 1922, and 2,616 in 1921.

Depositary: Mr. Athanase Sinas, Bible Depot, Korytza (Kortcha).

This is the first year of the independent Albanian Orthodox Church, which now embraces rather more than 160,000 members. There are now Bishops for Kortcha, Berat, and Durazzo, and in the near future there will be another for Argyrocastro in the south. These bishops, by the Church law, must be Albanians, and there are few men who can fill these positions. The Church services are conducted in the language of the people. Christophoros, Bishop of Berat, told his congregation that God has blessed the English Churches and nation "because they work according to the Gospel and its teachings." As an ardent patriot he desires similar blessings for his people. Fan Noli, Bishop of Durazzo, remembered in England for his able defence of the Albanian claims before the League of Nations, is a very erudite man. On the day he was ordained he preached from Matthew xvi. 24, "If any man will come after Me, let him deny himself and take up his cross and follow Me." The sermon lasted two hours, and the whole congregation listened with wrapt attention, none leaving till the service was finished. The Albanian nation expects great things from this man.

In spite of frequent sickness and fever, Elias Zarifzappas, the only colporteur in this country, has slightly increased his sales. During the greater part of the year he worked in the central districts, and from September concentrated his efforts on Tirana, the capital, a town of 12,000 inhabitants, situated in the north.

Mr. Sinas, says; "One day I had a long talk with a high functionary, a Muhammadan, to whom I had sold a copy of the New Testament. He is an admirer of Paul the Apostle. He said to me, 'I am full of sorrow and astonishment that there are many so-called Christians as well as the Muhammadans, who persecute the readers of your books. They ought to do their best for its distribution among the people. There is no better book for the education and improvement of mankind.'"

On another occasion Mr. Sinas read to an Orthodox churchman the Ten Commandments from the Book of Exodus. He was much touched on hearing them, and with joy he bought six copies of the Scriptures and said, "I will cause my children to read me a portion of these books every evening."

Page 111
Near the Albanian Frontier

Colporteur Vasiliou is carrying on his work at Yannina, and he is the only worker who has been continually occupying the same field for the last twenty-eight years. He has canvassed the cafés, shops, offices, and many houses, with fair results. His sales were, 73 Bibles, 248 Testaments, and 899 portions—1,220 copies in all—or 215 copies less than in 1922.

Page Appendix 9
Colportage Statistics

Colporteur Elias Zarifzappas has served in Albania for 13 years and for the year worked 52 weeks and sold 6 Bibles, 44 Testaments, and 2,134 portions.

121st Report, 1925

Page 2

The languages now number 572 in which our Society has helped to produce or circulate the Scriptures. The list is made up of 138 Bibles, 138 New Testaments, and 296 portions. By "portions" is meant not extracts, or anthologies, but complete books of Scripture. In 1915 the number was 487: so that during the last ten years the Society has published the Gospel in one fresh language on an average every six weeks.

Page 95
In Old Serbia and Macedonia

On the famous plain of Kosovo, where the Turks fought their desperate battle with the Serbian forces under King Lazar in the summer of 1389, our old pensioner, Stanko Mladenovitch, is still at work. The population is sparse, and the neighbourhood wild, but the old man holds out a light in a dark place. It is a Muhammadan district, but he has sold 471 copies during the year.

In the city of Monastir, which has never recovered from the awful bombardments and prolonged agonies of the war, another old pensioner, Nahum Stoikovitch, still works,. He writes: "I am thankful to God that He keeps me still alive and able to serve Him by distributing His Word. I have sold 616 copies during the year."

Pages 108–110
Albania

Circulation last year, 2,137 copies, as compared with 2,997 copies in 1923, and 3,040 in 1922.

Depository: Mr. Athanase Sinas, Bible Depot, Korytza (Kortcha).

Of Albania, Gibbon remarks that a country "within sight of Italy is less known than the interior of America," and that remark even now calls for little qualification. When "Childe Harold" threaded his way amid manifold perils from Yanina to Argyrocastro more than a century ago, to sing of the Arnaouts, or Albanese, "Fierce are Albania's children, yet they lack not virtues," it was not without some regrets and real affection that he bade farewell to that "rugged nurse of savage men." It was also Lord Byron who described, in prose, how the Albanians were dreaded by their neighbours. "The Greeks," wrote Byron, "hardly regard them as Christians, or the Turks as Moslems; and, in fact, they are a mixture of both, and sometimes neither. Their habits are predatory; all are armed." The lapse of one hundred years and more has not availed to put the report of the poet-wanderer out of date. Whether in individual and family, or in tribal and national life, unrest, surprise, uncertainty, upheaval still continue to be dominant features of Albanian history. Nor has even the past year passed without its revolutions; indeed, the Albanian is not more disturbed by a revolution than is the West European by a General Election.

Events of the Year

Early in the summer of 1924 the Government of Elias Bey Vrioni fled precipitately to the coast, and escaped abroad, before the forces of Archbishop Fan Noli. But within six months Ahmed Bay Zogou was engineering a counter-revolution, and without meeting any resistance worth mentioning, he successfully established himself in Tirana. Whereupon Mgr. Fan Noli, the late Prime

Minister, emulating the discretion of his predecessor, fled by way of Valona to Italy.

Circulation

The troubled state of affairs during 1924 has had a very prejudicial effect on Bible-work in the country. Moreover, our one and only colporteur, Elias Zarifzappas, suffered from illness during the early months of the year; and, as he is now well past sixty years of age, it has been impossible for him to cover more than a small area of North-Western Albania. The circulation shows, under the circumstances, a surprisingly small decrease of only 860 volumes.

The Depositary

Mr. Sinas, who was for many years depositary for the Bible Society in Monastir – before that Mecca of Macedonia became incorporated in the Kingdom of the Serbs, Croats, and Slovenes—took up quarters in Kortcha after the war. He has now brought to completion his translation of the Bible into Albanian. His work is being subjected to a final revision, and it is hoped that is may be sent to the press with the dawn of 1926. If this shall be the case, a long cherished hope of the Albanian people will then be realised – and how much would that not mean to a race which possesses so little literature!

Mr. Wiseman's Tour

In the Autumn of 1924 Mr. Wiseman, the assistant secretary, made a journey from the Macedonian frontier by way of Argyrocastro to the Adriatic coast. There are no railways, of course, but petrol and the motor engine have penetrated even to the wildest passes of the Albanian mountains. To get a place in a solid-tyre motor lorry one has to rely upon the merchants who charter the vehicles for the transport of goods from town to town. If you are so fortunate as to get a front seat by the driver, amid the dust, the steam, the jolting and jiggetting and the spurtings of dirty oil, you enjoy first-class travel. If not, you will sit or crouch upon a short plank, a box, a bundle, a barrel, a roll of leather, or anything else that can serve the purpose of a seat, and wedging yourself into a corner, you hang on tight – thinking not too much of the precipices down which a few months before (or it may be only days) a whole lorry went hundreds of feet to destruction. The roads are bad; happy he who does not also find them slippery through rain. The drivers are splendid; always very young men with no nerves. Crossing fifteen mountain ridges along by majestic chasms, plunging upward, downward, roundward, in inky darkness, punctuated only by the zig-zag lightning flash and in silence broken only by the reverberating thunder, one realises that some pats of the work of a Bible Society Agent are not "mere book distribution."

122nd Report, 1926

Page 106

Albania

Mr. Athanase Sinas, who, having reached his sixty-sixth year, retired from the Bible Society's service on March 1st, 1925, was seized with a stroke a fortnight later, and has been confined to his bed since then. He had completed twenty-five years of valiant service.

Colporteur Zarifzappas was to have retired on February 28th, 1925. No news has been received of him. It has been found impossible to appoint successors to these workers.

Since no figures are forthcoming, we are unable to say what the circulation, if any, has been.

123rd Report, 1927

Pages 108–109

Albania

It is with great thankfulness that we record an improvement in the condition of our ex-depositary for Albania, Mr. Athanase Sinas, who, having reached his sixty-sixth year, retired from the Bible Society's service on March 1st, 1925, and was immediately afterwards afflicted with a stroke which caused much apprehension to all his friends in Korytza, where he had charge of many thousands of copies of the Scriptures in the Albanian language. These books lay very near to his heart, for he had taken the keenest personal interest in the production of many of them; had done much valuable revision work, and was engaged at the time of his illness in the completion of the translation of certain portions of the Old Testament which have not as yet been published in Albanian. We gratefully record the steadfast interest which has been shown by the relatives of Mr. Sinas in the work of the Society during the last two years, throughout a perplexing and trying time. Special thanks should be rendered in this connexion to the son-in-law and the daughter of Mr. Sinas, namely Mr. and Mrs. L. Kristo, who have teaching posts in the Lycee at Korytza; and also to the Rev. and Mrs. Phineas B. Kennedy, of the mission school, Korytza, who, since the American Board has been obliged to retire from Albania, and no other Mission Board is as yet ready to take over the work, have been doing right noble service in the Tosk districts of Albania.

A successor to Athanase Sinas has yet to be found; meanwhile Mr. L. Kristo is kindly acting as depositary for the time being. He has taken charge of the stocks in Korytza, and is seeing through the press a revised edition of the Albanian Psalms. It is worthy of note that this new edition of the Psalms is being printed inside the Albanian Republic.

If the position of depositary in Albania calls for a man who has really heard the voice of God summoning him to such a work, so also does the vocation of colporteur in this wild and rugged land. Colporteur Zarifzappas, who was to have retired on Feb. 28th, 1925, has vanished no one knows where. No news had been received of him by Feb. 28th, 1927, when this report was written, nor was there up to that date any suitable man upon the field who was willing to come forward as his successor. There is no country in the whole of South-East European Agency where the toils of colportage partake less of mere bookselling than they do in Albania.

It is owing to the conditions above described that we are unable to publish a table of circulation for this country, though we know that, since Mr. Sinas was taken ill, 122 Testaments and 350 portions of Scripture have been supplied from the store in Korytza, and 82 Testaments and portions have been asked for outside of Albania.

Mr. J.W. Wiles, who visited the country at the end of the year, wrote on Dec. 7th, 1926: "Though the Albanian people do not yet possess the whole Bible in a convenient form, the Bible Society has provided them with a fine New Testament, and with a good proportion of the Old in small and handy booklets. Bearing in mind the wild character of the country and primitive life of its mountaineers, the British and Foreign Bible Society – as Father Vasil Marko, the President of the High Ecclesiastical (Orthodox) Council, remarked to me in Korytza only a few days ago – has kept well ahead of the reading capacities of the Albanian tribes."

It has also to be remembered that many Albanians can read without much difficulty the Greek, the Serbian, or the Italian Scriptures, and in not a few cases even the English, French, or German Bible. Until some real hero of a colporteur is raised up, the fanatical northern districts may for all practical purposes be ruled out of the reckoning from the point of view of systematic distribution.

Page 111
Greece

The Scriptures have been circulated in thirty-three different languages, the chief of which have been: Modern Greek, 35,003; Ancient Greek, 13,601; Graeco-Turkish, 1,662; Hebrew, 848; Judaeo-Spanish, 772; Armenian, 716; French, 434; English, 270; Ancient Greek with Modern, 254; Armeno-Turkish, 223; Turkish, 53; Syriac, 51; Albanian, 45.

124th Report, 1928

Page 96
The Strength of Islam in the South-East European Agency

Apart from the Turkish Republic, which as a result of the very strict and careful census taken during the autumn of 1927 was reported to have a population of 13,650,000 souls, the strength of Islam in South East Europe has been made out as follows:

Albania	560,000 Moslems
Bulgaria	750,000 Moslems
Greece	180,000 Moslems
Yugoslavia	1,337,687 Moslems
Rumania	250,000 Moslems

Page 97

The Colporteurs

Bible Society colporteurs come into contact with the focal points of Moslem life just enumerated, and a public tribute has been paid to their patient work by that most indefatigable and faithful evangelist amongst Moslems, Dr. S. M. Zwemer. At Tirana, the capital of Albania, 75 per cent of the inhabitants are Muhammadan, and there are thirty-four mosques in the fanatical town of Elbasan— far away from Western influences behind its bastions of mighty mountains, as one gradually approaches it from Korytza, where is the Society's depot for Albania. Yet it was amid the mosques of Elbasan on a dismal drenching autumn day the Colporteur Pandeli Sinas was discovered by our Secretary for South-East Europe – getting wet to the skin. Trudging from village to village with books in these parts is no pastime.

Page 98

Visit of Dr. Zwemer

During the early summer of 1927 Dr. S. M. Zwemer paid a visit to Yugoslavia, where there are nearly twice as many Moslems as in European Turkey, inclusive of Constantinople. Dr. Zwemer visited the Moslem section of the Ministry of Religion in Belgrade, had long conversations with distinguished people there on two district occasions, and was throughout treated with the greatest courtesy by the head of the department, Mr. Hasan M. Rebac.

Pages 101–102
In Macedonia and Old Serbia

Our two old pensioners, Nahum Stoikovitch in Monastir, and Stanko Mladenovitch in Old Serbia, near the Albanian border, write of their great joy in being allowed to serve God in old age. The two old men have made many journeys, and judging from the testimony of those who have met them, one can only conclude that the Scriptures they have spread, seasoned with some salt of wisdom gained through long years in war-ridden parts, have been a joy and blessing to many. Mladenovitch writes how in the ancient city of Petch (full of stirring associations for every Serbian soul) he was welcomed by old friends, who were delighted to see him alive and hale and still carrying his wallet of Scriptures. It is in regions such as these that the colporteur exercises a real "cure of souls" ...

From the Belgrade Depot there went forth: *Serbian,* 17,505 copies; *Croatian,* 4,790, *German,* 3,297 ... Wandering Albanians took 12 portions and 3 New Testaments.

Page 116
From Vodena to Florina – and towards Albania

Colporteur Mistakides has had the requisite faith, hope, and love, as well as the necessary physical energy and stamina, to visit all the principal villages of his extensive field, with splendid results. His headquarters are at Vodena. He goes out towards Florina and the Albanian frontier on the one side, and down towards Salonica on the other.

Pages 117–118
Albania

The Society's circulation last year in Albania was 466 copies, against 472 in 1926.

Acting Depositary: Professor Loni Kristo, Korytza (or Kortcha), S.Albania.

Introduction

Professor Loni Kristo has kindly acted as depositary in Korytza throughout the year. He has a plentiful store of Scriptures, but 'depot sales,' in the ordinary sense of that term, are practically nil, and it was only in August, 1927, that the Society, after much seeking, found a man of the necessary physique, experience, and character to undertake the arduous work of colportage in the Republic of Albania – which presents a vast complex of mountains without any railways whatsoever.

Colportage

The volunteer for this work is Mr. Pandeli Sinas, a son of Mr. Athanase Sinas of Kortcha, the Society's former depositary for Albania, who is now close on seventy years of age, and is suffering from the effects of a stroke. Mr. Sinas, junior, who is thirty-five years of age, has renounced his position as teacher in a village school to do this work of colportage in his native land. Our Secretary of South-East Europe visited him in October, 1927, and found him under drenching rains and amid swollen mountain torrents. He had just reached the "out and out," not to say fanatical, Moslem town of Elbasan, famous for its cream-

coloured felt fezzes. The decrees of Mustapha Kemal
Pasha, the "Grand Gazi" of the Republic of Turkey, have
caused some Moslems in adjacent lands to do some hard
thinking, and the puzzle in most places now is to find a
fez whose wearer is not feeling a little diffident about it!
But in Elbasan the puzzle still is to find an ordinary hat
whose wearer is not half-ashamed of it. The Serbians
on the Albanian borders often like to tell one that *svaki
pochetak yé tezhak* (all beginnings are difficult), and most
Albanians are ready to admit the same truth. Certainly
Mr. Pandeli Sinas has found it to be so in his country. He
had not been on his wanderings with pack and wallet
for many weeks before he was arrested and thrown into
prison. As many prominent people in Albania—including
at least one Muhammadan of education and influence—
have been particularly courteous and complimentary
on several occasions recently to representatives of the
British and Foreign Bible Society, Mr. Pandeli Sinas was
both pained and perplexed at this sudden contretemps.
But he maintained his good temper, and things eventually
came round all right. For one's comfort, in certain parts
of the Balkan Peninsula, it is well to bear in mind that a
man is generally assumed to be guilty until he can prove
himself innocent! The local gendarme does not like to be
suspected of "weakness." In this particular case, after a few
days many kind things were said about the Bible Society,
"which so nobly served our people and our literature
during the Ottoman reign," and the Ministry of Public
Instruction has now commended Colporteur Sinas to the
kindly protection of the Ministry of the Interior—which is
another way of saying that he is quite rehabilitated in the
eyes of the gendarmerie. All the same, such experiences
are not pleasant while they last, and sometimes they are

very damaging to one's health. "Endure hardness" is an exhortation always apropos in Albania. During these few weeks of work, and of interruptions, Colporteur Sinas has sold 2 Bibles, 15 Testaments, and 258 portions, amid a sparse and scattered population which is largely illiterate, often unsympathetic, and sometimes actively hostile.

New Edition of the Psalms

The Society has printed and issued through the Korytza depot a new edition of the Psalms in the Tosk dialect of Albanian, and it is hoped in the near future to print the Book of Leviticus separately; Albanians of the south and centre, not omitting Moslems, generally hail these Old Testament single books with real delight.

The Korytza Depot

Nineteen Testaments and 172 portions have been sold from the Kortcha Storeroom during the year 1927.

125th Report, 1929

Page 54

South-Eastern Europe

In view of all the racial and religious complexities which this Agency presents, to say nothing of the difficult and rugged character of so much of its terrain – making no small demand upon the devotion and the stamina of our colporteurs – it is a great satisfaction to be able to report that the circulation for 1928 exceeded that of the year 1927 by 5,084 copies. Marked increases are chronicled by Yugoslavia and Bulgaria, as well as by Albania and Turkey.

Page 63
Albania

The Society's circulation last year in Albania was 2,156 copies, against 466 in 1927.

Acting Depositary: Professor Loni Kristo, Korytza (or Kortcha), S. Albania.

The Republic of Albania has been made a Kingdom under the sovereignty of King Ahmed Zogu. But these changes up in the tree-tops do not much affect the ground below, and the problems of the colporteur amid his rugged and mighty mountains remain what they were. Owing to the labours of Mr. Pandeli Sinas, whose father is sometimes styled the Tyndale of Tosk Albania, during 1928 the circulation increased nearly fivefold.

126th Report, 1930

Page 67
In Macedonia

In Mr. Voislav Arsitch we have a recent addition to our staff. He began work in October, 1929, in Southern Serbia and Macedonia. He has been very active, and has already entered the prisons and hospitals in this part of the kingdom. Though he finds a desire for the Word of God, he regrets that nearly 85 per cent of the people in his area are illiterate, and finds this inability to read and write a great drawback in his work.

In Macedonia we have two old pensioners, both in the seventies, who cannot find it in them "to linger feebly or stay sick," as the Montenegrin Bishop said, but who must be up and doing to the best of their powers. Nahum Stoikovitch works in and around Monastir, now generally called Bitolj, which has over 40,000 inhabitants. He says: "I pray to God to spare me still for several years, for I have not yet finished my work for my Lord and Saviour." The second aged pensioner is Stanko Mladenovitch, who lives in Prishtina, hard by the famous Kossovo Field, concerning which some of the most striking and beautiful ballad-poetry in the world has been written. This aged servant writes: "This earthly body is weak, I wish I could do more, but I cannot go far, nor move about as I used to do thirty years ago."

Page 80–81

Albania

   The Society's circulation last year in Albania was 2,280 copies, against 2,156 in 1928.

   Acting Depositary: Professor Loni Kristo, Korytza (Kortcha), S. Albania.

   The Kingdom of Albania is the haunt of the eagle; indeed, that is the meaning of the name of the country in the vernacular, *Shqipria*. The reader of *Childe Harold's Pilgrimage* will remember Byron's picture of the wild Albanian with shawl-girt head and ornamental gun, and gold-embroidered garments fair to see: "fierce are Albania's children, yet they lack not virtues, were those virtues more mature." Albania, with her mighty mountain masses and labyrinthine gorges, will never be a land of railways. But modern progress has brought the motor-car, and you may reach the capital by aeroplane too. Education is increasing steadily, and there is a greater demand for the printed page than formerly. An Albanian Moslem in Tirana – who spoke French and German perfectly – asked the Society's Secretary for S.E. Europe if he would see that *Uncle Tom's Cabin* was translated into Albanian! During the past twelve months *The Story of Mary Jones* has been put into the vernacular by Prof. and Madame Loni Kristo, and at the time of going to press with this report a very handy Albanian New Testament is being given to Central and South Albania. The Orthodox Church has shown some official interest in the question of the completion of the translation into 'union Albanian' of the Old Testament, but such work progresses very slowly. Mr. Athanasius Sinas, however, has provided the whole of the groundwork for such a translation. Meanwhile, his son, Mr. Pandeli Sinas, who gave up the vocation of a schoolmaster in order to join the ranks of the Society, has laboured unremittingly with his wallet over hill and dale throughout the year. ... The figures for 1929 indicate a slight increase over those for the previous year.

127th Report, 1931

Pages 90–91

Albania

The Society's circulation last year in Albania was 1,841 copies, against 2,280 in 1929, and 2,156 in 1928.

Acting Depositary: Professor Loni Kristo, Korytza (Kortcha), S. Albania.

Agriculture is the principal occupation of the Albanians. The harvest of 1930 will be remembered as the worst for many a decade. The tillers of the soil who borrow money have to pay usury, 80 and 100 per cent in some cases; indeed, the Royal Government has taken special measures recently in order to protect the peasant-farmer.

The financial crisis in America has had its echo even in wild Albania, the land of the eagle, of mountain gorge and precipice; for many thousands of Albanians working in the United States have not been able to help their kinsfolk who have remain in *Shqipria*, as Albania is called by its own people. Two bad earthquakes have also caused great terror and distress.

Albania is notable as the land of no railways; but the Government has been working very hard at road construction. A sum of 40 million francs has been exhausted in the construction of over 1,000 kilometres of road and a number of large bridges.

Colportage

Mr. Pandeli Sinas, formerly a village schoolmaster, now the Society's representative as a colporteur, has been striving hard throughout the year to spread the Scriptures in his native land, and if one were to count in the number of copies of the new *Story of Mary Jones* in Tosk Albanian which he has so diligently circulated—and which the mountaineers have so much joy in perusing—it would be found that he had really done better than last year—especially in view of all the handicaps. Nearly 100,000 Roman Catholics inhabit the more northerly districts of Albania. They are a fine people, speaking the Gheg dialect, but fanatical and almost inaccessible to ordinary colportage.

The Rev. P. and Mrs. Kennedy carry on a patient, capable, and far-reaching educational work in Kortcha in Southern Albania, in which a real knowledge of Scripture is made an important item.

128th Report, 1932

Page 94
Near the Albanian Border

Colporteur Stoelides, whose seat of operations is at Jannina, spent the second half-year out in the Province of Arta and Preveza. It is gratifying to note that his sales for the year consisted of 84 Bibles, 549 New Testaments, and 2,884 portions – total 3,517 copies, 221 more than last year.

Pages 96–98
Albania

The Albanians are divided into two principal groups— the Ghegs, further subdivided into clans, who live in the north, and the Tosks, who live in the south.

The total population is about 1,003,000, according to the census of 1930, 68 per cent being Moslems, 21 per cent members of the National Albanian Orthodox Church, and 11 per cent. Roman Catholics, of whom nine-tenths inhabit the northern Gheg territory. The Moslems are found in the preponderating numbers, of course, wherever one goes, while the adherents of the Orthodox Church are found mostly in the south.

The Society's circulation last year in Albania was 1,472 copies against 1,841 in 1930, and 2,280 in 1929.

Acting Depositary: Professor Loni Kristo, Korytza (Kortcha), S Albania.

On the initiative of the B.F.B.S. the Gospel of St. Matthew in Albanian was, for the first time, printed in 1824 by the Ionian Bible Society. In subsequent years the B.F.B.S. issued its own editions and distributed them.

Introduction

Even Albania, which is as a strip of rugged Scotland placed along the sunlit waters of the Adriatic Sea – a land, moreover, whose strongly differentiated mountain folk are engaged for the most part in the primitive culture of the soul – even such a country has not escaped the consequences of the world depression. Remittances from emigrant Albanians who have been wont to assist parents or kindred in the home country have been few and far between in comparison with the years gone by, when things were going better with the world at large.

Changing Albania

Albania used to be notable as an impenetrable complex of glen and gorge and mountain. That old impenetrable area or mountain and precipice has gone – or rather it has been transformed; the bold peaks remain but they are now threaded by hundreds of miles of good road, which have been linked up by many good bridges. The mere scenery of man's life may quickly change without so quick and corresponding a change of psychology. But it is easy to see that the long motor-routes along which trundle big lorries, often fuller of human beings than commodities, and crowded omnibuses connecting village with village, are having their due effect in the modification of mentality. But mere physical "machinery" will not produce in Albania, any more than in Knightsbridge or Kensington, a deeper sense of God or a quickened desire for communion with Him, nor any intensified persuasion that He is a rewarder of those who diligently seek Him. Our Albanian colporteur, who was once a school-master, can now avail himself of the motor-omnibus; he finds, however, that spiritual positions still have to be spiritually attained, and that he is as dependent as ever upon the guidance of God in his excursions among men.

Peoples and Religions

Amongst the Gheg tribes of Northern Albania, who are all staunch adherents of the Roman Catholic Church, no Gheg colporteur has yet appeared – he would need the special vocation as much as any prophet of old – but the Roman Church circulates some special Scripture portions with annotations for the people. The Ghegs have their own dialect.

The main aggregation of Moslem life and interest is to be found in Central Albania, and the town of Elbasan, with its minarets and its lowly roofs and clusters of open, bazaar-like shops, whose owners sit cross-legged upon their counters and look out with keen eyes from under their characteristic 'white' Albanian fezzes upon a leisurely world not overburdened with any kind of book learning. You must go to Elbasan, this Mecca of Albania, before you can ever taste its atmosphere; it really has an atmosphere that can be not only felt but tasted. These Moslems of Central Albania do not speak Tosk, which is the dialect of the south, nor do they speak Gheg, which is as peculiar to the Northern tribes as Gaelic is to the remoter Scottish Highlands.

Now that the whole of modern Albania has been supplied with a 'nervous organisation' in the form of its network of roads for the passage of the motor-omnibus, there will doubtless appear more and more a tendency towards a 'Union Albanian' speech.

There does not yet exist a complete Bible in any Albanian form of speech. There is a good 'workable' New Testament, well printed and strongly bound, which finds acceptance more especially amongst the Tosk-Albanians, and many parts of the Old Testament are to be had in portions. It is an interesting fact that any Albanian who really wants to 'study' the Bible is almost invariably a master of some other language besides his own native dialect; it may be Italian, French, German, or English. Connexions with the United States provide a strong impulse towards the learning of English. When will come forward the Albanian scholar who in educational equipment, in spirit and mind and heart, shall be found worthy to answer the call to complete the Albanian Bible? The kernel of the problem is not financial but spiritual.

Circulation

The circulation is still of modest dimensions, 1,472 volumes, as against 1,841 in 1930.

The Scriptures were circulated as follows: Albanian 1,179 copies: Modern Greek (79); English (76); French (53); Turkish, in the new Latin script, (34); Osmanli Turkish (28); Italian (16); and Ancient Greek (7).

Mary Jones

The Story of Mary Jones has now been published by the Society in Kortcha. It was translated into the vernacular by Professor and Mrs. Loni Kristo, and is already a popular booklet. Colporteur Pandeli Sinas circulated nearly 200 copies during the year 1931.

English Bibles Given

On behalf of the Society, Professor Kristo, of Kortcha, had the pleasure of handing over to the Rev. Phineas and Mrs. Kennedy, who carry on a devoted educational work in Southern Albania, fifty copies of the B.F.B.S new one shilling Bible for use in the Kortcha Mission School. The pupils of this school are thoroughly grounded in English, and the volumes, so handy in form and so clear to read, found a right joyous acceptance.

Page 320

Editorial Report Summaries – Albanian

It was hoped that Mr. Sinas's translation of the N.T. Published first in 1913, printed in roman character, called National Script, would prove a union version of the Gheg and Tosk dialects. This has not been the case. The version would more properly be described as Albanian Tosk, roman character.

129th Report, 1933

Pages 82–83

Yugoslavia

The work of the B.F.B.S. for this country began in 1818, when a grant of £500 was made for a translation into the everyday speech of the Serbian people....

Moreover, Yugoslavia is a veritable happy hunting-ground for the philologist. For here are spoken: (1) Serbo-Croatian, Slovene, Slovak, all Slavonic idioms; (2) Greek and Albanian; (3) German, mostly in dialect; (4) Italian, Rumanian, and Kutso-Vlach; (5) variants of Romany, and also (6) Magyar or Hungarian, spoken by those Hungarians in the Voivodina who came within the limits of the Yugoslav Kingdom after the Great War.

Pages 102–103
Albania

The Society's circulation last year in Albania was 1,079 copies, against 1,472 in 1931, and 1,841 in 1930.

Acting Depositary: Professor Loni Kristo, Korytza (Kortcha), S. Albania.

Introduction

Twenty-five years ago Albania was as little known to Englishmen as parts of Central Africa. The mention of the name brought to mind a picture of wild and revengeful mountaineers who seemed to be generally engaged in tribal fighting. In Constantinople, from which centre Albania was governed, or misgoverned, Albania was thought of only as the recruiting-ground of the regiment of wild but loyal bodyguards of the Sultan. When Albania was definitely severed from Turkey, the latter's rulers probably gave a sigh of relief to be rid of such a troublesome and unproductive vassal State, whilst European Cabinets groaned over the prospect of another problem added to the already long list. Thirty years ago the Society's present Assistant Secretary in Turkey visited Albania. Travelling then was either by horse or native carriage over rough roads, or across open fields when the road was too bad. Few foreigners had ever ridden across the whole country, and those who had done the dangerous trip were obliged to take an escort.

Albania Today

But what a difference to-day! Modern motor-cars dash across and up and down the whole country in a few hours. A regular service of aeroplanes operates between Italy, Albania, and Greece. No escort of soldiers is needed, for

Albania is safer to-day than a country road in England. Good roads and bridges have been made all over the country, and the native chauffeurs, some of whom have had to return from the United States owing to the crisis and unemployment there, think the correct thing to do is to show how good the roads are by racing at fifty miles an hour, and over that when the road is clear. With all this mechanical progress, it is questionable if the people are any happier or more prosperous. The motor transport, however, is made good use of by our colporteur to carry the Scriptures to men in various parts of the country that he would otherwise be unable to visit.

Christians and Moslems

Albania is still divided into three zones as regards religion. The northern part remains strongly Roman Catholic, with the inhabitants using as their language the Gheg dialect. Our colporteur has not yet been able to penetrate into this stronghold of Roman Church. The centre parts, with the towns of Tirana and Elbasan, are mainly Moslem, whilst the south is mostly attached to the Albanian Orthodox Church. Kortcha is the principal town in this zone, and in addition to the Albanian dialect, Tosk, many of the people speak Greek. The Society's depot is in Kortcha, and its single colporteur sets out on his journeys from this centre.

For a long time the Society has been circulating the New Testament and some portions of the Old Testament translated into the Tosk dialect, and the reprint of the New Testament recently produced in Berlin has met with much appreciation, but it has been felt for some time that it is necessary to give Albania the whole of the Bible. The late Mr. Sinas, our depositary for many years, was able to complete his translation of the Old Testament before his death, and his manuscripts are at the disposal of the Society; but the language has changed during the last few years and the orthography with it. The manuscripts will therefore need careful attention to bring them into line with to-day's requirements.

In Kortcha there is also an American Mission school that has done excellent work for many years under the Rev. P. Kennedy and his wife. Mr. Kennedy has been using the Society's Tosk New Testament and available portions of the Old Testament as textbooks in his school from its beginning, and he also uses them in his Sunday afternoon open-air meetings. The Moslems of Albania, particularly of the south and in Tirana, are generally broadminded and tolerant, and Mr. Kennedy often proceeds to the outlying villages after his Sunday service in the Mission and talks to the villagers on Bible subjects. These meetings are well attended by Moslems, and his words are listened to with great respect. This feature of tolerance is very noticeable in Albania today. There is no feeling against Christianity, and several marriages have taken place between Moslem youths and Christian girls and vice versa. This breaking down of religious barriers between Moslems and Christians is bound to have important results later on if it is maintained.

Spread of Education

Under the old Turkish rulers, comparatively few Moslem Albanians could read or write, and families desirous of educating their children sent them to Constantinople, whilst Christian parents who could afford the expense sent their children to the American colleges in the same city. This reproach can no longer be made. Education is compulsory and everyone has the opportunity to learn to read and write. American schools have been founded, and it is no longer necessary to go to Constantinople to learn English. The King is deeply interested in education and encourages young men of promise to study science and economy, and has sent some at his own expense to continue their studies at the London University.

There is still a lack of books, and as one common language is not spoken by the whole nation, progress is somewhat hampered. Perhaps the most interesting place in the capital at Tirana is the Library presented by the Countess of Carnarvon in memory of her son, Colonel Aubrey Herbert, who devoted himself to the freedom of Albania for many years. The Librarian is a member of a famous Albanian family which has done much to improve the literature of its country, and one of whose members recently gave up a distinguished career as ambassador to open a well-equipped bookseller's shop, with the object of interesting his fellow-countrymen in good literature and in this way furthering their education.

130th Report, 1934

Page 3

With heartfelt thanks to Almighty God the Bible Society is able to report that the 130th year of its life and work has been marked by further progress in its task of placing the Word of Life in the hands of men and women in nearly all parts of the world. …In South-eastern Europe, where poverty is so appalling, 171,000 volumes of Holy Writ were sold, a decrease of 18,000. In both Yugoslavia and Greece sales dropped by 12,000, and in Turkey by 3,000. In Bulgaria and Rumania, however, there were increases of

6,000 and 3,500 respectively, and in Albania there was an advance from 1,000 to 1,500.

Page 80

In South-Eastern Europe the main religious groundwork is perhaps Greek Orthodox…, but there are also strong Roman Catholic interests, for about 40 per cent of Yugoslavia's fourteen millions owe allegiance to the Papal See; while in Bulgaria, Rumania, and Albania there is a vigorous and persistent Roman work of which but a feeble idea could be gained from mere arithmetical statements.

The Moslem world of the sunlit and diversified Balkan Peninsula is also by no means negligible. Few people realise that there are nearly 1,400,000 Muhammadans in the Kingdom of the Southern Slavs; or that in Bulgaria there are 789,000 Moslems; while in Albania, still practically unknown to the ordinary tourist and traveller, 68 per cent of the population still bow in the mosque for the worship of Allah. But mention has not yet been made of another country included in this Agency, and that is Turkey; Turkey with her wonderful capital of Istanbul – which the world still finds it hard not to call Constantinople.

Times have changed. In Istanbul there is now neither Sultan nor Caliph, and even the red fez, that once most typical item of all Moslem attire, is now nowhere to be seen.

Pages 108–110
Albania

The Society's circulation last year in Albania was 1,494 copies, against 1,079 in 1932, and 1,472 in 1931.

Acting Depositary: Professor Loni Kristo, Korytza (Kortcha), S. Albania.

Introduction

Albania, being a small country situated off the route of international railways and inhabited by a sturdy independent race of mountaineers occupied principally in agricultural and pastoral pursuits, should be the last to feel the effects of the world crisis, but the visit of the Assistant Secretary, Mr. Russell, to the southern provinces in August, 1933, showed that even in these parts the trade depression in America had its repercussions. The reason for this is that formerly many Albanians emigrated to America, where they found work chiefly in boot and shoe factories. These good people then remitted money regularly to their relations at home, and the circulation of this money helped much to keep many families in comfort. Most of these emigrants now found themselves out of work and several have returned to their native mountains. If it were better known that there is security in Albania, where the gendarmerie forces are trained by British officers, and that the main roads are excellent for motoring, many more visitors would go there and help the country by spending money in hotels and in visiting places of interest. The employment given to a great many men on road building has now practically ceased, as the major part of the routes has been made, and this lack of work, added to the normal poverty of the people, greatly hampers the success of the Society's colporteur, Pandeli Sinas. It says much, therefore, for the willingness of the inhabitants in the south and middle provinces and for his untiring efforts that the sales this year have been more maintained, the total showing an increase over those of last year.

Education and Mission Work

The Government has been able to carry through its road construction policy owing to a loan from Italy. Unfortunately, as the finances of Albania have not allowed the Ministry to pay the interest on the loan, Italy has withdrawn her help, and also ceased to buy cattle and agricultural products, which form Albania's principal exports. By way of retaliation, Italian schools in Albania were closed, and in order not to make an exception, American schools in the country were also closed. This included the long- established Kennedy Mission School in Kortcha, which has done so much good for the youth of Albania. This trouble has now been settled, but in such a way that the education of the youth of Albania, on leaving the ordinary school, will be more than ever influenced by Italian circles. This will strengthen the position of the Roman Catholic Church in Albania, where it has some 100,000 adherents amongst the brave but fanatical tribes of the northern parts, people who have always been inaccessible to the colporteurs of the Bible.

Albanian Bible

Several books of the Old Testament still remain unpublished. Professor Kristo, in charge of the Society's depot at Kortcha, is now engaged in preparing the MS. of the two Books of Samuel.

Circulation

Our circulation of 1,494 copies, as shown in the appended table,1 shows a gratifying increase of that of last year, in spite of all adverse circumstances. Colporteur Pandeli Sinas, who has circulated over 1,300 copies in 'The Land of the Eagle,' has toiled with a steadfastness which declares him a 'chip off the old block,' for his father was traveller, scholar, and Bible translator.

Floods and Distress

Professor Loni Kristo, of the Kortcha Grammar School, the Society's Acting Depositary, states: 'There is no improvement in our economic and financial situation though, thanks be to God, there is no fear that our people will starve. We have a growing export trade with Greece, in corn, beans, hides, etc. The months of October and November have been very wet, and the people have not sown at all, especially in the plains, which are still under water. An inundation has caused great damage in the town of Hermeti; a mountain stream in flood has destroyed over twenty houses and drowned twenty-eight persons, among them a nephew of our family, who left behind a wife and five young children. The whole of Albania has suffered serious damage from the continuous rains. Our colporteur has visited this flooded district. Here are a few sentences from the log-book of Colporteur P. Sinas:

> The year 1933 has been very critical for us Albanians. We have suffered a great deal. In Tirana, the capital city, hundreds of labourers have been standing every day before the Municipal Offices in hope that somebody might engage them, so that they might earn the daily bread. Tradesmen lolling behind their counters and killing time take an opiate against despair by smoking

endless cigarettes. I dared to ask one of them about business, and he answered: 'If things go on like this for another six months we are lost; we shall have to close our shops.' In the provinces the situation has been worse. Had not the Government grated corn free the population would in great part have perished from hunger. Thank God the harvest this year has been good. But where can we sell our corn, olives, cattle, and hides? Greece does not buy much on account of her depreciated currency, while Italy offers very low prices. Many Albanians had emigrated to Egypt, Rumania, Russia, and the United States of America; but now they are home again cultivating the soil and rearing cattle. In the wretched situation in which we find ourselves, is there anybody who thinks of asking God to give us His blessing and save us by the Saviour Jesus? The Bible brought joy and gladness in the old times when people used to believe it. A young man was telling me how the times have changed. I read to him and to a number of his friends Acts xix. 14-18. The same fellow used bitter language at first and called us 'adventurers,' but he repented afterwards when he saw that his friends scolded him severely for the insult. I reminded them also of Matt. xxv. 1-3. Finally, many portions were bought. On another occasion a group of young men were discussing the use of sacred books and the work of our Society. 'Is not the New Testament written by men?' some asked. I tried to explain to the what kind of men the Evangelists were, and read to them from the Epistle of John i. 1-4. They were satisfied and I sold a few copies.

One day a young man was sitting before the door of his house. When I got near he called me. During our conversation he complained to me that twice in his life he had gained considerable sums of money, all of which had slipped through his fingers. 'What is the matter with me?' he said. 'I am able to make money, but incapable of keeping it.' 'Have you ever read the Scriptures?' I asked. 'No,' he said. So I gave him a New Testament to read, adding: 'If you live according to the teaching of Our Lord Jesus Christ, you will not have occasion to complain like this; you will have a heavenly contentment.' He was glad to listen to what I had to tell him.

131st Report, 1935

Pages 84–85

South-Eastern Europe constitutes a most diversified, picturesque, and motley field of labour. Its main religious groundwork is perhaps Greek Orthodox, or, as it is expressed in the Slav countries, Pravoslav. Greece, Rumania, and Bulgaria are Orthodox lands, while Yugoslavia can show quite 47 per cent of her population as Pravoslav, and even Albania reports that more than a fifth of her people are members of the National Albanian Orthodox Church. Moreover, in South-Eastern Europe there are also strong Roman Catholic interests, some 40 per cent of Yugoslavia's 14,000,000 owing allegiance to the Papal See, while in Bulgaria, Rumania, and Albania there exists a vigorous, ably-organized, and persistent Roman Catholic work, of which but a feeble idea can be gained from arithmetical statements.

Then there is the Moslem world of the colourful, sunlit, forest-clad, and mountainous Balkan Peninsula. People who pass comfortably through Yugoslavia in luxury trains on their way from Paris and Milan to Constantinople— or Istanbul as we must remember to call it now—scarcely dream that there are about 1,400,000 devotees of Islam in the Kingdom of the Southern Slavs, or that in frugal and hard-living Bulgaria there are 789,000 Moslems; while in Albania, still a closed domain to the ordinary traveler, no fewer than 68 per cent of the population continue to bow in the mosque with thoughts winging eastward towards Mecca, and backwards through the centuries Mahomet and Medina; with lips murmuring adoration of Allah. And even then we have not thought of Turkey.

Pages 89–90

In Macedonia

The Society has a colporteur in Southern Yugoslavia who is endowed with pleasant manners and a lively wit. He describes the poverty prevailing in many of the villages in 'Macedonia,' as it is still often rather vaguely called, though it must be remembered that Macedonia does not end with the Yugoslav frontier. ... This happy and agile servant has distributed during the year 1934 no fewer than 6,229 Bibles, Testaments, and portions, and he writes: "I shall try with God's help to do better next year." He says that often in the villages people have not a penny in their pockets, and offer him instead fresh eggs or some fruit for a Testament or a Gospel, which he sometimes takes in exchange, though not always, for there are limits to the carrying power even of a colporteur's wallet.

Don't be a Donkey!

Here is another page from a diary: "I have travelled this year through many villages in the mountain regions of the Shar Planina, in the district near the Albanian frontier. Here one can find Orthodox Christians, Roman Catholics, and also many Muhammadans. It is interesting to notice that most of these Muhammadans cannot speak Turkish, but only Serbian, and that the Roman Catholics are frequently able to speak both Serbian and Albanian. The Roman Catholics who speak Albanian well are as a rule very fanatical, though I have often put into their hands many portions of Scriptures. Not seldom, however, they have come back to me, saying that they have been told by the priest that 'these books are not good!' One day a young fellow, who had taken a Testament from me, came to tell me that he liked the book very much, but that his priest had taken it away from him, telling him that it was not a good book for him to read. Then I said to this young man: 'But why did you not tell the priest to show you the wrong parts or the wrong places in the book? Do please go and ask him where the book is bad, and do not be treated just like a donkey. God has given you a mind and intelligence, and now He has also given you the opportunity to read His Word; you are not a donkey to be tied by a rope and pulled about from one side to another.' The illustration was apt enough, for not very far off were two or three donkeys with heavy loads on their backs being pulled about here and there with a rope, and the young man looked the colporteur in the face very earnestly for a while and then looked upon the ground; turning things over in his mind, he suddenly exclaimed: 'This is right. Why should I not read the book? I will go and ask the priest to give it back to me.' And with this determination he said good-bye. I know from many experiences, adds the colporteur, that many of these Albanian-speaking Roman Catholics have found great joy in reading the Four Gospels, and they have often told me so with bright and open faces."

Pages 109–111
Albania

The Society's circulation last year in Albania was 1,499 copies, against 1,494 in 1933, and 1,079 in 1932.

Acting Depositary: Professor Loni Kristo, Korytza (Kortcha), S. Albania.

Introduction

Albania used to be a country of the greatest risk and the wildest romance for the foreign traveller. Much of the romance remains, but most of the risks have vanished, for there is now excellent policing and almost exemplary public order, and there are very good roads. No trains, of course – the wild mountains and deep valleys naturally put railways out of the question. But motorcars and motorbuses and innumerable lorries make full use of modern highways in Albania.

The year 1934 has not been specially prosperous, but we are glad to report that our circulation has not declined.

Colportage

The following extracts are from the diary of Colporteur P. Sinas. He reports a considerable difficulty in selling the Scriptures, owing to the continued poverty ruling in Albania. The country remains on the gold standard and is unable to compete in exports with neighbouring countries with cheaper money, and as the majority of the people are engaged in agriculture, farm products fetch a very low price and no profit. Amongst his experiences Mr. Sinas relates the following:

> During my travels through the country I came to a village where a Moslem, attached to the Court as a secretary, bought a Bible in French. Some time after, while passing through the same village, I met this man

again, and he told me his Bible had been taken from him by a friend who, on looking through it, asked to be allowed to retain it. This friend was so pleased with the Bible that he preferred reading it to any other book. The Moslem bought a second copy to replace the one he had given his friend. This, however, was not the end of the story. A follower of the Christian Orthodox Church happened to be standing near us when the Moslem buyer made this statement, and he became so interested that he also purchased a Bible.

A man from Dibra, Orthodox by religion, who is at the same time a merchant in the capital city of Tirana, had the previous year purchased a Serbian Bible from me. When I met this man again this year, he began to talk against the Scriptures, and told me the Bible was not an important book. He had a friend with him at the time, and I read to them part of St. Matthew XXIV. Both of them became interested and satisfied, and the man then told me he had given his Bible to his brothers to read. I lent him another copy of the Bible in Serbian to look at, and the following day he paid for it. Since then we have been good friends, and every time I visit him he tells me he is reading the Bible regularly.'

In one of my visits to Kavaja I joined a group of men, both Christian and Moslem, who were discussing religion. One of the men, an army officer and a Moslem by religion, said, 'God is full of pity for every one, including Christians, Moslems, Jews, and pagans.' I thought these words were directed at me, and I said to myself: 'How can a man who does not believe in Christ be prepared for the Last Judgment?' I then read part of 2 Chronicles XX, saying, 'God loves all alike, but at the same time He manifests His power against those who do not follow rightly in His ways.' The officer was very pleased, and this incident resulted in my selling a Bible in Greek to one of the listeners.'

Some Insight into General Conditions

The Rev. Phineas B. Kennedy of Kortcha, in giving a report on "The Bible in Albania for 1934," writes to our Secretary for South-Eastern Europe as follows:

The Albanian Evangelical Mission located at Kortcha is the only Evangelical Mission in Albania. More than a year ago the Albanian Government closed the day- and boarding-school in connexion with this Mission on three counts: that it was conducted by foreigners, that it was supported by private funds, and that it taught the Bible in all of its classes. The work of the mission continues as an Evangelical Evangelistic Mission. Sabbath preaching and mid-week services are regularly maintained, and the attendance is encouraging. The only Sunday School and the only Christian Endeavour Society are in connexion with this mission. We appreciate the help of the B.F.B.S. in supplying us with copies of the Albanian Scriptures, such as are printed in the Albanian language for the work of our Sunday School and other services, either free or at reduced rates, and in allowing us some copies for free distribution when we hold services at the hospital or the prison. In holding these services at the prison we and our band of singers and speakers are received at the office of the director, and conducted to an open verandah, where we address the prisoners on an opposite verandah or in the open space below. We are not allowed to come into personal contact with the prisoners ourselves, but entrust such copies of the Scriptures and other literature that we have taken to the director to distribute later. At the hospital it is our joy to hand portions of Scripture to such patients as are able to read. This we have been doing ever since we came to Albania in 1907.

After my return from my last furlough I found, in going out to the villages to hold public services, that the local sub-officials hesitated to give me permission without a direct authority from the governor, and that he hesitated to give me permission even to speak at the hospital or the prison as well as in the villages, unless allowed to do so by the Central Government. Our young Albanian preacher, Mr. Cheno, and we missionaries, Mr. Jacques and myself, have filed several petitions, and more recently Mrs. Kennedy and I have visited Tirana, the capital, and called on several of the Ministers, but as yet we have had no reply whatever from the Government.

Pages 343–344
Review of the Year, Europe

Two books of the Old Testament, 1 and 2 Samuel, in the translation (or revision) made by Mr. Sinas, a depositary of the Bible Society, are being issued in Tosk Albanian. The manuscript was read by Professor Loni Kristo, a graduate of Harvard.

Page 355
Summaries

Albanian – The two books of Samuel are being printed. The translation was made by A. Sinas and read through by Professor Loni Kristo.

132nd Report, 1936

Page 82

The principal vernaculars of South-Eastern Europe distributed during 1935 were, in round figures: Rumanina (39,000 copies; Greek, Modern (33,000); Greek, Ancient (12,000); Serbian (Croatian) (31,000); Bulgarian (14,000); Albanian (3,000); Turkish (2,000).

Circulation in Albania

Bibles	Testaments	Portions	1935	1934	1933
51	325	3,323	3,699	1,499	1,494

Page 85

A colporteur in the South writes:

While visiting some villages on the famous Plain of Kosovo, where the Turks fought their great battle, which was the beginning of the enslavement of the Serbian race more than five hundred years ago, it began to thunder and to rain heavily, so that I was obliged to ask for shelter in order to save my books and myself from getting wet. I was welcomed kindly and found many farm workers, who had also been caught by the rain. So we sat and talked. There were Montenegrins, Serbians, Albanians. They were interested in me and wanted to know what sort of books I had, so I told them, and began to speak to them about the message which we have in the Gospel. They became more and more interested and wanted to hear something from the book. Then they ordered a Turkish coffee for me, and said that they would get me a meal if the rain did not stop soon. They then went on to ask me many question about religion and the Bible, all of which I had to answer very slowly and clearly. So the time was taken up till we suddenly found that it was raining no longer. So I gave to each of them a small Gospel and bade them farewell.

Page 86

Colporteur Djuro Lukac, a faithful servant who has long served his Master in association with the Bible Society, writes:

> The need for the distribution of the Holy Scriptures is emphasised by the crisis existing in the world and the great need in consequence of it. ... Travelling by boat in Dalmatia to the famous Bay of Cattaro, I encountered several Albanian, Montenegrin, and other fellow-passengers. While I was offering my books to the sailors, one of them asked me to read them something out of them. I prayed in the Spirit for the right word at the right time. All who were with me in the ship surrounded me in order to hear the living Word of God. It impressed them so much that, after I had read to them the 24th chapter of St. Matthew, they bought bibles, Testaments, and portions and I was able to rejoice greatly.

Pages 103-105
Albania

The Society's circulation last year in Albania was 3,699 copies, against 1,419 in 1934, and 1,494 in 1933.

Acting Depositary: Professor Loni Kristo, Korytza (Kortcha), S. Albania.

Introduction

It will be seen from the Table of Circulation that the year 1935 has been a very gratifying one. The large increase was due principally to the Albanian Evangelical Mission at

Kortcha sending the Rev. Edwin Jacques, assistant to the Rev. Phineas B Kennedy, to make a tour all over Albania. Mr. Jacques had a very successful season and circulated over 1,000 copies of the Scriptures, most of which were Gospels. In this work he was ably seconded by the young Albanian preacher, Mr. Cheno. It is interesting to note that this year Colporteur Sinas was not able to sell many copies in the Shkodra or Northern district, where the inhabitants are mostly Roman Catholics, although last year he sold over a hundred copies there. On the other hand, Moslems in other parts of Albania bought more freely.

The result of these increased sales has been that the stock of the Gospel of St. Matthew was sold out and a new edition had to be printed. The Gospel of St. Mark is also being reprinted, and the translation of the Books of Samuel by the late Mr. Sinas having been approved by the two leading authorities in the Albanian language, these will soon be added to the books of the Old Testament already printed.

Great changes have recently been made in the administration of the country. The King continues his efforts to advance the interests of his country and is making use of the younger men whom he had had educated in England and Western Europe. The Government of Mr. Mehdi Frasheri, composed mainly of leaders new to party power and of University graduates, has succeeded Mr. Pandeli Evangeli, the head of the Government of the Elders. The whole of the administration is now in the hands of men whose education, character, and serious nature inspire the people with confidence in the future of the country.

From Day to Day in Albania

Colporteur Pandeli Sinas, in describing some of his experiences during 1935, writes:

At Vlora, while going my rounds from house to house, calling out "Buy the Word of God; get the Word of God," a Moslem woman asked me what I was selling. "The Gospel of Christ," I replied. "But we are not allowed to read that," she said. "Then buy the Book of Job," I continued, "as in that book the writer is speaking of God only, and both you and I have and believe in the same God." The good woman then bought a portion and went away smiling.'

When selling my books in the hotel at Vlora, I came to a group of men sitting round the table in the dining-room, some of whom were in a position of authority in the town. I showed them the various books I was carrying, and they looked at them interestedly. One of the men asked if I had any copies of Omar Khayám."No," I replied, "our Bible Society has translated the Word of God in hundreds of languages and, in doing so, at the same time created many literatures. In buying the Scriptures and reading them, you learn not only the right way of God but you encourage our Albanian literature." The men then purchased with pleasure two copies of the New Testament, which they said were very acceptable.'

On another of my trips I met two Moslem schoolboys in the street. I asked them if they would like to read the Life of Jesus Christ, our Saviour. One of the boys replied, "Yes! I love Jesus Christ. If you come home with me, perhaps you will convince my father to buy me a copy of the New Testament." So I accompanied the boy to his home, where I met his father. I said to the father, "If you buy a copy of the New Testament, your son will read to you from it every evening and tell you the true Word of God, and you will be inspired and guided by the Life of Jesus Christ." Finally the parent bought a copy of the Gospel of St. John.'

When taking leave of my friends in Vlora, a boy came and asked me to go to the National Bank, as there was a man there who wanted to buy a copy of the New Testament. I thought at first that the boy was only playing a trick on me, but, nevertheless, I decided to go. On entering the building I asked if there were a man there answering to a certain name given me by the boy. Immediately a gentleman came forward and greeted me politely and bought the New Testament.

133rd Report, 1937

Pages 105–107
Albania

The Society's circulation last year in Albania was 2,108 copies, against 3,699 in 1935, and 1,419 in 1934.

Acting Depositary: Professor Loni Kristo, Korytza (Kortcha), S. Albania.

Introduction

The year 1936 in Albania has been a difficult one for the poorer classes. The economic situation has been at times almost critical, and the price of wheat and corn rose very high owing to the action of speculators. The Government came to the rescue and allowed corn to be imported duty free, with beneficial results to the nation. Government efforts were made in other ways to help the unemployed, and three hundred labourers in Kortcha were engaged to work on the road to Devolli, between Kortcha and Elbasan. Nevertheless there is still much poverty and the Society's representative in Albania, Professor Loni Kristo, points out that there are many people who would gladly purchase a copy of the Scriptures, but are too poor to do so.

Valued Friends

The Bible Society will miss greatly the assistance given to its Albanian representatives by Mr. and Mrs. Kennedy, of the Albanian Evangelical Mission at Kortcha, where for a great many years they have worked, under difficult political and financial conditions, teaching the Scriptures and educating Albanian boys and girls. During all these years Mr. and Mrs. Kennedy have worked in a voluntary capacity, increasing the circulation of the Scriptures received by them from the Bible Society, and it is very gratifying to learn that their work will be carried on by their successors, Mr. and Mrs. Jacques and Mr. and Mrs. Conrad. Mr. and Mrs. Kennedy have retired and settled down in their home outside Kortcha.

Colportage Experiences

Colporteur Pandeli Sinas, in describing some of his experiences during 1936, writes:

> One day I entered a cheap coffee-house where many young men were playing cards. I suggested that many of them should buy the New Testament and so learn the Word of God. No one seemed to be interested, when all of a sudden the coffee-house keeper bought a copy of the New Testament. One of the young men asked me for another copy. I was so glad to sell, in such a place, two copies of the New Testament.

As I was passing a bus station the agent asked me whether I had sold any of my books. 'Well,' I answered, 'I do my best, but even my friends don't help me. You say you are interested in my work, but you haven't bought a copy of my books.' 'We studied the Bible in school,' he said, 'now we are too busy to read it.' 'Well, my friend,' I said, 'what you learnt in school is forgotten; the Bible is as necessary to refresh our spirit and sentiment as the food for our body,' 'We Orthodox people,' he said, 'have our Bible which is different from yours, the Protestant one.' 'No, my friend,' I said, 'our Bible is the same for all Christians, for Catholics, Orthodox, and Protestant.' The agent then asked me for a copy of the New Testament and left me feeling very glad to have sold a copy of it."

On visiting Kuchova I saw that a small town had sprung up lately because oil had been discovered there by the Italians. The town is built at the foot of a hill. There are many wells, round which there are houses for the labourers and engineers of the Italian Petrol Oil Company. There are seventy wells in a small radius. The houses are far from one another, while all the stores are in a square. On visiting the stores I was able to sell a few books. In one store I found a Greek who was very much interested in the Bible. He bought a Greek Bible and he said to a bystander, 'Buy a Bible, because you will find there all the events from Adam to Jesus Christ recorded.' 'No,' said the bystander, 'this Bible is different from ours.' 'Not at all,' said the Greek, 'this Bible is the same for all Christians, buy it and I will explain it to you.' Two other store-keepers also bought a few copies of the Gospels from me."

To the south of Hushnja there is a monastery by the name of St. Theodora. Round about there are a few small villages called Kadi Pacha. On Feb. 5th a fair is held here, which Christians and Moslems attend. I went first to the village of Bubullima. The stores are small, low buildings. The salesmen come only on that day, as they live elsewhere. I began to visit the stores. To the first proprietor I quoted from Exodus vi. 6-7, the duty of a father is to speak to his children about the word of God. The good man said, 'I don't know how to read, but my boys go to school and I will buy two of your books.' He bought a copy of Deuteronomy and a New Testament."

At Elbasan I saw in a house a new Testament translated into Greek-Albanian by the late Mr. Kristoforides, in which I found this remark, 'Oh, how good is the Bible Society! It is to it that I owe this wonderful book in which I can read the Word of God, it is through this Holy Book that I have known God and our Saviour Jesus Christ.'"

A Moslem merchant asked me, 'What do you sell?' 'Why,' I said, 'these are the Holy Books called the New Testament, in Albanian. It is the life of our Saviour Jesus Christ.' 'What is your purpose in selling these books? You are trying to spoil our religion.' 'No, my dear sir,' I said. 'Our aim is to spread the Word of God according to the command of Jesus Christ. If you read these books they are full of interest for everyone, no matter whether Christian or Moslem.' I handed him a copy of Genesis, but on seeing the Gospel of St. Matthew he said that he preferred it. So I gave a copy to him, and smiling, he paid the price and went away."

134th Report, 1938

Pages 86–88

Albania

The Society's circulation last year in Albania was 2,831 copies, against 2,108 in 1936 and 3,699 in 1935.

Acting Depositary: Professor Loni Kristo, Korytza (Kortcha), S. Albania.

Introduction

Albania is about the size of Belgium, and difficult to get at. It is most easily accessible by sea from Italy; the Yugoslav and Greek approaches are through wild and very rugged country. Albania is the most solidly Moslem State in Europe, and a colporteur needs to be an expert 'apologist' to work from day to day amongst such people.

Revival of National Feeling

During the closing days of Aug., 1928, all the steps necessary for changing the republic of Albania into a monarchy were legally carried through, and on Sept. 1st Ahmed Beg Zogu, who had been President of the republic since 1925, was proclaimed King. Thus Albania became a democratic, parliamentary, independent monarchy, without any State religion; the King himself, however, is a Moslem. There now began a phenomenal recovery from the five centuries of Turkish bondage, which had been first broken in 1912, when the London Conference of Ambassadors agreed to the principle of Albanian autonomy, though, as a matter of fact, the independence of Albania had already been proclaimed at Valona three weeks earlier. Almost a year before the proclamation of the President as King, a defensive alliance for a period of twenty-five years had been signed between Albania and Italy. Italian influence was growing, but the slogan of the young patriots was *Albania for the Albanians.* Young intellectuals were hustled through Continental universities, and returned to displace foreign professors in all educational departments. The end in view was the attainment, in a very real sense, of Albanian unity, and it was demanded on the ground of nationalism. Thus it came about that divisive influence due to religious rivalries were everywhere frowned upon and the leaders of the two dominant faiths, Islam and Orthodoxy, responded to kindly patronage.

Albanian Schoolmasters for Albanian Schools

Mr. Pandeli Sinas, the sons of the late Mr. Athanasius Sinas (who did so much devoted work in the translation of the Scriptures into Albanian), has for some years represented the British and Foreign Bible Society up and down Albania. He was a teacher in an Albanian village school before he decided to occupy himself exclusively in taking the Word of God into the remotest and most sequestered corners of his native land. It was not long after the proclamation of the President of the republic as King that it became evident that the educational system must somehow be made to serve as a stouter bulwark against foreign influence. All foreign schools, therefore, were suppressed, and the Mission School, originally founded by the American Board in 1908, suffered the same fate. This all too drastic measure has been modified since, though the reopening of foreign schools is hedged about with very strict conditions.

Religion a Fundamental Necessity

It is significant that at the present time there should be in ruling quarters in Albania a strong conviction that it is culpable folly to neglect to provide religious instruction in the public schools. It would seem that a fear of a godless Communism spreading amongst Albanian youth has bought about the order on the part of the Government that Moslem, Orthodox, and Roman Catholic children shall be taught religion in the schools. And is there not a certain wholesomeness and breadth of outlook in this compulsion? It is at least a recognition that some acknowledgment by man of the great Upholder of the Universe is of cardinal import for the moral and social life of the people.

The Authorisation of Colportage

The Government has definitely and expressly authorized the distribution of the Scriptures by colportage since the year 1934. Bigotry there sometimes is, on the part of individuals, but it is a matter for thanksgiving that the Government itself rises above it. Though Evangelicals have no legal standing nor any legal right to propagate the faith which appears upon every page of the New Testament, yet the preaching of Christ is not challenged or suppressed, and such work is continued by the benevolent tolerance of the Albanian Government.

Colporteur Pandeli Sinas has been able to circulate 1,081 copies during the year: 28 Bibles, 144 New testaments, and 909 portions.

The total circulation for the year 1937 amounted to 2,831 copies.

Page 322
Summaries

Albanian – Correspondence has been conducted with the Metropolitan of Kortcha in regard to the revision of the N.T., which he desires to see done.

135th Report, 1939

Pages 72–74
Albania

The Society's circulation last year in Albania was 2,265 copies, against 2,831 in 1937, and 2,108 in 1936.

Acting Depositary: Professor Loni Kristo, Korytza (Kortcha), S. Albania.

Introduction

The Albanians call their native country "the Land of the Eagle." For centuries poets have sung of the rugged inaccessibility of this mountain realm and of the not less rugged character of its untutored inhabitants. The Albanian has long enjoyed the reputation of his rocks, travellers reporting him as hard to knock up against, steadfast and indomitable at his best and sometimes stubborn, pugnacious and truculent.

Nowadays, however, scarcely any land can be described as inaccessible or sequestered, and if Albania is still the land of the eagle with scarcely a single puffing locomotive in an area equal to that of Belgium, it is fast becoming the land par excellence of the motor lorry, the heavily laden omnibus doing all the duties of a goods van, and even more of the aeroplane.

Albania for the Albanians

This is an enthusiastic slogan expressing the patriotic ideal. Yet geography, if sometimes favouring it, is often against it. It is true that the Yugoslav and the Greek approaches to Albania lead through wild and difficult country, but the Adriatic Sea provides an easy approach from Italy, and it is obvious that Italian influence is strong in the domains of King Zogou. There is in existence a defensive alliance between Albania and Italy: it was signed for twenty-five years and still has many years to run.

Circulation

The Government has definitely and expressly authorized the distribution of the Scriptures by means of colportage since the year 1934, and the Society's colporteur, Mr. Pandeli Sinas, who was formerly a teacher in a village school, has been going up and down the land, all through the year. He distributed 17 Bibles, 115 New Testaments and 842 portions of Scripture during the year, while 24 Bibles, 124 New Testaments and 1,135 portions were circulated from the depot.

In Many Tongues

Of the total circulation, 1,869 copies were the Albanian language, 140 in Turkish (either in the ancient or the modern script), 87 in Modern Greek, 43 in French, 42 in Italian, 24 in Yugoslav, and 23 in English, 13 in Bulgarian and 4 in German. Twelve complete Bibles were distributed in Modern Greek and eleven complete Bibles in Italian.

Progress and Reconstruction

Correspondence with our representatives in Albania would seem to show a relatively bright and heartening outlook for this Switzerland of the Balkan Peninsula. The marriage of the King to a Countess of Hungarian-American origin is heralded as a harbinger of good. The nuptial celebrations took place amid enthusiastic acclamations, the Albanian people being most fully represented by delegates of both sexes from all over the kingdom. As to education, the number of pupils in the elementary schools has more than doubled during the past twelve years, and there are now eighteen secondary schools with some 6,000 pupils, of whom 1,500 are girls, while more than 400 Albanian students are studying, in order to help their country, in various Universities abroad. Much needed measures have also been taken by the Government to stimulate and improve agriculture. An Agricultural State Bank has been created to extend credits to farmers, and stock-breeding and the culture of olive and fruit trees has been improved. Attention has also been devoted to the promotion of better irrigation, for in Albania one gets reports of a shortage of grain nearly every year owing to lack of water. The King has unfurled the banner of goodwill, sound education on a religious basis, and a wisely directed progress on peaceful lines, and he calls upon his people bravely to follow him.

Page 283

Summaries: Albania

The Bishop of Kortcha (Greek Church) has offered to make a new translation of the New Testament if we are prepared to finance the work.

136th Report, 1940

Page 47

Circulation in South-Eastern Europe

The Scriptures were circulated in over thirty languages last year. The circulation in the more important languages was as follows: Hungarian, 172,622; Rumanian, 134,499; Serbian, 58,317; Croatian, 39,063; German, 6,945; Slovenian, 5,055; Albanian, 2,200; Russian, 1,797; Hebrew, 1,624; English, 850; Slovak, 733; Polish, 615; Ancient Greek, 372.

Pages 54–55

Albania

The Society's circulation last year in Albania was 2,925 copies, against 2,265 in 1938, and 2,831 in 1937.

Acting Depositary: Professor Loni Kristo, Korytza (Kortcha), S. Albania.

Introduction

The world was startled on Good Friday, 1939, to hear of the seizure of Albania by Italian troops, and of the flight of the Albanian King Zog and his Queen and infant child born but a few days earlier. Albania, which is about the size of Belgium, has now become an Italian province, and the Adriatic Sea an Italian Lake.

Religious Situation

Albania is the most solidly Moslem State of Europe, though the Moslems are of the more tolerant Sunni type. In ruling quarters there is a strong conviction of the need for religious instruction, and the Government has, therefore, ordered that such instruction should be given in the schools, whether Moslem, Orthodox Church, or Roman Catholic.

Circulation

There was a circulation of 2,925 copies of the Scriptures during the past year, a slight increase compared with the figures for 1938. Of these, 2,003 copies were circulated through the depot, while our single colporteur, Pandeli Sinas, was responsible for the circulation of 922 copies.

137th Report, 1941

Page 4
The Situation in Europe

Although most of Europe lies in Hitler's power, with the consequences that religious liberty has been seriously curtailed on the Continent, it must not be supposed that the work of distributing the Scriptures has been discontinued. ... In Yugoslavia there was a circulation of 59,000, and in Spain (where the work has been suspended) 9,000, while in heroic Greece the work appears have been well maintained.

Page 7
Summary

Since its foundation in 1804 the Bible Society has issued more than 532,544,000 copies of the Scriptures. Of these, about 129,284,000 have been in English.

Page 40
Albania

We have no report of the work in this county, and the news which has filtered through to us is contained in a letter from Mrs. Kristo, wife of our Superintendent in Koritza, saying that her husband had been arrested by the Italians, and that she had heard no news of him since. No funds had come through from Rome, and her position was a difficult one. As this letter arrived after the downfall of Greece, it has been impossible for us to help her in any way.

Report for 1942–1943 (Wartime)

Page 28

We have to record that our greatest difficulties have been in the securing of Scripture supplies, both of printed books from outside and of materials on which to print inside. Paper is very scarce, of poor quality and most expensive. But in spite of all the difficulties, we are managing to keep going and replenish to a large extent our stocks.

Page 31

Persecution of the Jews

The persecution of the Jews on the Continent of Europe has aroused world-wide indignation. Hitler's avowed intention to exterminate the Jews has been partially carried out, as the wholesale massacres in Poland and other places bear evidence; and there is no hope of this inhuman slaughter being stopped until the Axis has been finally defeated.

Report for 1944–1945 (Wartime)

Page 33
Bible Lands Agency, South

With the liberation of Greece and of most of the Balkan Peninsula by the Allied Nations the sense of security of the lands forming this Agency has further increased, bringing with it the removal of the black-out and the relaxation of other war-time restrictions. ...

The work of Bible distribution has continued throughout the Agency, and besides catering for the cosmopolitan populations of the Agency we have supplied Service people of the United Nations with the Holy Scriptures in their own languages. ... Prisoners of war and civilian internees have been given free grants of Scriptures in Italian, Albanian, and Greek.

Report for 1946–1947

Page 33
Yugoslavia

Yugoslavia was proclaimed a Republic on November 29, 1945.

We were delighted to receive news from our Superintendent, Mr. V. Jeremitch, in October 1945, that he was safe and well. He also reported the safety of Mr. Bogdanovitch, our depot assistant at Belgrade. Both had been imprisoned by the Gestapo for six months in 1941, and suffered very much indeed.

Report for 1948–1954

No information pertinent to Albania except tabular information.

Report for 1955

Page 165

Translations Report

Albanian – The Archbishop of the Albanian Church in America says the present Tosk version needs revising.

INDEX

This index is not keyed to the page numbers of this book, but to the years of the annual reports. It must also be remembered that the annual reports record information from previous years. Therefore, for example, when this index shows: "Abdul Hamid (sultan), deposed, 1911," this does not mean that the sultan was deposed in 1911 (he was deposed in 1909), but only that the event was recorded in the annual report for 1911. That is, this section must be used only as an index to this book, not as a chronological reference tool.

The original British and Foreign Bible Society logo

British and Foreign Bible Society Headquarters, London

The Bible House, Istanbul

Monastir June 26 1897

Rev. T. R. Hodgson

My Dear Sir

Some days ago I received your wel-
come letter of the 18th inst. but was unable to answer it
because I was busy with the accounts. Last week I sent you
the accounts and hope that you have received them in
time. To day I am through also with the Colporteur's
reports. Last week mr. Luka started for Scodra, he is
to go also to Berat where he is going to rent a house
for his family. In Autumn when ....

— 9 —

work, but do not be discouraged if you have
no sales, let us pray to our Lord and He will
open a wider gate for this sacred work. He bought
a Testament, but he had not sufficient money so
left it and got it on the morrow.

I met another young in boy with his father and
wished to buy a Testament, he asked his father for
the money but he said that they are Society's books
and they ought to give them without any money, but
his boy said don't you think father that four piasters
are as four paras for this precious book. In your
childhood you would have given 20 piasters still you
could not get it, but thanks to our Heavenly father that there are people who pour their money
so that we can buy them. His father gave him the
money, and the boy with great joy took the Testament.

Tsiko's Report.

In December we worked in Scodra and Durazzo when
the sales were very low on account of the flood that
brought a great damage to the market. The accident
took place before we reached the place. In Scodra the
sales have always been low. There we have to meet
persecutions by the Catholic church who continualy
speak against .... are bound there and
are trying to ....
who plainly ....

— 10 —

the bishops and priests. Our Bible is considered as
uncomplete. though their colporteurs get them
from our Society and sell them dearer.

With kind regards
Your most obedient
S. B. Kyrio

A Call from Albania.

Mr. George Kyrias, our depositary at Monastir, is himself an Albanian. Letters in Albanian, mostly anonymous, have been addressed to him full of gratitude and thanks for the work of the Bible Society. The burden of all the letters is to implore the Society to complete the Albanian translations, and to give to these people in their own tongue the precious boon of God's Word. Would that the Turkish Government might be led to remove the prohibition which alone prevents us doing this! Colporteurs Sinas and Laka, who have worked and travelled exclusively in Albania and whom no dangers daunt, send the same appeal in every report. Albanian men and women, they say, are hungry for the Word of God, which in a foreign tongue gives them neither comfort or pleasure. When the time comes for the Scriptures in the Albanian language to be circulated freely, the results—so both men agree —will give cause for thankfulness and joy.

From Saul to Paul.

Thus colporteur Christoff describes the case of 'a fierce and vicious youth,' who from a persecutor became a follower and helper of the Gospel. One day in the house of a friend he found an old and well-worn Bible, and borrowed it out of curiosity. After reading it he brought it back to his friend and said, 'This is the real Orthodox Bible and no "Protestant" book.' 'My friend,' said the man, 'that is what you call the "Protestant" Bible which you have so long persecuted.' Whereupon, says the colporteur, this youth from an enemy became his warm supporter, all through reading that tattered Bible . . . , 'by his assistance I was able in a few days to sell 59 copies of God's Word in that place—a rare event in our work.'

Facing page: a report to BFBS headquarters from George Kyrias, depositary at Monastir, written on June 26, 1897, with information from coloporteurs' reports. These reports were summarized in the annual reports.

Above: forty-four of the BFBS's annual reports and a sample page from 1905.

COLPORTEUR ELIAS, IN TROUBLED ALBANIA, WHO WAS
ARRESTED AND DETAINED FOR A TIME LAST YEAR BY
THE TURKISH MILITARY AUTHORITIES.

One of the many colporteurs of the BFBS, Elias Zarifzappas.

INSTITUTE *for* ALBANIAN & PROTESTANT STUDIES

The mission of the Institute for Albanian and Protestant Studies is to promote the discovery of Albanian and Protestant history and thought. This book is part of the 500/200 Series published in commemoration of the 500th anniversary of the Protestant Reformation in Europe, the 200th anniversary of the Albanian Bible translation project, the 150th anniversary of the publication of the Gheg Albanian Gospels, and the 125th anniversaries of the Albanian Evangelical Brotherhood and the Albanian Girls' School in Kortcha. The titles in this series include:

- *My Life: the autobiography of the pioneer of female education in Albania, Sevasti Kyrias Dako*
- *Gerasim Kyrias and the Albanian National Awakening, 1858–1894* (John Quanrud)
- *Captured by Brigands* (Gerasim Kyrias)
- *Albania and the Albanians in the Annual Reports of the British and Foreign Bible Society, 1805–1955*
- *Albania and the Albanians in the Annual Reports of the American Board of Commissioners for Foreign Missions, 1820–1924*
- *Travels in Albania, Selected Writings from British Authoresses, 1717–1878*

www.instituti.org

Publisher's Cataloging-in-Publication data

Names: Hosaflook, David, compiler and editor.

Title: Albania and the Albanians in the annual reports of the British and Foreign Bible Society, 1805–1955 / compiled and edited by David Hosaflook.

Series: The 500/200 Albanian Protestant Commemorative Series

Description: Includes index. | Tirana, Albania: Institute for Albanian and Protestant Studies, 2017.

Identifiers: ISBN 978-1-946244-13-0 (Albania: pbk.) | 978-1-946244-14-7 (pbk.) | 978-1-946244-15-4 (ebook)

Subjects: LCSH British and Foreign Bible Society–History–19th century. | British and Foreign Bible Society–History–20th century. | Bible–Publication and distribution–Societies, etc. | Balkan Peninsula–History–19th century–Sources. | Balkan Peninsula–History–20th century–Sources. | Albania–History–1840-1912–Sources.

Classification: LCC DR43 .H67 2017 | DDC 949.602/8–dc23